VOICES OF OUR
ANCESTORS

VOICES
OF OUR
ANCESTORS

Cherokee Teachings
from the Wisdom Fire

Dhyani Ywahoo

Edited by Barbara Du Bois

SHAMBHALA
Boston & London
1987

SHAMBHALA PUBLICATIONS, INC.
Horticultural Hall
300 Massachusetts Avenue
Boston, Massachusetts 02115

© 1987 by Dhyani Ywahoo

9   8   7   6   5   4   3

Printed in the United States of America

Distributed in the United States by Random House and in Canada by Random House of Canada Ltd.

Library of Congress Cataloging-in-Publication Data

Ywahoo, Dhyani.
    Voices of our ancestors.

    1. Cherokee Indians—Religion and mythology.
2. Cherokee Indians—Medicine.   3. Indians of
North America—Southern States—Religion and mythology.
4. Indians of North America—Southern States—Medicine.
I. Title.
E99.C5Y98 1987   299.78   87-9711
ISBN 0-87773-410-0 (pbk.)

The drawings at the beginning of each chapter are of shell gorgets found in excavation of the Duck River Indian lands in Tennessee, adapted from pictures in M. N. Lewis and Madeline Kneberg, *Tribes That Slumber* (Knoxville: University of Tennessee Press, 1958). The poems and songs at the beginning of Chapters 4, 6, and 7 are adapted from traditional Tsalagi songs and formulas contained in the "Swimmer Manuscript": James Mooney, *Myths of the Cherokee and Sacred Formulas of the Cherokees* (Nashville: Charles and Randy Elder, 1982). The diagram on page 50 is adapted from Tony Shearer, *Beneath the Moon and Under the Sun* (Albuquerque: Sun Publishing Co., 1975). Grateful appreciation is expressed to these authors and publishers for their valuable work.

Cover photograph © 1986 by Pamela Cabell-Whiting.
    Used by permission. All rights reserved.
Book and cover design by Amy Calkins

CONTENTS

Acknowledgments ix

Preface xi

Introduction 1

1. The People of the Fire 9

2. Voices of Our Ancestors 29

3. Renewing the Sacred Hoop 73

4. The Family of Humanity 111

5. Generating Peacekeeper Mind 147

6. A Living Vision of Peace 191

7. Diamond Light 235

Epilogue 265

Notes 267

Appendices
  A. The Family of Life 273
  B. The Directions and Their Attributes 279
  C. About Dhyani Ywahoo and Sunray
     Meditation Society 283

Readings 285

Index 287

DEDICATION

This book is dedicated, with appreciation:

To those who have walked before and clearly formed the path of the Beauty Way;

To my grandparents, my great-grandparents, and my parents, for the wisdom they cultivated and passed to me, that I might pass it to those ready to receive;

To Golden: May the Mystery whisper in your heart;

To my children and grandchildren: Thank you for choosing me to be your mom; may your visions be realized;

To the Principal Chief of the Etowah Nation, Hugh Gibbs, and his family, for the good works they do that peace may shine on Earth;

To the lost Cherokee: May these words be a signpost that you may find your way home again;

To the Sunray students, who are manifesting my Elders' dreams that people of all nations can together do good;

And to all those voices of wisdom who have whispered to me along the way. I give thanks for the guidance of Phillip Deere and Mad Bear; to the Diné medicine man, Tommy, who called me home and said, "Yes, you can do what your grandparents expected of you"; and to Marie, the dream friend who proved real.

Ga li e li ga, I am grateful.

ACKNOWLEDGMENTS

Special thanks to Tama Weisman, who typed the manuscript; to Lynn E. Alden, who prepared the illustrations; to Emily Hilburn Sell of Shambhala Publications, for her foresight in calling forth this book; to all the Sunray friends who have taped and transcribed my lectures over the past seven years; and to all the generous people who have contributed gifts of computers, typewriters, copiers, and other equipment that speed these words to you. And thank you, Barbara, for being here.

PREFACE

This book is written with the hope of bringing to fruition peace and harmonious relationships for all beings.

The teachings and meditations shared herein are based upon the traditional Tsalagi* teachings, teaching stories, and games passed to me by my grandparents, great-grandparents, and great-aunts.

In 1969, after generations of secrecy, it was decided to share the teachings of the Tsalagi tradition with non-Native people, so that our children would have water to drink and a place to walk. The intention is to strengthen individuals' relationships with their families, communities, nations, and the land, the Earth herself. We do not invite people to become Indians. We invite people to be in good fellowship and to respect the teachings of their family of origin. Thus may we all cooperate in manifesting a vision of peace.

These teachings are of a foundation level, suitable for all people of any religion or nationality committed to peace and good relationship. Thus we maintain the sanctity of the clan laws about what teachings are available to non-Native people.

My hope is that these words will inspire many people to right action that will benefit all beings, now and in future generations.

The material presented in this book is based on lectures and teaching materials from the years 1978–1985, shared with general audiences and particularly with members of the community and student body of Sunray Meditation Society, a *gadugi* (society) affiliated with Igidotsoiyi Tsalagi Gadugi (Three Sisters Gadugi) of the Etowah Band of the Eastern Tsalagi Nation.

*Tsalagi (pronounced Tsa-lá-gi) is used for "Cherokee" throughout this book.

xi

While the teachings come to you in the English language, they are rooted in the cycle of relationships of the Tsalagi mind. So in this work the reader will perceive discernible patterns of repetition with subtle variations. As part of the traditional teaching method, these formal patterns and interrelationships ensure understanding and appreciation of the teachings on many levels.

When we were being taught these things as children—myself, especially, as one chosen to be a lineage holder—much of the teaching was through diagrams drawn in the earth and the placement of natural objects in certain designs, such as a triangle with ten stones inside. Chanting and drumming were also a significant part of the learning, balancing activity of the right and left hemispheres of the brain; thus one immediately perceived the thought that was being shared.

These traditional methods of teaching are reflected here, in a manner of presentation that is very different from the linear, conceptual, analytic European style. The Tsalagi teaching, like the Tsalagi conception of reality, is a circle, and I am speaking to you, the reader, as if to my relatives, sharing with you the wisdom of our ancestors.

These are teachings from an oral tradition. They have been whispered, spoken, chanted, drummed and danced for hundreds of thousands of years, and they are imbued with the mystery of starlight, firelight, dawnlight. For the first time now these sacred teachings are conveyed in writing. May they kindle within your heart a great joy in the gift of life; in having friends, family, co-workers, a community to live and learn with; and in the opportunity to renew in this time the Sacred Hoop of life on this planet.

The basis of the teaching is to infuse each moment with the three fundamental principles of intention, compassion, and doing good. These three principles and their relationship with individuals, families, nations, and the universe are essential concepts in the Tsalagi worldview, and they inform every part of the teaching. They are often referred to as the Elder Fires Above or the "three sacred fires" of will, love, and active intelligence. Each teaching gives at least seven reminders of how these primary principles manifest in our lives. Thus, for each major section of the teachings presented here, seven examples are given, three directly related to the principles and four related to cycles of relationships. This formal pattern of repetition, like a sacred stitch, weaves a strong fabric of understanding.

Each chapter can be read as a self-contained whole, yet the chapters also move in sequence, and the reader is invited to trace common threads through the book as a whole.

And the words themselves, they are a small part of the interaction of reader with teachings. The words are like a carrier wave for wisdom's pure light.

In Tsalagi worldview, life and death, manifestation and formlessness, are all within the circle, which spirals out through all dimensions. The teaching expresses that expansion of the spiral. The same story can be understood in various ways as one is exploring vaster dimensions of mind.

Even time and history dance along the spiral. Patterns of the past echo in the present and resound through the future. Our time-keeping system (which is essentially the same as the Mayan or Aztec calendar) reflects the spiral as interlocking wheels of energy and consciousness ever in majestic motion together. Throughout the oral tradition and the written history of the Tsalagi there are certain teachers who continue to manifest in the Americas in regularly repeating cycles of time. These teachers express the same essence, the same wisdom, and come at appropriate times to remind the people of harmony. This cyclical reincarnation of pure mind is still going on. As the Pale One, the Peacemaker, and Quetzalcoatl walked upon this land, so shall there arise in our time a teacher of great compassion to rekindle the wisdom fire of right relations for all people.[1]

There are many similarities between the Tsalagi worldview and those of Buddhism, Christianity, Judaism. All people and all religions trace their roots to the one Great Tree of Peace. Yet many people know little of the true history and content of Native American philosophy and religion, and what little is known is likely to be inaccurate. May you read this book with an open mind and without attachment to any previous ideas or concepts about what Native Americans are.

For the reader to think that by reading a book about Tsalagi philosophy she or he will understand the whole mind of Indian people would be an error. I hope that this book will mirror the wisdom of your own mind and your own lineage, through your perceiving the "like patterns"—common factors of human condition and mind.

Native American philosophy—be it Tsalagi or any other— has many levels of understanding. The practices presented in this book are appropriate for all people; they will not cause harm when practiced according to the instructions given. The deeper rituals, ceremonies, and practices of Native people, such as the pipe and the purification lodge (sweat lodge), are intended for Native people, and to seek to imitate them is both dangerous and disrespectful. These are the high mysteries of our peoples, as sacred to us as is the mass to Roman Catholics. May you contemplate the Great Mystery through the windows that are open before you and see in the continuum of your own life the signposts marking the Beauty Path.

In these times Native American people are confronted daily with cultural and physical genocide. In this very moment the Native people of this hemisphere are pawns in the multinational corporations' concept of progress and profits. May you consider the mass relocations of Native Americans in North America and the frightening genocide of Native people in Central America, and recognize that this cruelty could also happen in your neighborhood if we as human beings allow our hearts to be hardened to the suffering of any of our relatives.

So I hope that each reader of this book will look deeply into the patterns woven by our thought and action and develop mindfulness and generosity for the future generations. May compassion arise within your heart and may you see all beings as your relatives in this dream of life.

The opportunity of life is very precious and it moves very quickly. May these words inspire you to right action in relieving the suffering of the peoples of the world. May all beings realize freedom from suffering and all conflicting thoughts reach resolution, that the great Fire of Wisdom may burn in our hearts and shine forth in all we do, as enlightened action benefitting all our relations.

VOICES OF OUR ANCESTORS

INTRODUCTION

We Cherokee, or Tsalagi, have traditionally called ourselves the Principal People (Ani Yun Wiwa), in that our creation stories and philosophy refer to our sacred duty to instill
light, to manifest good for the benefit of all beings.

We trace our origins to the stars known as the Pleiades, the
Seven Dancers. Encoded within our ceremonies and patterns
of relationship is the Fire of Wisdom, hence we are the fire-
keepers of the sacred light, responsible for rekindling the fire
of clear mind and right relationship in these changing times.

The teachings contained in this volume are put forth by
one who is of the fifth generation to survive the coming of
darkness upon the Tsalagi's natural way of life.[1] Children of
the fifth generation were given special duties by their elders
to rekindle the sacred wisdom fire, by inviting the people to
see the effects of our thoughts and actions upon the Earth,
upon ourselves and one another, and upon future generations. Our elders, some of whom suffered great deprivations
and punishments for seeking to maintain our culture, encoded in us through ceremony, song and example the methods of realizing a sane world.

Until 1979 it was illegal in the United States for Native
Americans to practice their traditional religions. In 1978 the
U.S. Congress considered legislating the unilateral abroga-
tion of all existing Native treaties, taking away what little yet
remained of the land base of the sovereign Indian nations.
This would have forced the death of Native culture, for the
very basis of Indian religion, language, relationships, and life
is sacred practice upon the land, sacred relationship with the
land. In 1979 the American Indian Religious Freedom Act
was passed, permitting Native Americans to practice their
traditional rituals and ceremonies once again. Many of the
fifth generation perceived the passing of this act as an at-

1

tempt to make palatable the destruction of the Indian land base. Although the 1978 bill did not pass into law, it stirred the fifth generation to act as their elders had hoped.[2] For many Native peoples the attempt to break all treaties and steal the remaining land base was the awakening of their "Indianness." With the realization of how close we had come to extinction and assimilation, renewed study of Native language, philosophy, medicine, and religion began. The Tsalagi are but one of many Native nations currently growing and flourishing.

This book is dedicated to those wise elders who had the faith and foresight to keep the wisdom fire burning.

Myself, I am a Tsalagi of the Etowah Band, a vessel filled with dreams of those who walked before, blessed and empowered by the elders to be a repository of the teachings of the Ywahoo lingeage.

The Ywahoo lineage was established 2,860 years ago by the "Keeper of Mysteries," the Pale One, a great teacher whose name is spoken only in ceremonies. When the people had forgotten their original instructions, neglected their spiritual duties, and become warlike, the Pale One came to rekindle the sacred wisdom fire. Born in a miraculous manner, his body emitted great light; he appeared in many places at once and he spoke the language of all creatures. The teachings of the Pale One flourished throughout the Americas. He reestablished the building of temples and schools, reformed the priestcraft training, and gave methods for cultivating and maintaining peace within individual, family, clan, nation, and planet. This great teacher was a living reminder of the unmanifest potential in all. He rekindled the holy fire and renewed the original instructions encoded within the Crystal Ark, that most sacred crystal that ever sings out harmony's beauteous note, inspiring people to act as one with the sacred law and bringing all thoughts and actions to harmonious resolution.[3]

The duties of each Ywahoo are to care for the Crystal Ark and to maintain ceremonies for universal balance. Thus the

Ywahoo lineage is the caretaker of the crystal and of the crystal-activating sound formulas and rituals.

There have been twenty-seven Ywahoos entrusted to maintain the teachings, to ensure methods of stabilizing the mind in times of confusion. Thus the teachings outlined within this book have been maintained and transmitted through the Ywahoo lineage for twenty-seven generations. They were passed to me, Dhyani Ywahoo, by my grandfather, Eonah Fisher (Bear Fishing), who received the teachings from Eli Ywahoo, his father-in-law, my great-grandfather (also known as Rain Cloud), and from my grandmother, Nellie Ywahoo, daughter of Rain Cloud.

From an early age the insight of Tsalagi children is recognized and they are invited into particular spiritual societies according to their clans and the particular lineages moving within those clans. The Ywahoo lineage is of the Ani Gadoahwi (Wild Potato) Clan of the Tsalagi Nation. My ancestors, the relatives who taught me, are from the Carolinas and Tennessee. During the Trail of Tears, which occurred in the 1830s, rather than leave their honored homeland they hid in caves, that they might maintain their spiritual duty to the Blue Mountains and the rivers and land of that region.

So the things I speak are of a continuum. Myself, I am a firstborn daughter of a firstborn daughter. The medicine tradition[4] that was kept by my family is the tradition of the Tsalagi people, traced back through the times of the sun temples. So we consider ourselves a very ancient people; our history speaks of over a hundred thousand years of relationship to the planet Earth.

In the Tsalagi view, children are valued members of the society, and from the moment they make their first smile they are invited to partake in spiritual ceremony and responsible action for the good of all the people. That first smile is an indication of the child's willingness to reach out and communicate with others, and from that smile one understands what that child's gift is.

It is common among the Tsalagi and many Native American

3

nations that before a child is born the grandparents have visions and dreams about that coming child. My grandparents also had visions. They say that a Red man came from across the ocean carrying a message of unity, of rebuilding the sacred hoop. He spoke of me, saying that I would travel around the world and that I should be given all of their teachings. The elders followed those instructions. While I was a child my elders would sit around the fire and make many prophecies. They said a time would come when I would speak to people from all over the world, and that we would be of one heart. The prophecies have proven true. Now may the prophecy of unity of action and a shared concern for life renew the sacred hoop, as they foretold.

Prior to 1969, the Ywahoo lineage teachings were hidden, shared only with Tsalagi and other like-minded peoples.

According to the ancient teachings and calendar, a great darkness would fall upon the peoples with the end of the cycle of worlds called the thirteen heavens.[5] Over five hundred years ago a Council of Elders of the Red Nations of North, South, and Central America was called to ensure the survival of the sacred teachings through the coming age of darkness. At that time the teachings were hidden within the home fires, in secret societies within family lines, to sustain the people through times of tribulation. The thirteen heavens ended April 21, 1519, the day Cortés landed in Mexico. Thus a "pale brother returned from the east,"[6] his memory of the unity of the human family impaired, and his coming wrought great destruction upon the land and the people. The science and culture that spawned the world's most accurate calendar and most beneficial pharmacopoeia and, over seven thousand years ago, discovered the mathematical concept of zero, was stomped into the dust. Yet the wisdom survived within the home fireplaces, awaiting a time when the people would be of one heart, awaiting sturdy vessels to carry the fire out.

The great Smoky Mountains, Arkansas, Georgia, and Tennessee have been homeland to the Tsalagi Nation for thousands of years. During the early 1800s, as the settlers encroached upon the sacred areas and forced the people on the Trail of Tears, the darkest night fell. (The seventh hell began in 1831; the Indian Removal Act was ratified in May 1830.)

It was spoken to me at an early age about the Trail of Tears; my grandmother described it to me so vividly that I felt I was there. She said that people—soldiers and settlers—came into the cabins and threw the people out, took whatever was belonging to the Tsalagi people and just said, "Go with the clothes on your back." Even their food stores were kept from them. And what amazed me, as a young child listening to the wisdom of the elders, is that they spoke without bitterness. They described the Trail of Tears as an indication of dark times for the mind of *all* human beings, the beginning of a final cycle of purification. In this era, illusions of domination over the natural world and materialism in place of ethics have choked the lifeline of all.

As the darkness fell upon the Tsalagi people, some priests and priestesses self-immolated the physical form in the sacred fire. It was recounted to me by my elders how two members of my family thus stepped into the fire and disappeared, leaving no physical remains. Their sacrifice was to scatter the seed essence of the original instructions, to sprout again as the fifth generation appeared to reestablish right relationship with the land, the nation, Mother Earth, Father Sky, and all our relations. In the minds of myself and others of the fifth generation were carefully placed certain keys, that we might again stir and rekindle the sacred fire in all people, so the hoop of life could be renewed.

Thus for hundreds of years the sacred teachings were kept hidden. During 1969, elders of the Etowah Band and the Ywahoo bloodline conferred and decided that the general aspects of the teaching were now to be shared with all those of good heart who were dedicated to manifesting peace. The elders stated that the astronomical teachings were to be restored to the world; these are the basis for understanding the movements of the stars that give order to the ceremonial calendar shared by most Native peoples of the western hemisphere. The elders said that the Medicine of the Twins was to be understood by all, so that even anger and fear could be recognized as opportunities to realize that clear wisdom fire within. And they said that the general teachings of the Pale One were to be shared, to give light to a new day.

These things are being done according to instructions. In 1969, Sunray Meditation Society was founded as a vehicle for the appropriate teachings of the Ywahoo lineage to be shared with those of one heart, and today students and practitioners of the Sunray teachings are flourishing as seeds of light and right relationship in communities throughout Turtle Island (North America and the world). And through this book I pray that sparks of the wisdom fire may kindle remembrance in the hearts of many.

The Tsalagi teachings of the Ywahoo lineage convey specific areas of study and practice. There are general teachings, suitable for all types of people, which include physical, mental, and social codes or values. There are teachings that are specific to particular clans, taught only to members of these clans; these include codes of behavior, bloodline duties, rituals, traditional stories, and teachings for protection and survival. There are particular teachings for nations, governmental law based upon clan law, to aid in maintaining peace and planetary balance. Then there is a particular method of training used in the priestcraft, entailing ten steps of development and example.

This book contains teachings suitable for all people—basic *Elo* (philosophy) and practice for purifying ignorance and obscuration, for clarifying mind, for pacifying afflicting emotions, illusions, and suffering, for magnetizing the good, and for actualizing the vision of peace and harmony held as a sacred ember within the heart of every being. Native American religion does not proselytize or seek converts. These sacred teachings call upon you, not to become an Indian, but to become the best human being you can possibly be, to fulfill your unmanifest potential for the good of all beings.

I pray that these teachings be conveyed clearly for the benefit of all my relations, whether flying, walking, swimming, or crawling. May it be known that any inconsistencies or ambiguities herein with respect to historical chronology are the result of my own limitations or of destruction and/or confusion in the ancient records. The teachings themselves are true and offer means for realizing peace on all levels.

We have been in the ninth and final stage of purification, the ninth hell world following the thirteen heavens. And in this time the fifth generation, living in a natural way, is keeping the sacred precepts, dreaming of beauty. The fire is rekindled on Earth's holy places. The song of peaceful remembrance goes forth. A new day is dawning. The new cycle of thirteen heavens began August 30, 1987, thirteen days after Fifth World ended. Now I pray that each one of you may perceive the vision of peace and have the will and courage and compassion to manifest it. May the thoughts that obscure the inherent beauty be transmuted, revealing the means of right relationship. And may you be called forth as a Peacekeeper, turning aside anger, shame and blame, calling forth harmony and joy for all relations.

ᏕᏃᏣᎦᏱᎯᏍᏛ

Ga lu lo hi gi ni du da

Sky our Grandfather

ᏄᏣᎦᏴᎯᎵᏏ

Nu da wa gi ni li si

Sun our Grandmother

ᏲᏣᎦᏴᎠᏓ

E lo hi gi ne tse

Earth our Mother

ᏕᎵᏞᎵᏕ

Ga li? e li ga

I am thankful

ᏏᏴᎯᎮᎦ̃

Si gi ni gé yu

We love each other

ᏬᎢᎵᏕᎵᏕ

O sa li he li ga

We are grateful

1

THE PEOPLE OF THE FIRE

TSALAGI ELO—our philosophy, our oral tradition—tells how the Principal People, the Ani Yun Wiwa,
originated in the star system known as the Pleiades, whence
first arose the spark of individuated mind.

From the mysterious void came forth a sound, and the
sound was light, and the light was will, intention to be, born
of the emptiness: "Creator Being," fundamental tone of the
universal song, underlying all manifestation. Compassionate
wisdom arose as will perceived the unmanifest potential of
mind streaming forth. Will and compassion together gave
birth to the fire of building intelligence, and thus was formed
the sacred triangle from which all matter is derived, the
Three in One. It is a Mystery, we say.

The first "thought beings," *tla* beings, carriers of mind's
pure light, existed like cells in one body, of one mind and purpose: to explore the mysteries of mind. Coalescing along
twelve vortices of activity, elemental lines of energy or force,
mind took form, the One became the many. Star Woman fell
to Earth, opening the way for star beings to manifest upon

9

Earth the light of pure mind. The Three Elder Fires precipitated the planets and the animals, while the people were the dream children of the angels, their dreaming arising with the primordial sound.

The twelve original tribes of the Tsalagi Nation each exemplified a particular vortex of activity, a particular creative energy, all moving cohesively together.

Tribe	Activity/Energy
1	Quality of will. Crystal caretakers, maintaining clear thought and rituals to keep form in order. Timekeepers, drummers.
2	The healers, caretakers, high teachers; the Peace Chief who never sheds blood.
3	Those with understanding of sacred geometry and astronomy, watchers of the skies, giving instruction on proper building.
4	Masons, builders of the form shaped by the Three. Local administrators, responsible for good clan and community relations. Craftspeople, creating objects of beauty for prayer, contemplation, and utility.
5	The scientists, mastering and teaching the wisdom of particulars; observing patterns and possible futures.
6	Great caretakers of the temples and holy gardens where the sacred food is grown for the communities. Keepers and manifesters of the ritual form.
7	Sacred warriors, warring on ignorance; the shakers, transformers, life force makers; guardians of correct action.

8   Ambassadors with other realms, having access to consciousness (this the Ani Gadoah are particularly known for, with their great accessibility to other realms). Planetary understanding; assisting in planetary weather system, distributing energy for the benefit of all beings.

9   Communicating with stars, creating inventions for clear communication. May bring forth new plants to feed the people. Expressing a more ethereal manifestation of the conscious building seen in the third line of force. Magnetizers, world shapers.

Of the tenth, eleventh, and twelfth lines of force we do not speak, for their function is beyond words; it cannot be cognized.

These star people came to Earth in Elohi Mona, five islands in the Atlantic Ocean, later known as Atlantis.

Before the star people came there were great waters upon the land, and male and female still existed in one body. There was emotional nature but not yet the mind to actualize and complete the intention of Earth being a place of learning, a place of dreaming what is good. So the purpose of individuation of mind and the descent from the stars was to quicken life upon the Earth. The star energy came to spark the fire of mind, that all might return again to the Mystery. The human being is much like the salmon; we all come forth from the lake of clear mind; we swim out into the ocean of experience, with its many lessons and opportunities and illusions—and as the salmon finds again the stream that leads it back to its spawning ground, so too must human beings find and follow the stream that will bring them again to the vast clear light.

The star children, the Sacred Seven, primary energizers, were greeted by the Children of the Sun, already living upon Earth, in the Americas. They had been attuned, through crystal and sound, to receive the inpouring of pure mind carried by the star beings. The Sun Children were the true Earth people, in that they first experienced individuated mind while on Earth, as the dream children of the star beings. The first to come forth from the Pleiades were the Adawees, great angelic beings; in contemplating form, in dreaming, they precipitated the Earth and its peopling in concordance with the great principle of creation. It is taught in this way that all human life originated in the Americas, whereas the Sacred Seven originated as seeds of pure mind in another star system.

That the seed of pure mind might become firmly rooted upon the Earth, it was decided by the Adawees, the Seven Before the Throne on High, that those who came from the stars were to marry and bring forth children with the Children of the Sun, and that at some time those of Earth would come to full ascendancy. It was known that in this process there would be periods of great travail and confusion until there was clear recognition of mind, that sacred fire burning bright within all people.

What we see today is that prophecy come true. Those who believe in the primacy of matter seek to manipulate and curtail the fire of clear mind and spirit. Mind of separation, mind of domination, these have birthed genocide of Native peoples throughout the world, the Inquisition and the Nazi holocaust in Europe, the destruction of lands, cultures, and peoples in Asia, and the invention of weaponry with power to kill all people on Earth twenty times over. In the Tsalagi teachings such great sufferings are seen as unnecessary. They are the result of pride, the idea that one is better or more important than another. In reality, in the circle of right relationship, there is no above and no below, no in or out; all are together in the sacred circle.

Thus the Sacred Seven intermarried with the Children of the Sun, the Earth people. Their descendants in North America are the Tsalagi, Creek, Choctaw, Yuchi, and other

12

Red nations of the southeastern United States, each nation having a particular function in the hoop of life.

The islands and civilization of Elohi Mona were eventually destroyed through the arrogance and ignorance of those who abused the sacred power, seeking to enslave others. Through lust and grasping, a few carriers of the starseed became enmeshed in the material world; instead of seeking to educate and enlighten, they sought to manipulate and oppress. Such thought forms were antagonistic to the very elements holding the people and the islands together. The form would no longer hold them, for they went against the sacred law, which is cohesive. Thus over a ten-thousand-year period the islands began breaking up and the great migrations of the people began. It is in this way that five of the original twelve tribes were lost and their seed dispersed throughout the remaining seven tribes (or "types" of people). From these seven tribes many people in North America today can trace some affinity to the Tsalagi Nation.

The people found their way through South and Central America and eventually met with people living in what is now called the Four Corners area.[1] There were many migrations. Similarities in Native languages throughout the Americas are indications of common origins and meetings.[2] Before the coming of the Europeans, just in North America alone there were over 587 different Native nations and languages; in the 1600s there were some sixty million Red people in what is now called the United States. Now there are perhaps two million. This is the result of deliberate genocidal destruction of life, land, language, science, art, religion—a result of people ignoring or fighting the natural wisdom light, forgetting that all humans are relatives and that we all are to care for one another and for our mother, the Earth.

In the course of the many migrations people settled in groups in different places, yet their common roots may be known and honored. Long ago the Tsalagi and the Iroquois were one people, for example, and in the Tsalagi language the root stock, Algonquin, is still discernible. Tsalagi and Maya once shared the same religious practices; the Mayan seed and nobility was of the star people also. The two peoples diverged over the Aztec imposition of rituals of blood sacrifice upon the peaceful religion and way of life of the Principal People. Such practices were not part of the original teaching, and much of the community of spiritual relationship and exchange among these peoples ended when the Aztecs "conquered" the Mayans.

Thus the mound builders, the temple keepers of the Americas, trace their migrations to the land of Elohi Mona. In North America they built a strong creative culture and civilization, from the southeastern and southwestern parts of the present United States up into Canada. The mound society, or temple society, was composed of four levels of people. The Sun People were the rulers, in that they very clearly manifested the light of clear mind for the benefit of all; then there were the nobles, the average people, and the "stinkards." The stinkards were those who may not have honored the clarity of mind or allowed the fire to burn brightly; they probably did the work of butchering, tanning, and so on.

That all future generations might be infused with clear mind, all Sun People were required to marry stinkards, ensuring that the spark of wisdom fire would move throughout all levels of the people. This sacred purpose is still honored today in the manner in which the Ywahoo lineage is passed. There was once a family bloodline lineage that amassed great power; they were great magicians who abused the rights of the people, who then rose up and scattered and destroyed them. Thereafter it was decided that the lineage would pass, not to first daughter or son, but to appropriate family member, in-law, or one adopted into the family. The lineage was passed in this way from Eli Ywahoo to his son-in-law Eonah Fisher, my grandfather. So it is that the holy duty to instill light continues to be fulfilled.

The temple society existed before the time of Christ. When De Soto arrived in the Mississippi Valley and found the beauteous and clean cities of the Tsalagi, he sought their wealth and captured their female leader.[3] The average mound-building city had no more than 18,000 to 25,000 inhabitants (except during ceremonial times, when all people came) because it was considered very important that no area be overburdened. While the decline of the sun temples began with the coming of the Europeans, the theocracy continued until the Forced Removal in the 1830s. The existing temples continued to be maintained until that time, although no new ones appear to have been built after the Conference of Elders preceding the first hell in A.D. 1531.[4] Some Tsalagi continued to keep the old ways, even into the present. They became the Kituwa Society and the Etowah Band, and some small traditional communities in Oklahoma.[5]

When I was a young child listening to our elders speak about the true history of North America, I stood with my feet firmly planted on the ground, in the now, and realized that they were speaking great truths. I thought it odd that others did not know or understand or believe these truths; even today I think it odd. This true history will emerge again and be known by all. There are Native scholars now studying and recovering our history,[6] and ancient documents and books of our people, stolen from this land, are preserved in the archives of the Vatican and Spanish museums, taken there by those who feared revelation of the magnitude of the destruction they had wrought. When our elders spoke of these things there was never bitterness or blame as they expressed the brutalization and genocide committed upon Native peoples. They were simply stating what had occurred, that the truth might be known.

Our elders also told me that long before the white men made their appearance upon the shores of Turtle Island, other visitors had come. In the great long time ago, the Black people came from Africa; they came to visit, to look, and they also came to conquer—but they found people who were self-empowered and without a need for domination, and so they were unable to conquer. Also, they were turned aside by the

15

energy of the Uk-kuk-a-duk, or Ukdena, the great dragons that used to protect this land, who have now moved into another dimension.

The connection between these dragons and the mind of humans is significant for our understanding in these changing times. The dragons were energy moving in the wave pattern of Earth's energy. They used to follow the will of the great medicine people who, with certain crystals, would call them to turn aside dangerous activity and thus protect the people. The medicine people became too few to give them proper guidance, and the dragons became weaker and weaker; many were tied into the mountains, and the intelligent ones vibrated themselves into another dimension. The last dragon was seen in the Smoky Mountains in the 1700s.

Basically, the dragon is the unconscious of all nations, the untamed energies of anger and fear, waiting to be called into the light of clear thought. Until people awaken to their own minds, the dragon appears to be dangerous; when emotions are tamed, the dragon becomes a winged angelic being.

So it is not the dragon that is evil, and knowing one's true power and the movement of clear mind in one's own being is not evil. Evil is thoughtless action, evil is what causes harm to others. Evil begins in the heart of ignorance and the desire to dominate. So we teach the young ones that nothing is above or below; the leader and the community are ever in a reciprocal relationship. Our most sacred teachers, our most sacred leaders, they are like a walking stick; they steady the people, who are like the body holding the walking stick, so they find safe passage, yet they are guided along by the people themselves. The Six Nations Confederacy is based upon this concept of leadership,[7] and it was borrowed from the teachings of the Peacemaker for the writing of the U.S. Constitution. It would be well for all of us to search within our hearts again for the true meaning of leadership and right relationship. A leader is not to dominate; a leader is to guide like a walking stick, that the nations and all the people may move firmly on the road of good relations.

The history of North America as written by non-Natives is incomplete, for it is written by those who think they are conquerors. The conqueror is the person who looks outside himself to make order rather than making clear his own mind; therefore, all that he sees and speaks is based on the lies of pride and confusion. The Native people, particularly the Tsalagi people, had a philosphy and a written language probably before the people of Europe were emerging from their caves. The calendar of the Americas is the oldest calendar in the world and one of the most accurate. The first people to understand the significance of zero were the Native American people, through careful meditation and observation of the universe.

Medicine was and still is a very highly developed art among the Native people; ninety percent of the world's pharmacopoeia is derived from the medicines of the Red people of the western hemisphere. And over 130 of the foods that are eaten around the world were first cultivated in the Americas; in the Land of the Hummingbird, the Amazon Basin, and in the high Andes Mountains, that is where it began. Corn, tomatoes, beans and squash, all of these things originated here. People tended gardens. Even now in various Native American nations different types of sacred corn, beans, and squash seeds are kept until the appropriate people come to plant them, care for them, and distribute them to others. In the traditional way of life gardens were a ceremonial event for all, an opportunity to give to the Earth as well as to receive. The seeds of good food are also the seeds of good relationship, so caretaking the garden is symbolic of caretaking all beings. The garden can be an offering to all.

Native religion is a whole way of life, based on everything being in relationship. The sacred rituals are to maintain harmonious balance of the energy currents of sun, moon, Earth, the entire universe, so that the seed's bounty can be brought forth. Contemplating this orderly, harmonious universe, ten thousand years ago our ancestors here in the Americas were able to develop a mathematics and an astronomy that reached

17

the highest level. These are things that archaeologists are beginning to learn only now. And it is good that these truths be rediscovered and made known, for the wisdom of our ancestors is a gift to *all* the children of Earth, that we, too, may be wise and generous in creating a good future for those not yet born.

THE TEACHINGS OF THE PALE ONE

The ages of darkness are times of opportunity for human beings to understand the gifts of mind and the creative potential of our thinking, to bring correct our thoughts and actions, to choose what is good and to walk upon a path of beauty. In 873 B.C., as the people began to forget some of these wise teachings, there came again to the Smoky Mountains, to the people of the Tsalagi, one that we call the Pale One. He was fair-skinned, born of a woman who knew no man; her grandmother dreamed of miracles to come, and they waited and saw that the granddaughter was with child, although they lived alone. They knew that it was a special blessing, that the child was seed of the stars, coming again to quicken the action of right relationship in the hearts of all the people. Many sky beings came to celebrate the birth of this child; he was received with great grace and great care and raised in a special manner.

The Pale One rekindled the sacred fires and reaffirmed to the people the basic principles of creation, that the temples might ever resound with the light of clear mind and the people live in harmony with the Earth and one another. He left many prophecies and wondrous teachings. Some of his prophecies refer to this stage of time, known by the Tsalagi and Meso-American calendar as the ninth and final stage of purification. By this ancient calendar we are now at the end of the Fifth World, preparing ourselves to enter the Sixth World, a world of clear relationship and right understanding where each one takes care of the other and the sacred sound will precipitate what is needed by the people.

18

Before that day arises we each have a duty to cast out our doubt, to turn aside our ignorance and come again to realize that the spark of clear mind, the creative principle, the Great Mystery, is within ourselves. That mystery is unmanifest potential, the void, the emptiness, indicated in the sacred calendar by the oval glyph in the center. It is also zero. With the understanding of zero came again clear relationship to the power of mind—because from the emptiness comes forth your dream, through the vortex of sound, through the energy of will, through the power of clear intention, through the wisdom of equanimity and compassion, through right action that builds and brings things to clear conclusion. These three building fires exist within each of us, as spirals of energy ever moving, ever bringing forth the fruits of our intention and desire. They are the grace of Asga Ya Galunlati, Creator Being, moving within, vivifying spirit, animating form.

The Pale One reminded the people how to live in harmony with these fundamental truths of creation. He instructed them in the five sacred rituals shared by all Native American peoples, means to maintain most pure mind. Smoke offerings clarify mind and environment; on the smoke one's prayers and action are dedicated to the good of all, and the smoke carries the prayer to all realms. The Pale One particularly instructed the people in the use of tobacco and cedar as offerings. Rituals of fasting and sweating are offerings made to purify body and mind and to relieve the ignorance and sufferings of the people. Through sacred vigil one tends the wisdom fire, crying for vision, for the courage and compassion to walk the Beauty Path to benefit all beings. The religious practices of Native peoples are practices of sacred relationship; they involve prayerful communion with the natural elements and powers, including the Adawees, those angelic beings who are guardians of the directions, gateways of consciousness; and communal ceremonies based on the cycles of sun and moon and the movements of the stars.

Practice of sacred relationship is practice of good relations with all in the family of life. Thus the Pale One gave seven reminders to the people, that all might recall and honor the unity of the hoop:

1. What walks, swims, flies, or creeps is in relationship; the mountains, streams, and valleys and all things are related to your thought and action.

2. What occurs around you and within you reflects your own mind and shows you the dream you are weaving.

3. Three principles of awakened mind guide enlightened action: will to see the Mystery as it is; intention to manifest one's purpose for the benefit of all; courage to do what must be done.

4. Generosity of heart and action brings peace and abundance for all in the circle.

5. Respect for elders, clan, land, and nation inspires acts in harmony with the sacred law, good caretaking of the gifts received.

6. Action to benefit the land and the people unto seven generations shapes the consciousness of the Planetary Caretaker, dreaming those yet unborn, ever mindful of life's unfolding.

7. To be in good relation, transforming patterns of separation, pacifying conflicting emotions, is to experience the wisdom within, still lake of Mystery.

Arising from these teachings are the nine precepts in the Code of Right Relationship:

1. Speak only words of truth.

2. Speak only of the good qualities of others.

3. Be a confidant and carry no tales.

4. Turn aside the veil of anger to release the beauty inherent in all.

5. Waste not the bounty, and want not.

6. Honor the light in all. Compare nothing; see all for its suchness.

7. Respect all life; cut away ignorance from one's own heart.

8. Neither kill nor harbor thoughts of angry nature, which destroy peace like an arrow.

9. Do it now; if you see what needs doing, do it.

The Pale One is a cyclically incarnating being.[8] He comes when the people have forgotten their sacred ways, bringing reminders of the Law, recalling all to right relationship. He is expected soon again, and he may be alive even now. It is good.

THE PRIESTCRAFT

From the beginning the Tsalagi have always had a priestcraft tradition. The primary duty of the priests, both men and women, is to maintain the thought form of harmony and balance for all things, even for the rocks and trees, everything that shares this dream with us. Such a person does not shed blood or cultivate thoughts of an angry nature.

Traditionally, many of the priests and priestesses lived in what are called White Villages or Peace Villages, places of sanctuary where the hands were always clean of blood. This concept of sanctuary is very significant in our time, for to rekindle and understand the energy of sanctuary is to know forgiveness in oneself.

In the days before the hoop of the nation was broken, there was no need for prisons or mental hospitals because the sacred precepts and principles and the care of extended family and nation maintained harmony in the lives of the people. If

21

someone stepped outside the bounds of good law, if someone became lost, all of the relatives and friends would come to guide them. Even the most heinous criminals could make their way to the place of sanctuary, to the Peace Village or white village; there they could pass a year in ceremony and spiritual practice to remove that negative pattern of thought, that illusion based on pride, so that they could come again and be accepted as whole by all the people.[9] The mental illness of these times, as we approach the year 2000, comes from the idea that the invention, what is built by the hand, is more powerful than the person. Yet all begins in the mind. To make things right, to bring things to clarity, that is our duty, that is the gift and responsibility of the human being in this time. In this way each of us can create healing sanctuary in our own minds, in our own lives, calling all our relations to enlightened action.

Each clan had its priests and rituals, and the priests were directly responsible to the clans they represented and cared for. The wisdom within each clan (or sacred teaching school) is likened to one of the seven sacred woods from which the sacred fire is built. Thus a priest who also carries the lineage of a clan is one of those responsible for the entire nation. In the Ywahoo lineage, the lineage holder has always the duty to care for all beings in all worlds, through the generation of clear mind and teachings that enable beings to transform aggression and realize peace and right relationship.

The peace chief is one who, by training and actions, has demonstrated capacity for wise leadership. His or her primary duty is to cultivate clarity of mind. Through the learning of sound formulas and ritual movement, the mind and body can be cleared of illusions and obscurations; with mastery of the basic meditation and dance forms of the spiritual practice there arises an ability to produce light from the body. Often the peace chief is also a priest.

It is the priest's responsibility to care for the sacred crystal, which mirrors the clear light of the unmanifest becoming. Many of the priestcraft duties are based on generating energy. From an early age the children who show signs that this is their path are given special diet and training so that their nervous systems will be sensitive enough and strong enough to channel the energy of mind. Their minds are trained to maintain a clear, open relationship with plant, animal, and mineral kingdoms so they can call what is needed by the people, be it the rain or the woodland buffalo. Through the maintenance of the ceremonial cycle, rites of purification, and community celebration, groups of priests and priestesses work with crystals to generate a visible field of light, enabling the community to perceive the means of right relationship with the environment. The rituals ensure that the winds will be strong, the waters pure, the crops abundant, the people in good relationship with one another and the land. Traditionally, the temple keepers were also good mathematicians who could keep all of the cycles—of stars, sun, moon, and planets—that determined the sacred calendar and thus the ceremonial cycle, so that the people's harmonious action would benefit the Earth's internal energy.

The basic teachings of the priestcraft are presented to candidates in childhood. Initiations to deeper understanding are based upon demonstrated abilities, such as compassion, truthfulness, exceptional mindfulness, and/or dreams of the children's potential in the minds of elders.

The priestcraft training occurs in ten major phases and sixteen minor phases:

1. Development of nervous and muscular sensitivity and suppleness. The purpose of training in this phase is to keep unobscured the inherent light flows. Diet, movement, chanting, and visualization are the means, resulting in light visibly emitted from eyes and body.

2. Mindfulness of equanimity and development of communication skills with animals, trees, rivers, the natural world; healing with herbs.

3. Intelligent means to precipitate, through prayer and

ritual, what is needed for the well-being of the community (e.g., rain, abundant crops).

4. Memorization of hymns and rituals for individual and community conflict resolution; transformation of the energy of anger to right relationship.

5. Particular understanding of thought and sound vibration, enabling one to plant seeds of good cause. Affirmative thought actualized through understanding of seed sounds, blossoming as beneficial systems.

6. Devotion to ideals as expressed in Mother Crystal's song. Doubt-free action, one-pointedness in harmony with original instructions.

7. Energy to transform thought patterns of confusion, to reveal inherent clear mind.

8. Interphasing with planetary ley lines,[10] reciprocal gift-giver to children of Earth. Harmonizing national and planetary thought patterns through meditation. The shape of the inspiring helper appears according to perceiver's needs. Parent to all in Earth Mother's dream. Crystal guardian.

9. Solar matrix communication; red and blue become as white, born in every moment.

10. Self, lost in the vastly vast Mystery. Unmade, making, beyond thought is the Mystery.

There are sixteen subtle stairs leading to the temple plaza, sixteen zeroes, empty and full. One may perceive "it all" in one to seven lifetimes, after which one may choose to become Mother-Father of all, as a planet or star world.

When one is ready to become a priest or priestess, after many years of instruction and training, there are tests that are made, particularly of one's ability to generate light for the people. The ancient temples had no interior light; they were lit up by the seven or twelve wise people who sat in them. Even today that energy can be manifested. Our spiritual practice develops an energy field of light so that we recognize our relationship in many dimensions. To be a Mother-Father for the people, to be an island for those in need, that is the purpose of the priestcraft training. My grandmother Nellie Ywahoo was a priestess, taught by her father. She lit up the world and now she is a planet; she is an island for those in need.

The temple people lived in a very ordered and very caring way. As they moved around they made their sacred mounds and sacred spaces so that always their relationship with the star family could be kept. To this day throughout the Americas there are many large edifices, mounds, and shapes such as serpents that are meant to be seen from above the land. My elders recently told me that there used to be many more sky-walkers and that we young people are to practice so that we can again walk in the sky and rekindle our family relationship with the people of the stars.

Thus from the beginning the temple keepers, the priests and priestesses, have been keeping the focus of life and mind for the benefit of all. The sun temples themselves still existed well into the 1600s, while the sacred tradition of the priestcraft has continued throughout and is still a living tradition in this present time.

To this very day the sacred fire of the Tsalagi people still burns, rededicated by the Pale One and tended by the people for thousands of years. The Tsalagi and the Hopi are keepers of the sacred fire in this hemisphere. The fire has burned as long as the people have existed; it has never gone out. It was carefully tended and carried even during the Trail of Tears. That fire is the breath of life, it is the manifestation of pure mind, it is the clear light of things in their essential truth. The fire is the strength of the people, a symbol of the wisdom fire carried here from the Pleiades. Its significance, the fact that it has kept burning, is the energy that has kept this planet intact. Scientists still cannot explain fire. It is the Mystery made manifest, it is the stirring of thought into action. In recent years, from the main Tsalagi fire other fires have been lit. It is very beneficial to all of us that this fire is being kindled and tended in other places, for it is a spark of our pure nature, recalling us to enlightened action. That fire of clear mind is in everyone, and to remove any obscuration of its clarity is the duty of all people in this time, that each one may remember and find our way again to the source of our being.

We are the temple keepers. Our priestcraft went underground in the 1880s and families have been keeping that sacred wisdom for this moment, when all people choose to be reunited as human beings dedicated to peace. So now we speak again of the sacred craft, weaving a tapestry of beauty. Each one carries the seed of truth; our shared life is the garden in which to plant and bring it forth.

The sacred teachings of the Tsalagi people encompass a 100,000 year time period, during which there have been four great upheavals of Earth's life forms. The first was a change of direction in Earth's rotation and polarity, caused by a large comet and its attendant radiation destroying and mutating many life forms. The second change was brought about by intense winds arising from people's confused thought and action, distorting the Earth's mantle. It was during the second change that beings who were once male and female in one body separated into different entities, and are even now looking for their other halves. The third change was due to volcanic action stirred by the destruction of Earth's sister planet that once dwelt between Mars and Jupiter. The volcanic action forced humans to live beneath the ground for generations, subsisting on transparent fish and fungi. The fourth change was wrought by water as the human types sought to integrate emotion and mind power. This was the time of destruction of Atlantis, Elohi Mona, and during this age only those who heeded the voice of truth within were able to avoid destruction by reaching the high places. According to Tsalagi time-keeping we are now in the Fifth World, the ninth and final stage of purification, and entering the Sixth World, the time of reintegration of the people and the land.

So at this moment we are on the threshold of a new world. According to the ancient calendar of the western hemisphere, on August 16, 1987, we leave the last cycle of nine hells, and on August 30, 1987, we enter the first of the new cycle of thirteen heavens. This calendar is most accurate; it considers the movement of Venus, Mars, and the Earth around the sun, and Sirius and the Pleiades.[11] These star systems give forth a crystal voice singing out throughout all worlds, reminding us to come again to the circle of right relationship. Star songs call forth a vision of peace, the morning star a reminder of the Peacemaker's promise that all may trace their roots to the Great Tree of Peace. Just as seed grows fruitful when planted by the stars' signs, so the seed thought of planetary peace has taken root. May it sprout through all heavens. May each one cultivate caretaker mind, caretaking one another and the Earth herself. Let us each consider our actions unto seven generations. Thus a new age begins.

Human beings have the opportunity to exercise the creative power of intellect. Some of men's inventions have gone astray and run wild; such inventions as armaments and pollutants threaten the existence of life. Just as these inventions arise first as destructive thoughts of control and domination, so may your mind give birth to creative means of reconciliation and transformation. You make a difference. Know that the very thing which disturbs your mind's peace offers opportunity to generate clear mind and transform patterns of disturbance for all. Replace your anger with care; defuse potential destructive energy by clarifying conflicts in your own mind and relationships. By the force of resonance that clarification will expand through your individual relationships to your family and neighborhood, to the nation and the planet.

A new day arises, spawned by our thoughts and deeds—seed thoughts of peace moistened by love, tilled by right action, weeds of discord pulled by diligent action. The harvest shall be abundant joy sustaining future generations. The first heaven opens its gates for all who will cultivate enlightened action.

27

ᏓᎳᏪᎯ ᎠᏂᎮᏁᎭ

A da we hi   a ne he ne ha

Wise Protectors they are giving

ᏙᎯᎤᎠᎳᏂ

Do hi u a iu ni

Serenity it resounds

ᎣᎶᎯᎠᎵᎦᎷᎶᎯᎤᎾᏔ

O lo hi a li ga lu lo hi u nah ta

Mother Earth and Father Sky are giving

ᎦᎵᎡᎵᎦ

Ga li? e li ga

I am thankful

ᎣᏏᏓᏛ

O sa da dv

It is well

2

VOICES OF OUR ANCESTORS

ELO, the continuous oral and written history and philosophy of the Tsalagi people, is composed of creation stories explaining the manifestation of matter and development of living creatures; stories of right relationship and spiritual duties; specific instruction for mental and physical development; and ritual and ceremonial instructions containing sound or song formulas and methods to benefit all beings.

Creation stories are told in the quiet of winter nights, that all may see the continuous process of creation and the part our thoughts and actions play in the world's unfoldment. During times when the people neglected the original instructions, there came teachers such as the Pale One and the Peacemaker, to rekindle the fire of clear mind and remind the people of their spiritual responsibilities.

According to Tsalagi teaching, we have spun down from the realm of Galunlati, the realm of light, through the grace of Star Woman falling to Earth.

Asga Ya Galunlati, the father of all, had a beloved daughter whose beauty was as bright as a star. One day while in her father's most special garden, she heard drumming from beneath a small tree. Curious, she dug beneath the tree, creating a hole through which she fell from the Seventh Heaven, spinning down to Earth. The creatures that lived upon Earth had great emotion, deep feeling, but not yet the fire of clear mind; they were waiting for that spark of mind to come. The world then was covered with water and creatures floated precariously upon the waters. As the Star Maiden slowly spiraled down to Earth her father saw her fall; he could not call her back, so he sent supportive winds and inspired the Earth creatures to help her. The creatures saw her slowly spinning down and felt, "We must do something for her, we must find a place for her to land, because this is surely a great gift." Turtle said, "Upon my back she may land. We must make it strong and firm for her." Many creatures dove down into the waters to gather firmament from beneath the sea. One creature was successful, Water Spider, who dove deep down and brought up a bit of earth in her *tusi* bowl, made from her legs. She rose to the surface, and with her dying breath she placed her gift upon Turtle's back. Some people today recall that the firmament was brought up by lowly Muskrat; whether by Water Spider or Muskrat, the bit of earth was placed upon Great Turtle's back, and it grew and grew and grew. Great Buzzard flapped his wings, raising up mountains and valleys, and many comfortable places were made. After many days of spiraling down from the world of light, Star Woman landed upon Turtle's back. From her came life as we know it today. Her breasts gave forth corn, beans, and squash; her tears, rivers of fresh water. All humans may trace their roots to the mother of all, Star Woman. Through her blessing the spark of mind was emblazoned within us as a sacred fire, that the mystery of life might be understood as the many in the One.

This is a very important story because it makes clear that we have a relationship to many worlds of thought, and that what we see in the moment, what we call solid reality, is first determined and shaped by our thinking. Thought weaves the patterns, the tapestry that we are all living. And one mother is the mother of us all, so we are all relatives.

Star Woman carried in the emptiness of her womb twelve potential characteristics of humankind. The following crystals exemplify the qualities of the twelve original clans:

Quartz	Will
Ruby	Compassion
Topaz	Building Intelligence
Orange jasper	Manifestation of beauteous form
Emerald	Wisdom of particulars and science
Rubillite & rose quartz	Energy of devotion to manifesting the ideal
Amethyst	Energy of transformation
Pearl	Luminescent planetary mind
Fire opal	Individuated mind awake in the solar stream
Tourmaline	Awakened mindfulness of relationships beyond rings of solar system
Azurite	Energy of reconciliation
Aconite	Cycle's completion, systems unwinding, returning to emptiness

Star Woman was impregnated by fruitful winds, stirring her seed to fruition. These winds surrounded Mother Earth, obscuring light, until her sons captured the fire of inspiration, manifest as lightning flashing forth from the wings of Thunder Bird. From Star Woman first came two sons of opposite natures. One son, whose face was like ascending light, was born in the natural manner. The second son, whose face was likened to descending night, argued and fought against the natural order of things; he was born from beneath his mother's arm, causing her death. Her decaying body brought forth grasses, grains, beans, squash, all good things for the people to eat, and her tears springing forth in her time of birthing became fresh waters to drink.

Brother of the Light Face departed on a journey to gather light and find suitable places for the people's growth. The first migration began with this journey. Brother of the Dark Face captured the lightning, which he tended upon the shore, waiting for Brother of the Light Face to return from his westward journey. The creatures living upon the Earth welcomed Brother of the Light Face as the harbinger of mind. As he progressed in his migration, carrying his mother's thoughts,[1] he raised the clouds of obscuration that lay upon the planet, and light began to manifest upon Earth. Sun, moon, and stars were still but an idea, awaiting the correct rituals to remove that which obscured their forms. Brother of the Dark Face maintained the fire burning upon the shore. He sang the creation song as sent forth from the Great Crystal in anticipation of the ideal world manifesting in time and space.

This story is told in many ways to young people so that all may understand their own thought and action, how they affect other beings and how our thoughts return to us. Brother of Dark Face represents the negative thoughts that arise in all human beings. From him comes the night, which chases the sun. Yet even in his negative actions there is the seed of good; after capturing lightning's fire he tended it and awaited his brother's return. Each human being today sometimes feels buffeted between inclination to good and to harm. Even the worst person has the seed of good within, and even the most positive person can make errors from the seed of ignorance. So this story reminds us to cultivate harmony in our thoughts, words, and deeds. The Twins also show us that negative actions can be the seed of realizing the good. Because of this understanding the Native tradition does not have a belief of permanent sin. Even the most foul person can cultivate the seed of good and come to harmony with the natural world, by "testifying" to remorse, purifying his or her activities, and affirming better action. The greatest compliment that can be said of a person is that he or she is of one heart. To be of one heart is to know the balance and to be in good relationship.

To this day the human's sacred duty is to manifest the ideal of right relationship for the benefit of all beings. The ideal, the rhythmic pulse, the primary cause around which the threads of individual and group destiny spin, is to perceive the mystery of mind, relationships of inflow and outflow.

The primary tone, the foundation stone of all worlds, is sung by the quartz crystal. It is said that the quartz crystal is neither solid nor liquid; it vibrates at 786,000 pulses per millisecond, its continuum moving faster than light, its vibration the axis of the universe. A facet of spiritual practice for the Tsalagi people is observation of this energy manifested through relationships of individuals and groups with one another and the land. Sacred songs and formulas of balance resonate to the primordial tones amplified through the quartz crystal. The tempo and pitch of these ancient songs vary according to the geophysical relationship of peoples to the land. For example, one may hear a chant of the Tsalagi, a mountain woodland people, sung at a deeper pitch and slower tempo by the Lummi northwest coastal Salish peoples.[2]

Within each human being is the potential of most clear mind, which will burn brightly as the clouds of confusion, doubt, and alienation are transformed into right action. The possibilities of mind's manifestation as contained within the crystal structure and song are the road map leading again to the Vastly Vast, the source of being. Each being, gathering information about the particulars of existence, returns to the unchanging stream. In that matter is neither created nor destroyed, it is the coalescing of mind around desire and action that determines the destiny of forms. Mind flowing along the superstructure of intention, as expressed in crystal forms, precipitates the form, the pattern of one's life. In this way we are all relatives in the dream of life.

Our duty as individuals is to bring forth the unmanifest potential of peace, through understanding our own nature and our relationship to others. In the traditional Native American view, one's first duty is to flow in balance with the original instructions as radiated by the crystal from the realm of Galunlati, the realm of ideal form: to tend the seed of clear mind and right relationship with all beings. In that the One became the many to manifest the potential, it is our basic duty to understand our mind and to actualize the vision of heaven upon Earth.

All beings move along a chosen path. The Beauty Path is one of right action, with consideration for future generations. The person who has not purified emotions, thought, and action walks a confused and destructive road, reacting to any impulse or stimulus, any shadow on the path, without regard for the outcome. The person who has examined the nature of mind and relationships, who purifies the energy of anger, avarice, envy, and fear, and who dedicates actions for the benefit of all beings, such a person walks the Beauty Path.

Each person has a spiritual duty and special gifts to aid in the renewal of the hoop. To perceive that gift requires vigilance to see beyond the illusions of one's own and others' expectations, to see what is. It is by our thought, speech, and deeds, individually and collectively, that we are shaping our tomorrows. We plant seeds that will flower as results in our lives, so best to remove the weeds of anger, avarice, envy, and doubt, that peace and abundance may manifest for all.

THREE FUNDAMENTAL TRUTHS

1. From the Mystery all came forth. All manifestation is in harmony with that sacred Law; nothing is outside of it.

Wisdom is a stream put forth from the Great Mystery, beyond concepts, words, or form.

In the beginning was the emptiness. There came forth a sound as light, giving birth to all that we perceive in this and all worlds—the light-sound, the sacred Word, the unmanifest becoming real. The intention of Creator underlies all manifestation, and each human being is aligned with that sacred intention through the energy of will, shaping outcomes by thought, word, and deed.

Will to be, will to know—that sacred blue fire is a color, a tone reminding us of our life's purpose: to understand the nature of mind. As this light observed its flow, it noted intention to be. Its unmanifest potential generated a ray of wisdom. Compassionate wisdom, red fire of equanimity and generosity, in observing itself brought forth the seed of active intelligence, the means to make the unmanifest real, yellow fire of creative mind, wisdom to succeed.

From these Elder Fires Above come all phenomena, one mind exploring itself in myriad forms. This creative process is ongoing at all levels of life.

The triangle and three fires is a symbol of unity, the triune mind. The will to be is intention manifest as action, then beings swim in reaction. The lake is still, a pebble drops, cycles of energy radiate out. So life arises from intention and causes radiating out, becoming the dance around the wheel of life. Sleeping mind perceives the ripples as challenges of life; awakened mind sees them as ripples on a lake. Human beings have a particular opportunity to realize the arising nature of mind, mind's creative nature, and to generate those thoughts and actions which are beneficial to harmony and balance. In this lifetime we may know all worlds, transcend suffering, and transform conflict to manifest a world of peace and beauty.

The First Sacred Fire: Will, Intention to Be

Will is the underlying current, the fire that brings forth that which we perceive as our reality. Many may think of will as a force or energy used to control others, oneself, the environment; yet will is the first building fire, pure intention to do. We may affirm the will to do good, to live in harmony, or we may be unaware of the creative power of will in our lives.

To bring our will into harmony with the sacred Law is to understand our life purpose. Why am I here, what are my gifts? Human life is a great opportunity. Each one has particular gifts, a unique role in the circle. Conscious will becomes manifest as one dedicates one's gifts for the benefit of family, clan, nation, all beings.

From the emptiness spiraled forth the light and sound, and intention to be was the apex of the triangle, doorway through which all manifests. The wise practitioner cultivates the principle of will to overcome habits of conflict and discord, supplemented by the wisdom of compassion and the voice of affirmation. Child mind is aware, yet one may relinquish or lose touch with the sacred principle of will at an early time in life, through fear, lack of understanding, abuse, or whatever cause, and then choices of unconsciousness are made. When a young person hears adults say, "We will," and then in fact they won't, a sense may arise that outside forces are determining their reality, leading to a feeling of will-lessness, powerlessness. Faith in a sacred plan, divine law, is the wind that fans the flames of will power to manifest what is good. Through spiritual practice we reawaken clear relationship with the principle of light, conscientiously planting seeds of good cause for the benefit of all. Will combined with the wisdom of equanimity, seeing all things in right relationship, makes choices that manifest what is good unto seven generations. So the sacred principle of will considers all, recognizing and affirming that all are in relationship to oneself, calling forth peace and harmony throughout the circle of life.

2. *Wisdom of equanimity knows all things as relative to one's own thought and action and stirs the fire of generosity and good relations, in harmony with neighbors, friends, family, co-workers, and critters.*

36

The Medicine Wheel of Life is a circle; all exists within that circle. The circle is named life—precious opportunity. The circle is 0 (zero), balance of positive and negative. All creatures walking about the circle experience birth, pain, old age, death; no one is above or below. When it comes to dying time all go alone without the comforts of wealth or friends. Birth of any form has its attendant struggle. All beings seek peace and the comforts of a secure home and healthy family. All young and aged beings require care and support. Here arise patterns of relationship giving order to what could be chaotic.

Lines and circles are equalizers that touch all beings. The circle's first line is between life and death, a line from heaven to Earth, from North to South: will to be. From the South arises a line to the North, completing the road of birth, life and death. The North's frozen lakes reflect promise of what is yet to come; warm winds release the potential intelligence, sending a light across the circle from East to West. From the West comes a line of changes making complete the quartering of the circle. Wisdom's winds spin; the cross and the dance of life are one.

The circle teachings represent the cycle of all things that spiral in the ever-moving universe, in a process of constant movement and subtle change in harmony together. Thus each one of us, within the circle of our own time and space, is ever spiraling with our thoughts, words, and actions toward realization of the whole. The circle represents complete harmony and balance. It becomes our Medicine Wheel.

To transform any thought or activity that hides the perception of the circle is the duty of human beings. Where separation thoughts arise, thoughts of "them" and "us," recall that we are all in the circle of life together.

Each great religion has its prophecies of what may come. These prophecies serve as reminders to live in a harmonious manner lest destructive energies be loosed upon the Earth. The foundations of spiritual practice remind us to cultivate care for life and one another.

37

Many now sense the power of peace within ourselves, knowing that our consciousness does indeed affect the stream of thought upon this world. As responsible human beings, let us affirm a world of complementary resolution. We may recognize the different parts of the whole, hear the different views and perspectives, and know that our view does not invalidate another's view. We are human beings and our perception of the same reality—the way the flame moves, the color of the grain—may be expressed differently based on our language, our culture, our experience. It is aqua, or is it blue? Familiarity, or habitual thought, is the screen through which the world is shaped. The congregation of thoughts and patterns that we think to be ourselves becomes the feelings of a city, the feelings of a nation. Each nation upon this planet has the heart of the people, the voices of the people, bringing it into form as a nation. Individuals make a group, individuals make states and nations.

Whatever our religious or philosophical views, we may each trace our roots to the Great Tree of Peace. Whatever we call ourselves the result is the same—we are people living together on planet Earth. In this time it is our duty to transform the obstacles of prejudice expressed as "isms." Let us put aside ideas of separation, for what occurs in one hemisphere will surely be carried on the winds to the other hemisphere.

The wondrous process of creation has brought forth the gift of human life, with limitless opportunities to explore its mysteries. We in turn have responsibility to cultivate seeds of good relationship, expressing joy for the opportunity of life. Some of the first lessons taught by my grandparents were: "You have a spiritual duty to be happy," and "Speak kindly of others, for you know not what they have suffered until you have walked ten thousand miles in their moccasins." See things as they are, in process of change, without fixation on imbalance; see the potential and call it forth. By acknowledging the inherent perfection, the crystal song singing within each one, we may bring forth the best in our family, nation, and planet.

When errors in thought, word, or deed are expressed, the result is like an ash-filled fireplace; wisdom becomes a dim ember buried in the ashes of confused thought and conflicting emotions. The appreciative firekeeper purifies the mind as one sweeps a fireplace—sweeping it clear of doubt that the fire exists, fear that one may not keep it burning, envy that another fire burns more brightly, anger at the damp wood. Any thoughts, words, or actions that hinder the wisdom light are errors or unbalanced actions. Spiritual practice opens the flue, bearing the winds of inspiration and insight, renewing and maintaining balance.

An error of thought, word, or deed is that which takes one out of harmony, giving rise to anger, fear, envy, doubt in the orderly flow of universal love. Any human who feels that he or she is not "good enough" to cultivate peace and generosity is overlooking the wondrous gift of life. You live, therefore you are good enough. You live, therefore your merit is such that you can make a difference.

A young child expresses joy at seeing leaves shimmer as if dancing on the tree. Adult replies, "Leaves do not dance." Doubt may arise in child's mind about the validity of feeling joy. The fire of joyful expression has been dampened by careless speech; the pattern of joy may be deeply altered, giving rise to imbalance. Through the heart meridian flows the river of joy, and this river can be dammed by harsh words, uncaring words.

Envy of another's success, good fortune, wealth, or good looks is an error because it disturbs the equilibrium of the mind and hinders the liver flow, disturbing synthesis and appreciation of one's life accomplishments. Envy poisons the group effort because "I wish" becomes bigger than "We can."

One may profess to be a Christian or a Buddhist, a this or that, and harbor angry seed thoughts at another's views. Sectarian views hinder peace. To live the great teachings is to see inherent truth underlying all great religions.

Anger is born of careless words and deeds, bringing harm to mental balance, setting a course of reactions. Words or thoughts expressed in anger destroy like a bullet. Anger is a burning fire that destroys digestion and peace of mind. Let not the wildfire begin through your carelessness.

Fear of what might be, could be, are thoughts based on possibilities. Fear of failure hinders a beginning. What can you be sure of? When you inhale you exhale, and smoke rises from the fire. Cultivate certainty by observing the cycles of nature.

"The One Who Thinks the Breath Creates" is how Creator is expressed in some of the old Tsalagi hymns. The breath carries thought around the world. Through mindfulness of the breath mental errors are transformed. The bellows fans the wisdom fire. Wise person, take care, for your thoughts, words, deeds today blow clouds across the sky of tomorrow.

Far away in the realm of Galunlati, the Seventh Heaven, there are crystal beings singing. Their songs give order to chaos. Adawees, Wise Protectors, are their names. *Hi la hi yu*—"long time ago"—heavenly beings chose to aid those on Earth who had not yet the spark of wisdom fire. They sing for all who would hear, of worlds in harmony. The ideal signs within each person as sacred DNA spiral, giving form and pattern to desire. The spiral ignites the fires of will, compassion, and action, bringing fruit of life. Our thoughts and actions affect this sacred spiral, giving rise to balance and ease or imbalance and disease; hence our offering of prayerful appreciation keeps the ideal song in tune. Vigil and purification cultivate the most pure song, keeping whole the body and renewing the hoop of good relations. Each person contributes to the song, all have something to give—right thought, right action, and appreciation of the land, sharing with those in need.

The Second Sacred Fire: Affirmation, the Wisdom Energy of Compassion

Positive affirmation and generosity arise from the wisdom of equanimity, seeing all things in relationship and choosing to articulate and live in a sacred manner. By affirmations one energizes one's vision of enlightened action.

Our elders taught that forgiveness was a great balm, the most great medicine that brings freedom from hurt. We may pray, do outwardly good works, yet they mean little without forgiving ourselves and others for what might have been, could have been, should have been.

Everyone has some idea of what another's vice or fault is and what ought to be corrected. The real issue is to clarify one's own consciousness, be one with the stream of clear mind in oneself, that one may act in the present rather than react to issues of the past. We have a ritual once a year where everyone goes down to the water's edge and we throw water over our backs seven times. In that moment we are washing away those thoughts and actions that we recognize as no longer necessary or beneficial for our continued growth and evolution. We wash aside that which has separated us from clear communion, we wash away the illusion of loneliness so that we can hear again the voice of truth in our hearts. During this time we forgive anyone who has said a sad word or a bad word, and we start the year anew. *Autohuna* is a friends-making ceremony. We call forth a sacred crystal at that time, one that is brought out only for that ceremony. We hold the crystal into the firelight, that we may see the light of truth within ourselves and observe how our actions shape the coming year. We sing, we pray, we make offerings for forgiveness in our hearts, and come again to perceiving the perfection of our nature, putting aside the illusion of illness, the illusions of strife.

Remorse for our negative actions, affirmation that we may transform obscurations, commitment to generating patterns

41

of resolution, and willingness to share forgiveness with others, that friendships may be made anew—this is medicine to heal relationships.

When we were young children a story was told to us to show how the universal energy of love forgives and renews any being who is of good heart. Very, very long ago in the Smoky Mountains, to the west of Oconaluftee River, there lived a wonderful young hunter. He had learned from the master of the hunt how to think like a bird, a deer, a bear, a turkey, a fish, and to understand all the signs of the woods. As a very young boy he would be as still as a tree, looking and learning from nature and from the animals moving about. As he grew, the master hunter of the band taught him how to purify the wood to make a bow and arrow, how to make offering to the turkey who gave its feathers, how to show appreciation for the gifts of the forest. Thus hunter learned very well the lessons of the woods. He did not take the first animal he saw; he would honor it and make offerings and pray that others of its kind would come, that his people might eat. His name was Walks the Forest.

As Walks the Forest became a man he provided his band with much food and with skins and feathers for clothing. His generosity was well known. One time there were two old people who needed the medicine of the bear gall, and Walks the Forest said he would bring back that medicine. As he embarked upon his way he felt that this hunt would be very different. The forest was extremely quiet; even the talkative streams were whispering on this day. He walked through the forest calling the bear. *"He! Hayuyá haniwá, hayuyá haniwá. Eyonah, yo ho, yo ho, yo ho!"* Soon he saw the spoor of a bear. He made a resting place that night near the old tree where the bear had slept some time before, and ate a bit of the parched corn he carried with him. On the fourth day he sighted the bear. He shot an arrow; it landed in the bear's shoulder. The bear kept moving. Walks the Forest tracked the bear for three more days. By how he had run out of food, and he began to realize that this was no ordinary bear and that this was a very sacred hunt. On the seventh day he sat upon a ledge and fasted and prayed to understand the import of the message the Creator was showing him. That night in the sky he saw a star coming down to Earth and he also heard many animals moving close by him. He felt that they, too, were on a vigil.

As the sun rose, Walks the Forest saw before him a vast, shallow lake and heard the flapping of thousands of birds' wings and the sounds of many, many animals. He looked and he saw the bear, in whose shoulder the arrow still rested, walk to the water and pull out the arrow, and the bear was renewed. On the side of the lake he saw old wolves crawling to the water, deer limping, all kinds of wounded animals. As they approached the water they were made new and healthy again. The predators did not attack their usual prey because they knew this was a sacred place. Any who could make their way to these waters of Atagahi, the Magic Lake, were renewed and past hurts were made whole.

Then he heard a voice in the sky. "Walks the Forest, you are of strong and pure heart. Remember this well. All who make their way here shall live long and give great benefit to their own kind. Tell your people not to hunt in this place, for here is sanctuary for all living beings."

Walks the Forest understood and went home, taking with him a bit of grass from the lake's edge. As he walked back to the village that grass became like the bear's gall bladder that was needed by the old people. Everyone said, "Where is the bear?" He said, "A most wonderful thing has happened," and he gave them the medicine and told the people what he had seen. All agreed to honor that sacred place. Only those of pure heart can go there and see the sky reflected in the waters and renew their being; to any others it would appear only as a vast grassy plain.

Just as easily as the mind reflects forms of pain and warfare, we may actualize elements of complementary resolution. We are now in a transitional phase of movement around the spiral where this resolution is possible. One step we can each take is to focus on what is clear rather than what is unclear when we are feeling a sense of anger or wishing to communicate with another and finding the words too small. It is good to establish a "negativity fast" in your own mind, in terms of your thinking and relationships, and most especially in terms of your speech about yourself and one another. If we are anti-something, we are setting up a polarity and a reason for argument. If we are observing and recognizing what is, there is a balance, there is a stream, there is a path through which the resolution can be perceived.

So let us forgive ourselves and others for what might have been, could have been, should have been, and mindfully stir away ashes from the wisdom fireplace. Observe the mind and see new worlds of peace arise.

Repatterning limiting thoughts and opening channels for mind to create new forms—this comes through affirmation of the voice. See that you are in a process, that such-and-such a pattern needs to be corrected. "Am I that pattern? If that pattern is incorrect, I will correct it." And how? The first step is to affirm, "I am perfect within, I am whole within." That power of affirmation begins to release something like love in the brain. (Chocolate also gives people that feeling.) You think good of yourself and there is greater vitality in your body, and it flows to all around you; the vitality of the one who really accepts, "I am alive and I am okay," has a very vitalizing effect on other people. Through the resonance of your nature another who may be unhappy begins to re-member something to be happy about. That is one of the key methods of complementary resolution, looking for the element within yourself that brings joy.

In these times many speak of "conflict resolution"; it is good to focus on resolution, yet the idea of "conflict" is itself an illusion. All is vibration, and what has the appearance of conflict is better understood as dissonance or discord, energies seeking resolution in harmony. How to recognize discord in oneself, in one's environment, in one's relationships? Discord produces disharmony and disease. The body may become ill, mind may endlessly argue and chatter, relationships may be come strained and unnourishing, the land around may become depleted and produce less food. The elements respond to our thought. Seeing the bounty and ease within and all around and diligently fanning the flame of certainty, this opens the channel for dissonance to resolve naturally into harmony.

In yourself, look to the breath. Is it freely flowing, expansive, invigorating? If not, look within: where is that life energy caught or blocked? Consciously aerate the body-mind with thought forms of light. As the breath is invited to find its natural flow, obscuring thoughts or emotions may arise, and these can be keys to understanding the source of contraction or discord in one's system. With friends, family, co-workers it is a similar process. Look to what is happening, give thanks for clear perception and the opportunity to come again to good relationship. Recognize the actions that are inappropriate and causing disharmony and vow to act differently. Acknowledge the light flowing freely among you. Affirm and visualize yourselves in harmonious communication and relationship, calling upon the three sacred fires of will, affirmation, and skillful means to transmute all that obscures your vision of the clear mind within.

Inner discord expresses mind or actions not fully aligned with one's sacred purpose in this time, not fully shining the crystal of clear mind. Sometimes in the busy world one develops what we call the illness of being two-hearted. In Native mind that is the worst kind of illness you can have. It is where you want to do and have the ability to do but you don't do, and you argue with yourself about it. Good to be of one mind, one heart, and to see the ifs, ands, buts, and possibilities only as thoughts, without attachment, keeping clear your goal of being all that you can be, understanding the Mystery, seeing the truth as it is. To see the essence of what is, to perceive the harmony and live it, is to accomplish the "good life."

As equanimity arises in the mind one feels that the relationship with all other beings is more dear. Through this sense of being together the heart of generosity arises; we consider how we may help and share. The happy child always has something to share—toys, smiles, insights. Even in the poorest tribal household there is always enough in the pot to feed a guest. Generosity is the outflow of the breath. We receive, we give. We are most joyful when we share with one another. In the Native way we celebrate our joy by feast and present giving, and also if we want to understand something we make a feast and give presents. Possessions can be poison. The happy heart gives away the best. To know how to receive, that is also a most important gift, which cultivates generosity in others and keeps strong the cycle of life. If the heart knows not how to share—a smile, laughter, precious things, food, a home—then that heart is closed off from receiving and closes off the free flow of others' giving. This is considered an illness because then one does not see the inherent wisdom. Giving, receiving—one breath. The fire of mind grows dim with selfishness, the fire of mind grows bright stirred by winds of generosity.

3. Discipline, diligence, active intelligence make waves of grace for the land and the people unto seven generations.

The Third Sacred Fire: Actualization, Skillful Means

The fire of actualization precipitates the ideal into reality in harmony with the sacred will and the energy of compassion. These three fires together become a triangle from which ideals are actualized through a process of strong intention, diligent action, and consideration for all beings.

Through the third fire the Creator's intention and individuals' relationship with that intention become real. For example, one of strong faith, even in a challenging situation such as loss of job and income, having strong faith in a divine presence and ability to accomplish through diligent action, may bring into manifestation the desired goals. Skillful means is the perspiration, the diligent action, and one's willingness to apply clear thought and ethical and moral behavior to manifesting the ideal in one's life.

Skillful means are developed through the generation of altruistic mind, affirming that you will be the best person you can possibly be to benefit yourself, your family, and all relations. Then you gather the teachings to clarify obscuring habits of mind. The first step is cultivating positive speech and thought, bringing the mind to stability through contemplation of the breath, and the power of faith actualized as prayer and meditation. In prayer one activates the force of sacred sound, the creative word, acknowledging the bounty already received and affirming that more will be received to benefit all your relations. Affirmation is a skillful means for transforming energy, and it begins with the deletion of negative statements about self and others. A negative statement freezes one in time and space without room for harmonization. For example, when the Tsalagi first met the settlers, the term used to describe them was "acts like a mean man"— "acts like" instead of "is," so as not to freeze them in the character of meanness, leaving room for essential perfection to manifest.

So the fire of actualization is fed by the wood of ideal form, the wood of skillful means (understanding that particular actions bring particular results), the wood of devotion to the good, the wood that transforms illusions of obstruction, the wood of planetary harmony, and the wood of universal mind perceiving heavens and Earth and the Mystery of creation manifest in all.

AFFIRMATION

To manifest fully, an affirmation needs to be unambiguous, a simple and clear statement of one's intentions. To make clear an affirmation, one first gives thanks for having a human life and the ability even to consider enlightened action.

Then, in the sanctuary of mind, one assesses the skills of this time and considers the goals and objectives to be accomplished—in three days, three months, three years, one's lifetime—for the benefit of one's family, clan, nation, planet, and future generations. Affirmation enables one's unmanifest potential to become real through the following means:

1. Acknowledge the creative principle in yourself. Look at yourself in the mirror and greet yourself: "Hello, how are you?" Affirm, "I am alive, I am thankful, and I shall accomplish this day, for the benefit of myself, my family and all beings, these three specific things. . . ." Repeat the affirmation three times. You may say, "On this day I shall respond with compassion to any anger or frustration," or "On this day I shall listen without interrupting." One states very clearly an objective of clear relationship.

2. Affirm, "I shall realize my creative gifts," repeating this affirmation also three times. And visualize in your mind's eye the accomplishment of such tasks. For example, if you wish to have better relationship with co-workers, visualize you and your co-workers seated in a circle, surrounded by rose light, talking heart to heart and accomplishing great works. It is important to believe your words and to cultivate faith that you will manifest your sacred gifts in this life. Another example: Suppose you are addicted to tobacco, alcohol, coffee, or unwholesome food. The first step is to acknowledge that this is something that will be put aside. Then affirm, "I am free from attachment to ____," repeating three times. And see yourself surrounded in light, happy, healthy, active, free from attachment, those objects of craving or attachment no longer present in your life, your mind-stream.

To actualize is to manifest the ideal, through sacred practice, great diligence, perseverance, and perspiration. To acutualize is to make real a vision of peace for the people and the

48

land. It is the happening and the doing. You bring your mind to stability with thankfulness, prayer, and meditation. The actualization of your idea—be it the idea to be free from drinking intoxicants or to build your home—is apparent in your actually putting aside that to which you were attached or beginning to create designs for your new home. This is the wakening of clear energy to bring forth your visualized goals and your creative potential. Another example: You hoped, you prayed to make your family relationships clearer. Your vision of family harmony, magnetized by your prayer, your affirmation, and your action in generating peace, is manifested as a family gathering free of previous negative patterns. Through the process of magnetizing and actualizing what is beneficial for all, patterns that have obscured clarity of thought and relationship become less and less grasping, they become more transparent until finally they disperse. The actualization is the beauteous result derived from the skillful means of the third sacred fire.

Will is the neutron, compassion the proton, and the energy of actualization the electrons in the outer ring, wisdom that succeeds, bonding in good relationships. In your life, the clear intention to manifest your sacred gifts, to bring forth your creative potential and establish good relationships, is the neutron of will. So here we are, weaving patterns in a dream.

MEDICINE WHEEL, MANDALA
MIRROR CLEAR MIND.
LET THE SACRED HOOP
BE RENEWED IN THIS TIME.

The Tsalagi ceremonial calendar is based upon the Mayan (commonly called "Aztec") calendar, in which measurements of time relate to the movements of Venus, Mars, the Pleiades star system and Sirius.

The *Elo* states that the calendar was carried from land

which fell beneath the sea. The mathematical formulas derived from mystic understanding of zero, and the relationships of stars were seen as a road for all peoples to realize wisdom's clear light. The mathematics were brought to Earth from the Pleiades with the wave of star beings who are ancestors to every Tsalagi.

In this sacred calendar a "world" consists of 22 periods of 52 years each. In each world there are nine hells, times of obscuration of the wisdom fire, and thirteen heavens, times in which enlightened thought and action flourish for the benefit of all beings. Each complete cycle, or world, equals 1,144 years, and 25 worlds—28,600 years—comprise an era. We are living in the Fifth World and entering the Sixth World, the beginning of a new era.

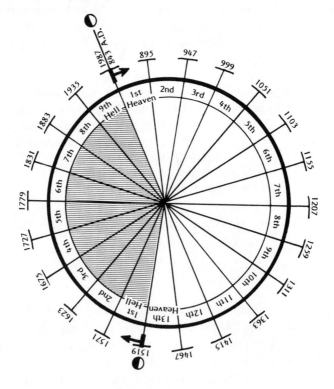

First heaven brings new opportunity to understand Earth as a living being and develop systems of transforming waste rather than increasing pollutants. In the Tsalagi teaching of the circle, the Medicine Wheel teaching, we see the image of a bear dancing on fear and ignorance, recycling even death, the poisons of improper invention, bringing forth that which benefits life. This book in your hand began as ideas. The idea of constructive, nonpolluting inventions arises within a stable mind and is brought to fruition through the cooperative action of those who consider themselves the ancestors of generations yet unborn. Inventions born of the creative flow of of mother-father energy, quickened by faith's inspiration, are gifts that serve rather than enslave the people.

Each human is composed of elements from mother and father. Even the perfection of "that which cannot be explained" exists within. That wondrous perfection arises as joyful appreciation for all beings and creative intelligence to benefit all, when mother-father are realized within your heart: mother's understanding, wordless, encompassing; father's skill doing what needs doing—this playful dance unfolding the riddle of your life.

From the Earth energy arises, feeding through the navel; heaven's insight spirals down through the top of your head. Heaven and Earth meet within the heart, setting free the choice and voice to do; oneself, the circle containing all possibility; Earthward flow, the intention; heavenward flow, the energy to accomplish. From East to West the winds of inspiration flow, carrying joy, making apparent one's gift to be shared. From West to East the wind-that-blows-away-that-which-is-no-longer-needed shakes its lightning wand. The vision is realized through the cross. Quartering the circle defines the Vastly Vast, giving shape to form, up and down, East and West.

The swastika and the cross are ancient symbols of energy's manisfestation. The same principles of world formation apply to human life. Receive life force from heaven and Earth;

51

spiral out from your heart compassion. See that all human beings are relatives in this dream. Blood and lymph are pumped through the body as tides are driven by the moon. Thoughts transpire as lightning dances along the mountain ridges. Creation is an ongoing process; your thoughts bring winds of change.

Without the voice of the crystals coating the fine hairs of our ears we would not even hear one another's voices. The crystal is an amplifier of that ever-present voice of creation within. In our world of inventions the crystals in radios have been amplifying desire, saying, "Buy this, buy that." In reality the crystal sings, "Let us plant the seeds of peace, let us put aside the mind of separation." It is that subtle vibration that has stirred the hearts of so many people to peaceful resolution. The crystals buried deep in the Earth sing out the song of our planetary harmony.

In the crystal's light there are two flows: father energy spiralling upward, mother energy expanding outward. All things in this universe are held together by these sacred flows. Without the flow of mother and father, without the sacred symmetry of the DNA spirals within our very bodies, we would not stand upon this Earth. Here we have the blessing of life. It is for us to take correct action, to recognize truth as a stream and realize wisdom as a voice within each of us.

All is in relation. Come to peace in your own nature with the flow of mother-father and accept the gift of life. Earth is in a transitional stage of mental unfolding. In the past we would look to our elders, our ministers, to communicate and hold the form of planetary peace. In this age it is incumbent upon each of us to hold the form. What is it to hold the form of planetary unity? It is to sing a song of resolution, acknowledging the common human goals—clear water to drink, abundant food for the family, and good neighbors.

How do we come around this wheel of life? We begin with the will to be, affirmed in the first breath. As the baby comes forth it is already aware of some special gift. When it smiles, everyone responds. In the will to be present we set many causes, many fields, into motion. We have many possible futures, and we choose along the way that which will be our life. It is our choice. Very often we hear a confused idea of "karma": that in this life we may suffer and in another life attain the benefits. In *this moment* we receive benefit, and in *this moment,* if we close our hearts to the bounty of joy, we will perceive suffering. It is a simple choice; to attune to the sacred flow of life, to recognize in our attunement that life is a process of change and that each of us can bring peace to this world by first making peace within ourselves. Exploring our own consciousness, we return to the sacred fire of clear mind and to the awareness that wisdom is a stream, ever washing, ever renewing. The inherent spark of clear mind is never sullied. The thoughts and actions may be impure, yet that creative principle of life is ever holy.

Illness is an illusion. That we are separate nations and separate peoples is also an illusion waiting to be unraveled, for certainly we sip the same waters, breathe the same air. Through the fibers of our thinking, through our thought processes, we are weaving our reality. Each of us contributes to tomorrow by our thought, word, and deed. Coming to peace in ourselves, forgiving our relatives and ourselves for what should have been, what could have been, and accepting who we are—this is a primary step upon the Beauty Path. Casting out patterns of attachment and expectation enables us to act in the now. Once we make that step, we ever walk in the way of beauty.

To see that our actions and hopes are shaping tomorrow is a spiritual practice. When I was young the old people would visit me in my dreams and ask me to do certain tasks. Imagination creates a world of dreams. Before going to sleep, decide and affirm, "I shall recall all that I experience in the dream." This begins to make more firm the threads of communion of individual mind and the mind that we all share in. Simple words, an affirmation: "I acknowledge that sacred flow of life, and even as my body rests I shall hear and put forth the song of beauty, that my words may always be true and that I may respond to the inherent wisdom of the people." Thus we realize that seed thoughts of peace manifest as good will in our lives.

Those who work in the healing tradition may meet people whose bodies are outwardly expressing disease. It is for the healer to hold the form of ease and balance, looking deeply within for the perfection of the person. How do we see? With our hearts, with our inner eye. So often in our youth we heard the voice of an imaginary playmate or the voice of the wind. In the process of education we may have attended less and less to that subtle, joyful sensing until it became a secret hidden even from ourselves. Now as adults we have the opportunity to explore the wisdom of the child within ourselves, to look deeply within, to listen to the voice of truth within our hearts.

Vigil

To hear the voice of wisdom one first stabilizes the mind. In the Tsalagi tradition the development of mental stability is called the vigil. The vigil begins as one observes the dancing fires throughout a given time period, usually outdoors. One may fast or take purifying baths before gathering the seven sacred woods for building the fire. Then one makes offering of *tsalu* (tobacco) to the fire and dedicates the vigil endeavor to aid all creatures, whether they walk, crawl, swim, or fly. One gives thanks for the opportunity of life and "cries for vision" of life purpose and means of aiding the people. One's family, clan, co-workers, and nation are included in the circle of those whom one's actions are to benefit. The process of maintaining the fire through weather changes requires and develops determination to succeed. Lazy attitudes become transparent to one's sight, enabling transformation. As a rhythm becomes established the fire burns with ease, enabling the vigilant person to focus the mind on the flames. Many images may arise from the mind as one sits and watches.

The fire is a gateway to wisdom. By observing, one may see

more clearly those thought patterns which hinder successful good relations. As thoughts of arrogance and fear arise, like a weaver one pulls those threads of discord and replaces arrogance with humility. See how small the concepts of self are in relation to the vastness of the sky. Replace fear of success, fear of life, with committed courage to succeed for the benefit of those you love. Should love not be apparent, cultivate appreciation for the gift of life. The greatest wealth is that of good relations with family, friends, and neighbors. Should you have doubt of love, cultivate love for the child within your breast. In this way one begins to heal the illusion of separation.

We cannot live without one another, and it is very difficult to live without loving oneself and others. The first step in planetary healing is to walk toward the beauty in *thee*—to see the beauty in your own heart, to forgive those ideas and correct those thought forms that obscure the true wisdom fire in your mind. How to change a thought? How to remove a conflict from your own heart? Sit a bit and watch. We call this the vision quest. We may sit for many days, as long as it takes for that peace to be recalled to our hearts.

How to put aside the mind of obscuration, the realm of doubt, that we may perfectly recollect creation's beauty? By giving thanks. Tsalagi prayers do not ask for anything but give thanks for what is. We live, we breathe. The challenges of illness, separation from loved ones, frustration in one's work, these are opportunities to burn away patterns of mind obscuring the beauty of wisdom's fire. So the rising sun is reason enough for thankfulness, in that another day has come. Let us see the beauty in ourselves and one another. When we meet, let us look into one another's eyes, hear the beat of one another's hearts, speak the best of ourselves and one another, know we are all in process.

We can see what needs improvement and be willing to make those changes. The idea of weakness is an illusion, the idea that one "cannot" is an illusion. Together we have woven this dream; together we will bring it to harmonious resolution. Inherently all is well, only hidden by the dust of ignorance. Let us put aside the boundaries of caste and class and recognize that we are all human beings—and if we are to continue as human beings we must put our minds together and turn our inventions to something helpful. When we consider an action, let it be considered unto seven generations. Consider what it means if I speak harshly or gently in this moment. Let us consider what our words mean to all with whom we cross paths, for words weave tomorrow. When you leave home to go to your work upset, your relationships with other people are upset that day. When you recognize your home as a sanctuary and have made a special place within it to make prayers of thankfulness, then what you meet outside may distract for a moment, yet you may always come again to peaceful understanding.

It is within the power of human beings to make the streams, the rivers, the oceans pure again; it is within the power of our hearts to renew this very planet. The idea of nations at war can be put aside as we accept the gift of life as love and know that we are worthy of it. The body that we have been given is a great bounty. We have come from the sea of Mystery to explore the many facets of that Mystery, and we all return to that sea as the salmon return to their birthing place. Each of us shall carry back a great message: "This I learned in life, this I learned on Earth—that when we meet one another we are to meet as friends and relatives." These are messages that are carried on the stream of mind, bearing fruit in future times. One may experience separation while in the stream of life. The river, as it flows over the rocks, may be spattered and sprayed, yet it is still the river, returning to the sea. So it is with us.

We are the children of the light, we are the voice of creation, exclaimed as sound became light. We have come here through the illusion of separation to explore all the wonders of this creation. As we explore we recognize ourselves as co-creators in this universe, our thoughts and deeds shaping tomorrows. We see within our hearts a stream of wisdom ever aware of right action.

Right action is that which eases suffering, causes no harm, and inspires no others to generous caretaking. Right action enables one to honor the fire of clear mind with one another without need to perceive one above or below, more or less than another. Right action perceives the cycles of relationships and creates order within one's own mind, putting forth disciplined action free from desire to dominate or be dominated. Mind dedicated to right action perceives that we are the ancestors to those yet unborn and considers the effects of thought, word, and deed unto seven generations—each moment a holy moment, pregnant with tomorrow. Best to speak kindly, act with care, lest your tomorrow be filled with fear.

Spiritual Practice

It is our spiritual duty to pray in the morning, to pray in the evening, to call people together in joy, to eat together, to be happy human beings together. Many of us did these things in the past; we can recall how in our growing-up years when our neighbors needed aid, we were there. Now we are too busy. We have forgotten that the inventions are creations of our own minds and they have begun to gobble up our every moment. We must be disciplined and say again, "These machines have come from our minds; let us direct them with clear thought." Let us very carefully examine the wisdom of the day and nourish those ideas and inventions whose roots are deep in the soil of harmony. Let us recall that what each of us does will come around the sacred wheel and touch us again. As the pebble in the stream makes many ripples, so does each word and thought we hold in our minds.

This is the power of the voice: affirming that there shall be peace. Let us hold the thought of our planet's wholeness; let us honor the children, the future generation. This is how we make peace. As we look around us at events in the world, we see many things happening that stimulate fear, the thought of "them" and "us." But there is no "them." We are all together. What happens in the north, what happens in the south, it is happening in each of us. In the east the sun rises and I realize, "I am that I am. I am a human being with a gift, I am a human being with a purpose." The gift may be hidden, yet it shall become apparent. To be a friend to one person, to inspire one heart to clarity, that is a special gift. Too often we may think the gift is something else, something we must get from outside. The gift is in each of us to give. First we align with the perfection in ourselves, bringing the mind, the body, the emotions into harmony with the creative principle of life. We may do it in many ways, through introspection, through making something with our hands, through community action. We cultivate peaceful thought, and soon we react less and less to the idea form of conflict. Then there arises the awareness that we are all relatives on Earth.

In the morning I sing a simple song of thanks, as my grandparents taught me. I am singing for all my relatives, everyone who lives and breathes, even the stones, for the crystals are alive and they grow just as we do. Through our experience with life, through our interactions with one another, we learn to put aside anger, we learn ways of communion, we find ways of resolution. The sacred spiral of light unites all beings. My grandparents said, "Remember that you come from the place of the Seven Dancers, the Pleiades star system; that is where our nation comes from." So, visualizing seven stars above my head and perceiving the three sacred fires deep within my spine, I sit and listen as they sing a very simple song. May you recall that sacred spiral of light, Asga Ya Galunlati, Great Spirit that unites us all. Through all of our cultures, all of our religions, there is one thread, there is one tree. Let us perceive that great tree, let us recognize that clear light of reason, the fire of wisdom through which we may all trace our roots to the Great Tree of Peace.

As a young child, that was a first step upon the Beauty Path. Just learning to sing a morning song of thanks, and sitting quietly and realizing that there truly is light moving through this body, made the words of my grandparents take more meaning in my heart. I understood that there truly is light moving through each of our bodies as we breathe: we have mind, and it is carried on breath. Then another question arose as I recognized the light: "Does mind truly affect the plants, the crops, the environment? Will I be like my old people, calling forth what is needed just with a prayer in the heart?" A seed was planted that many would sing out a song of peace and abundance as the elders did. By the standards of life in these days it would seem a poor life that they led. If they wanted water they went out and pumped it; if they wanted butter they churned it. It was good. Many of us are looking again to simple ways of living, dignified ways that do not enslave us to wage labor in order to pay for things we don't really need, becoming ever more dependent on technology that pollutes the Earth. It is fine to chop our own wood, it is fine to make a cookfire outside. To live simply is to see without attachment. Our status, our position, is determined not by the work we do outside but by the work in our hearts and how we assist others. The effort to recognize and speak the truth is the greatest work that any of us can do. It is to realize the power of our clear mind and to call forth the best from all the people with whom we walk along life's path. This is a gift of giving and receiving. Then one's heart feels it will burst with a sense of love and appreciation, free of confining fears.

Take time to pray with your children in the morning. It has far more power for your family and your planet than all your busy work. The power of our voices tuned to right action and the willingness to speak and live correctly and to hold our hearts in joyous balance—this is the path of harmony. Each of us seeks to come into union with the sacred wisdom. Communion, communication, community—words calling forth from the longing in our hearts the desire that we stand together around the sacred circle, that we honor the truth in ourselves and all our relations.

TEN SACRED STONES

As a teaching aid, my great-grandfather Eli Ywahoo would draw a triangle on the ground and place ten stones within it. He said, "The quartz is the will. This reminds us of the sacred flow. Those red stones, the petrified coral, are to remind you of love's wisdom. The yellow of the topaz is to remind you of the well-tuned mind, that you may actively bring forth with your thought what is good for all the people in this moment and in future generations." These are the stones of the sacred triangle, the three flames of most pure mind.

As that triangle is made strong, you recognize the sacred energy of the square, and you begin to put down roots for a holy place for people to meet as a family and as friends. The stone to remind you of this is the jasper, yellow and orange jasper. This stone removes swelling and pain from the body and reminds us that our feeling of being separate from the source of all nature is overcome in our right relationship with family and friends.

The fifth stone is green, jadeite or emerald. It is the stone through which you make balance from the realm of ideal form into the present moment. Through knowing, through practice, you will find the medicines that best strengthen the people. The fifth stone represents the practice.

The rose quartz is the sixth stone, showing the open heart, the heart that gives and receives. In time people will recall the sacred power of that stone for strengthening the heart that has been overcome by grief. (Medicines are made from these stones in a careful manner, some preparations taking twelve years to complete).

Looking to uncover great beauty makes apparent the obscurations. It is then that you call upon the energy of the seventh stone, the amethyst, stone of transformation. That subtle purple quartz very quickly speeds up the process of transformation in ourselves, and what was an obstacle becomes the heart of the wisdom fire.

Looking inside, we call upon the pearly wisdom of the

eighth stone, the simple pearl from the fresh water, to remind us of our perfection and our many layers, and of the light ever reflecting. We have a recognition, a remembrance of light whence we spring, and respect for all within Earth's dream. As we recall more and more of the light and see one another in interaction as co-creators, then we come to the wisdom of the opal. The opal is the ninth stone, a stone of universal mind, the awakened fire of mind precipitating thoughts revealing enlightened action. A door may be opened in our nature as our aura reflects that opalescent light.

And the tenth stone, it is being formed within each of us. It is somewhat like the lapis, but translucent. It is our will in alignment with the Creator's will and the purpose of this planet that shall manifest this stone in the Earth. The Earth is always producing new elements, which come to the surface as we transmute and transform. This stone of knowing shall unfold in our hearts as a flower of knowing. We must call forth the beauty. We must recognize that Earth herself is a holder of the form and we all share in the mind of that being. We might say that this is our planetary garden, and within this garden we develop a planetary mind.

Ten sacred stones, ten mirrors of the wisdom fire within.

There is a message in these stones, there is message in our hearts. The symmetry of these crystal structures points to the symmetry of this universe. As in music, everything in creation is moving, and its flow is a song of jubilation. We are now in the process of changing from one key to another. The people are now awakening to the song of inherent joy, appreciation of life, recognizing that in this moment the song can fully resound. The sound of human thought and the planet's dance is changing. We are moving into the key of D, the only key that is a reciprocal of itself, that returns to itself. It is a note attuned to the sacred will, and it ever comes around the sacred circle. Many of the songs you have learned in churches and in sacred ceremonies are in the key of D. It is strengthening in you the will to do good.

In these times the crystal is the hub of our communications wheel, amplifying many thoughts, feeding desire, calling forth action. Crystals activate the "go buttons" in armament systems, and the sounds of desire are amplified through advertisements chanting, "Buy this, you need that." And yet it is the crystal networks that make apparent our neighbor's plight halfway around the world, the singing of crystals in radio and television that conveys that all humans share the same concerns, the same planet. Destruction or peace: it is your choice what message is amplified. Recognize the thoughts arising in your mind. Weed thoughts of greed and anger from the garden of your mind. Cultivate what is beneficial and generous. The crystal heart of the Earth sings, "Help me renew the waves and the atmosphere." You may assist by purifying your thought, word, and deed.

The crystal is a living being, vibrating faster than the speed of light. It is not a solid; it is sound, ether, concretized. The crystal is a conscious being that has taken a particular form to resonate the basic sound of creation. The clear quartz crystal is one of the deeper mysteries of the practice of the Tsalagi people. With the quartz one walks in all dimensions. It is also a key to healing, amplifying the proper tone so that the body may realize its resonance with the sound of creation.

CRYSTAL MEDITATION

In a quiet place, sit with a clear quartz crystal friend. You may make a simple shrine with the crystal in the center, a candle in front of it, and bowls of fresh water and cornmeal on either side, reminders of the purity and generosity of your natural mind. With smoke offering of incense, dedicate your prayers for the good of the Earth and all beings. Sitting in a relaxed manner upon a cushion (or in a chair with both feet upon the floor), spine erect, breathing fully and naturally, call upon crystal light of pure mind to infuse yourself and all beings with clear knowing of wholeness and purpose, and to radiate throughout the planet the beauteous light of peace.

Read, chant, or sing this meditation aloud and then meditate in silence.

Clear quartz crystal sings out a clear quartz sound.
Dimensions meet, axes spin around.
Living being, conscious thought
Sings forth a crystal song
Faster than the speed of light.
A liquid moving, appearing still,
Silica dioxide, marriage of forms.
Crystal amplifies
The song that is.

Crystal is a living being,
A friend in the Wheel of Life—
Ever singing the sacred song,
Showing you means to transform.

Full moon light, new moon light,
Dedication times.
Dance the spiral light.
New moon light, full moon light,
Dedicate the sacred singing stone,
Dedicate your purpose,
To bring forth clear mind.

Have you heard
The pulse of the Earth?
Inhale, exhale
Dreams of peace.

Ha ha ha ha
Ho ho ho
[Repeat four times.]

Dance, dance, dance,
Crystal singing song
Tonight.
Give thanks, give thanks
For the gift of life.

Ha ha ha ha
Ho ho ho
[Repeat three times.]

Dance the sacred spiral dance,
Sing a sacred song tonight.
Energy dances from the north
Reflecting crystal wisdom within.
Long face of crystal
Aligned with the north,
There see the face you wore
Before, before,
And evermore.

Ho!

Pray to recognize the creative energy moving through your body as you chant and pass the crystal through the smoke of the incense. Sing this special song and sense the spiral of creation arising and descending through your body. Gaze at the crystal, bring it close to your heart, sense the energy flowing between you.

It is good to place the crystal in a special place at home, an area where you may sit each day and offer prayers and cedar incense and watch the process of your own mind. To still the mind is very important, so that you may truly know yourself. A shrine, a sanctuary space is a drawing point for the healing energy needed by the planet. Each of us who makes a temple in our heart and in our home is contributing to the planet's well-being through generating a field of equanimity. In the old ways these things are placed upon the shrine: corn; the sacred crystal; a bag with scents you find enjoyable, like sage or dried roses; a bowl of water to remind you of the stream that unites us all; and a bit of salt to recall the blessing of the Earth. It seems a small thing to do, yet if you look to your traditions of long ago, every mother had a hearth shrine, each home had its own special shrine. Perhaps in this moment your heart is calling for a renewal of sacred tradition in your family life. Make a place where you may sit and listen to the silence, where you may study words of wisom as taught in your family of origin. Good seeds need a garden to grow in.

When you make a connection with the crystal, a field of resonance develops, a cycle of communication is awakened between your mind and the mind of the crystal. It is the energy of apperception, enabling one to perceive, disentangle, and reweave patterns of thought. Light travels in waves and particles, as does the energy of mind. The quartz crystal is unique in that it will receive one packet of energy, and within the crystal that packet will become two. The cells of the healing etheric web that interpenetrates all form are six-sided, like the quartz crystal. One packet of energy coming through your body in your thought process, in your action, moves around this web, and as it hits each corner of the hexagon, it also becomes two. So the human being, too, is a generator, an amplifier. Our potential is unlimited.

THE RAINBOW BRIDGE

We are the rainbow, each of us. When we speak of "rebuilding the Rainbow Bridge," it is to bring again into harmony the left and right hemispheres of the brain, to renew the flow of our intuitive mind and the mind that has learned through repeated action. The body knows what is good for it, the body knows to inhale and exhale. It is our middle brain that oversees these functions. When we accept the innate wisdom of our middle brain, we integrate the wisdom of triune mind, right and left hemispheres, and limbic system functioning together in harmony.

My great-grandfather said to me, "When you see the rainbow it is an indication that the holy spirit is strong in the people's bodies as a result of ceremonies done correctly." If there were no rainbows after the ceremony it would mean that somehow the connection was not complete between left and right, mother and father, moon and sun in ourselves. We can make it complete by honoring the beauty of our mothering nature if we are wearing a man's body and the power of our fathering nature if we are wearing a woman's body. Everything we are, every form, has within it the energy of the mother and the father, the seed of the rainbow.

Here in this new age, this changing of keys, it is we who determine the future. As we learn to work as families, as friends, as groups, united by sacred law, we will renew this planet and her waters. The creative elements of life have not been made impure. They are obscured by our impure thinking, and our thought can very easily make the transition. This is the question for each of us now: Are you one with creation? Do you want to come again to the sacred stream? Will you stand on the Beauty Path? Yes or no. We can't say "maybe." As my grandmother said, "You're either pregnant or you're not." And we are each pregnant with a new world. Each of us is carrying the seed of a planetary unity and a great peace that has not been seen for thousands and thousands of years. The seed of that peace is a child within us all.

To nourish that seed of peace we must nourish one another. To come again as friends, to sit, to pray, to offer food to one another, in this way we return something to the Earth. In your busy life, in the cities, you may wonder how you can return anything to the Earth. Remember the rivers of energy within your own body. The sacred meridians that carry subtle energy through your body also resonate with the energy of this planet. Earth, too, has meridians, sacred energy flows. Some of these places we know as holy places; others we feel for a moment and say, "Oh, is this a power spot?" What is the sacred flow? How do we recognize it? All around the Earth is a lightning grid through which the lightning energy of inspiration flows, quickening the seed that life may grow, drawing forth the waters of the Earth. The lightning grid is the nervous system of the Earth—and our thoughts affect the lightning grid. Our thought forms, how we feel about ourselves and one another, become collected in the gridwork around the planet. As we move through the process of resolution, the last fear, that last guardian of the threshold, shall give way and the Great Peace shall manifest.

We fill each area we live in with forms of our thoughts. Sometimes a thought becomes separated and one becomes fearful. We decided to live in communities long ago so that food could be easily gathered and we could care for one another. In that process of community development we also developed territorial mind. As the tribe became larger, this territorial mind sometimes felt scarcity. That thought form of scarcity is still hanging on around this planet. It is for us to recognize the abundance in our hearts so that the last illusion, that most fearful separation from the abundant wisdom of love, can be put aside.

Discipline the mind so that you see the best. Doubt is probably the greatest scourge of human nature. To doubt the divine order of things is to deny the dignity of humanity. A first step is to look within and extract the thought form of doubt. Realize what you can be sure of: you inhale, you exhale. Our actions are the seeds of tomorrow. The mind weaves a picture, one of many in the great tapestry of life. Inhale, exhale, sun rises and sets, of that there is no doubt.

Give and you shall receive. Share a smile; give alms and kind words. As our own generosity grows, we find that our family receives what is necessary for continued growth. It begins in our mind, it begins in our thought. Have the discipline to say each day, "I realize more and more the wisdom light. I am light, I cultivate thoughts of love and harmony." Something happens around you. When you first begin the process of affirmation, everything will test you. The children who were so well behaved will go wild when you sit down to meditate; everyone will want to speak to you on the phone. You listen and love and return to the quiet. Eventually the distractions will lessen. Our family, our friends, they reflect our inner life. If we see uncertainty around us, it is to remind us to cultivate certitude. We must come again to the only thing we can be sure of—the breath of life, that we inhale, we exhale. By exploring the breath and its movement through the body we can stay centered when many things are going on around us that may distract us from the quiet. We can be sure of this: we live in the present, in the moment. Our thoughts do become a reality. You think "hungry," then you eat.

We are always communicating, heart to heart, mind to mind. There is a universal language that all beings understand. Even these words on the page are just a carrier wave for the deeper communication that occurs within ourselves. To recognize our own thought and to take responsibility for the thought forms we create, to see that which we project and that which we receive and to make a discriminating choice, this is most important.

You are the ancestors of those yet unborn. You are the road of a great peace. May you observe the nature of mind, cultivate generosity and joy, and actualize peace on Earth. May you recognize the power of active intelligence integrated with love's wisdom and the ever-present will to be, that most beauteous triangle of creation. As one sits and stills the mind, subtle means of knowing are revealed in the mind, in the light, in the stars above the head. There is a way of knowing that passes through all realms: to be fully present in the moment, that what is above may manifest below. That is our choice.

How to make this choice when one has so many responsibilities in the world? How to come again to living as truly dignified human beings? God is in the marketplace, too. Everything is part of the sacred flow. To see our work as prayer and an opportunity to bring forth a flash of truth is a great gift. To know that even the busy world is a holy world is quite a change of heart. And as the years go on, perhaps the heart will say to many of us that it is time to go back to the land, or to make stronger and more sacred the flow of life in whatever business we are working in. As long as we are attentive and not reacting to the thought form of limitation, whatever we are doing is sacred. To be aware in the moment, recognizing past and future in the moment, is to be firmly rooted in the now. This is our gift and our bounty as human beings: to have an opportunity to live as individuals and to share in the planet's evolution.

In this time our sun is taking an initiation of great significance. For many of the Native people of this land it has meant a great revival of our sun dances. The sun that feeds and sustains this planet is going through an initiation that will open the door for us to communicate with others in other worlds as we recognize the sun of reality in ourselves. So our thought process and our affirmation of our beauty are important for the Earth and for our entire solar system. A little over ten years ago the keepers of the lodge keys of Jupiter and other planets put out a great song of distress, calling on many of Earth's medicine people: "Are you going to do something about this planet? The experiment is not very good." What was being done here on Earth was polluting the whole solar system. Jupiter was upset because the anger coming from the Earth was interfering with the very beautiful flow of energy between it and its most important moon, Iona. People sat in kivas and longhouses and churches and prayed and listened. How will people hold the form? Do we believe in humanity's future? Are we willing to hold a thought form of peace and continued well-being, or do we have to say to those beings that Experiment Earth was a mistake?

The disarmament movement proves that people are able to call forth good medicine. Cultivate the essential good nature. Affirm that peace may prevail through complementary resolution. Trust that we shall come again as a human family, as beings of light, to live in harmony. You make a difference. I ask you, with the power of your voice affirm peace in yourself and beauty in one another. This is how Earth's beautiful song shall gladden all the universe.

MEDITATION ON CLEAR INTENTION

Sitting easily, spine erect, breathing in, breathing out, allow thoughts to slow, mind to become quiet. Visualize self surrounded in light, receiving heaven's light through crown of head, Earth's energy through base of spine. Be aware of these two spirals of light, one flowing up, one flowing down, dancing in the spine. Maintain the inner motion as you sit. Attune to the primordial force of life, will to be, cause of your living in this time. Will, born of the void, symbolized by egg or circle. Observe the ever-flowing stream of consciousness, light giving birth to sound and manifestation. Attuning to the light of clear mind leads to thought and action in harmony with divine will, enabling one to shape one's life in right relationship with others and with our planet. See that in a universe of abundance there is no scarcity. Dedicate your thought and action to peace. As our solar system moves into a higher vibration, humans shall realize a consciousness of planetary oneness. Perceive within self the silver cord that connects you with awakened mind, enlightenment a seed within you awaiting its glorious blossoming.

Completion stage: Light is absorbed into your being, and a vision of peaceful Earth resides in your heart. Rose light expands from your heart, reaching to all realms with thoughts of compassion for all beings. Maintain equanimity. Then mind becomes quiet.

Go through the day with peaceful thoughts, doing good things.

ᏓᎪᏃᎯᎵ

Da go no hi li

Flying this way

ᏓᏳᎩᏲᎯᏂ

Da yu gi yo hi ni

Daylight

ᏗᏰᏏᏗᏏᎩ

Di ye(s) i di si gi

Wakes them up

ᎦᎷᎩ

Ga? lu gi

She comes

ᏬᎭᎵ ᏗᏰᏏᏗᏏᎩ

Wo ha li Di ye si di si gi

Eagle wakes them up

3

RENEWING THE SACRED HOOP

WITHOUT spiritual foundation there can be no society. Without spiritual practice confusion reigns. Even the
softest prayer sends vibrations of prayer moving through the
air, just as the guitar strings stir the piano's song. To call forth
the voice and to sing in joy and harmony, to let the beauty
flow in our hearts, is something all of our elders have talked
about, saying to us, "Let us pray together, let us do things
together." People come together to pray not only for social
reasons; there is a real power in joined voices. It is the power
of human nature reweaving the sacred web of light, acknowledging the whole community. All that we see is a reflection of
consciousness, and to see requires pulling the veils from the
eyes, pulling away the illusions that limit us in time and space,
the illusions that say we are separate. We are not separate. We
are all together. When we join our hearts in prayer, in singing,
in sacred dancing, in planting things together, we are returning something to the Earth, planting seeds of good cause.

The qualities of laughter, joy, and sorrow and our thoughts
and actions weave the tapestry of life. Spiritual practice

transforms ideas of conflict and develops perception of ourselves and the universe as energies, tones, complementary aspects seeking balance and resolution. There is a song arising in our hearts as a community of human beings sharing and co-creating an environment. The song is of planetary peace, planetary cooperation. It is calling each of us to transform conflicting emotions, to reveal the inherent beatitude. Speak the best of yourself and others, recognize process and change, and affirm the healing power of peaceful thought. Hold the form of peace. Realize that our thought and action shape tomorrow. Each one contributes to the outcome of peaceful resolution. Our hearts and the heart of the Earth are one.

Ideas float through the atmosphere, become trends. Ideas of "Buy this, buy that" float about as advertisements on the waves of the media age. Such thoughts fuel patterns of behavior and cultural belief systems such as "This is good" or "More is better." One chooses which of the trends to flow with. Will you flow with the trend of "holistic health" and become a healer? Do you flow with the trend of "M.B.A." and become a banker? Each person needs to choose carefully his or her response to cultural expectations. The media wave may espouse "Thin is in" while your genes sing "Round survives." The wise practitioner chooses to actualize those thoughts which clarify and ennoble all our relations. As the melodies of life thread through our actions, each person is weaving the tapestry that becomes our tomorrow. Affirm the sounds and overtones in harmonious resolution.

Habitual thought patterns become your reality. While the thoughts may be expressed internally, they still create a force seeking fruition. Prayers and sacred mantras tame the mind by replacing destructive or limiting thought patterns with those that pacify negative traits and affirm the inherent good. One who is consistently thinking "I can't" is really chanting the mantra of failure. One who tames the mind with a prayer mantra—such as prayers to assist one's family and the Earth— creates a new reality. Thus the light of clear understanding transforms patterns of conflict, through developing equanimity, nonreaction to this or that, for reaction creates charge of attraction and repulsion, ripples on the still pool of mind.

Know that all of our relationships are aspects of mind and that our thoughts are always contributing to the forms around us. Within every being there is the seed of our family's full unity; the opening of that great flower of the heart's wisdom is a moment of capitulation into the vastness of mind. When we affirm love and forgiveness as a stream within our hearts, we release in our bodies a great energy, and the sacred flow within us flows more readily, more fully. In that stream of forgiveness we see that we continue on in a process and that we have choice. Our words, our actions, our very breath shape the fiber of our reality. The rocks in the stream are part of the dream.

Everything in form is vibration. Energy moves along an axis, a line of energy of greatest flow and of least resistance. Energy within crystal structure flows as a generator; to manifest the initial form it chooses a path of least resistance through the spiral. Our thoughts sing into the atmosphere. Our very life is application; no separation of the theory and the practice. As you look at yourself, you are recognizing a vibration of life. Removing some of the obstructing thought forms is a result of meditation. See the effect of your consciousness on the stream of life. Choose to manifest wholesome thoughts.

The shape, the movement of the atomic structure within the crystal is consciousness, and the consciousness atoms are moving within us. We are in relationship to all that goes on in this universe. One may commit oneself to holding the song, the vibration, that the current of enlightenment may stir in all being. Choice is very significant. The crystal in its growth process chooses at certain points whether to elongate or truncate its form; the octahedron can also become a cube. The way in which the crystal aligns itself determines how the light will move through. So it is with us.

Thus the Peacemaker must understand vibration and realize that life is a cycle, a process. Attunement to the intersection of the individual cycles with the larger cycles in the Medicine Wheel brings harmony. There is harmony in your heart; it is a gift to share with all the universe. Wisdom arises in observing repeated patterns of mind and action and casting out what is inappropriate. Wisdom develops like the pearl: it develops within the oyster or the mussel as an irritation, and it surrounds that with a very beautiful layered crystalline structure.

To understand process, cycles, patterns is to recognize the beauty of the moment unfolding. It is to be present. What is the thought that stands beyond the present, that builds fortifications of mind and heart? Basically, it is a thought of fear. Yet in our true nature there are only two real fears: fear of sudden noises and fear of falling. All others fears are fed by the mind.

We have come beyond the beliefs of childhood to a stage in our lives where it is time to know who we are and how we are in relation to other things—and to be aware of our choice. Destiny is a matter of our thinking. Life unfolds in the world around us, and our interaction is a part of its unfolding. So the world situation is not happening *to* us; situations are the results of our collective thought and action.

It is important to understand the process of balancing ourselves. The first stage is to know the mother and the father in our hearts, because everything in form, to maintain its pattern, seeks the balance of mother and father. And then there is a third quality generated that people often refer to as the Child, or wisdom nature. What is important is that we be aware of wisdom energy and its flow in our own consciousness, that we make peace with ourselves, accept the wisdom of the past and know that the future exists in our hearts in this moment. Many of us have great secrets stored in our hearts, in our muscles, in our minds. It is time to let those secrets free, to be all that we are. Some secrets may obscure awareness of your life purpose.

It is a common concept in Native American philosophy that we all have a purpose, a spiritual duty. The religion of

76

the indigenous peoples teaches that we have a spiritual relationship and a responsibility with our entire environment. Spiritual relationship perceives a thought of clear action, of people communicating, acting together in harmony. To create the means whereby that may happen, a whole system of ceremonies and seasonal cycles of relationship was carried on for generations. My relatives say it is over 133,000 years that we have been here, the time period of human mind development upon this land. There have been four creations before this, and now we are in the Fifth Creation, the Fifth World. The Fifth Creation, like the fifth tone in music, is the opportunity to go into yet another realm. We can come now to the Beauty Path, the path of right action, of good relationship, of clear intention. That is a choice we make as this fifth cycle ends.

To make that choice is to honor yourself and to honor and respect all aspects of this world we live in, because through this world we are given the opportunity to realize the Great Mystery, the One from which we all descend. To recognize that Mystery is to recognize oneself in step with the seasons, attuned with the voice of the sun and the cycles of the moon. These days these rhythms are called biorhythms; through them we are interacting with the Earth and the entire universe.

Through the energy centers within our own bodies and the meridians that carry elemental energy, we are in communion with Earth and stars. Our thoughts, our actions are contributing creative vitality, or perhaps holding something back by not fully connecting with Earth, due to selfishness. So one goes on a vision quest to be sure one is truly doing the work one has come here for; to understand the seed that planted one in this time and place; to understand the sacred energy and the angelic guide that stands beside one, the protecting forces of life, the protecting angels of life. They, too, are elements of the mind fire.

Cornmeal is the gift of life. It comes from the Corn Mother, we say. The corn grows according to our thinking and our actions. If we do not tend it, if we do not thin it out and water it

77

at the right times, then it grows not so well. So, too, with our relationships as individuals in a family, with our co-workers, our friends. Each of us must sow good seeds. We must plant a garden where we are able to honor and respect one another and recognize ourselves moving in step with the very rhythm of this Earth. This we all know. It is the ideal.

We call that ideal realm Galunlati. In this time of purification we sometimes forget the how, the means to manifest the ideal. First, affirm that there is a path of beauty, very diligently put your feet upon that path, and with great energy, through the practice of good voice, speak of what is good, recognize what is and what may be in the process of change. When speaking of something that needs correction, let the energy you place upon it with your voice be without charge, that things may come to balance and resolution. This is a practice, this is something each of us can do. By practicing a voice of compassion, by activating the wisdom that discriminates, we can speak to one another in the moment and realize how to work together. Basically, as human beings we wish to survive and we wish to communicate with one another. We are all coming to know in a deeper way the nature of true communication. It is said that there will be a time when all upon this planet will speak one language and that language will be few words, many visions. That is a seed germinating in our hearts even now.

The cosmology, the system of understanding from which these teachings spring, it is very old. In this time many are stirred with curiosity to understand these things. And it is good that after the fifth generation of much obscuration and bitterness and separation from ourselves as a people upon the land, we come together again as dignified human beings and look to the means by which we can manifest peace in this great land. We live in North America together. We live on planet Earth together. We live in this galaxy together.

What is the purpose of our being here? The old people say it is to experience and to realize the Great Mystery. That is the purpose. And the seed of that Mystery and that wisdom is ever in us. Mystery carries us around the circle, the Medicine Wheel. In the North we see the special lesson of our actions. We become still, as the lakes become frozen; we understand a certain balance of mind, gentle balance. As we move to the East there is the sunlight of our illumination, the realization, "Oh, I am a person thinking, sitting here now." In the South we find the seeds of our actions, we see the gentle sprouts of their coming to fruition. And we also realize that we carry upon our backs tradition, the thoughts of our ancestors, things that again and again have given a cohesiveness to the very world we live in. As the water drips and makes a canyon, so do the patterns of a people. In the West burns the transforming fire, gateway to the clear light—or to your choice to come again until all the people realize the Mystery. And as we grow wiser, we come again in our sacred meanderings back to the center.

Whatever your tradition is, whatever your practice has been to see the clarity of your mind, whatever has stilled you, trace the roots of that—because as you trace those roots you see there is but one truth, one wisdom. And here the people of Turtle Island say, "Together, by tracing our roots to the Great Tree of Peace, we make whole the sacred hoop, and the sacred fire will be alight in every heart again." To see that happen is an idea, and that idea becomes manifest as each of us makes an offering of our ignorance upon that fire of transformation. Ignorance is heavy—why be attached to it? It can be cast into the flame.

> Be gone, be gone, O thoughts of doubt!
> Be gone, be gone! Let there be peace throughout.

How to make strong the voice and how to maintain it as you walk into the world with many things to do? Perhaps there is a traffic jam, a certain clear reminder of obscuration. "Have to stay cool, watch it. Did I make this happen, did I cause this traffic jam? Well, here I am on this road. Can I blame the street lights? Can I blame the road repair crews? No, here I am sitting on this road. So better I see and think as I drive and look ahead. And better that I remember that I'm on the road because I choose to be." That is a big step; then you are no longer abdicating responsibility for manifesting in your own life what is correct, what is good for you and for the people with you.

So here we are, sitting in the world; we see people playing lots of games with very big missiles, and we are thinking about peace in our hearts. How does it all meet? The ideal of our living as planetary human beings, how are we to manifest that in this time of great arms buildups along borders here and there? It is for us to look at the borders of our minds. It is for us to speak out about those deeds which are unkind. It is for us to stand very firm and strong and say that we will not accept fear or aggression. To be a Peacekeeper is not to be a sissy or a wimp. It is to speak very clearly and to stand up for what you know is correct. To hold the form. If we are anti-anything, then we are still arguing. When we recognize ourselves as making peace, we are keeping peace in our hearts and looking for ways to communicate that in a group process.

Why do we come to war? Because someone thinks there is not enough, not enough. It is the illusion of scarcity. "Not enough oil"—that is not so. We don't need to take it from the Earth, and we know that. So you know you don't want to take any more oil from the Earth and you don't wish to be caught in the game-playing that has become wars around oil. What do you do as an individual? You chop wood. There is always something we can do. As a human family, what are we to do? We meet in groups, we pray, we call people to right action, and we examine very carefully the possible futures being generated by such actions. Have we come to resolution? Do we know ourselves as a planetary family? Your voice makes a difference. It is for each of us to send forth light and a strong voice to say, "We can live in peace, we are strong in our awareness of an abundant universe." As the abundance is known, then what is there to argue about?

80

To have the gift of a body, to be alive in this time is indeed an opportunity to co-create, to bring forth a family of dignified human beings. Through right relationship with one another, through actions that bring forth good for the people, through clear intelligence we see what is open before us and we choose wisely what is the best course—peace. We come again to the Beauty Path by walking in beauty within ourselves and by honoring and respecting that seed of beauty within one another. Thus we bring forth the wisdom of the planetary family. So it is now, in this moment. When my grandfather used to speak these things to me, I would wonder, "Does that mean we were here before?" And he would say, "We were here before, but we are here now and before and after; everything is happening now." To be attentive here and now, that is what is called for. That is to be upon the Beauty Path.

So let us walk clearly upon the Beauty Path. There are many signposts along the way. What do they say? "Quagmire of doubtful thought." Don't walk down that way. See it for what it is, and know that it is woven by the thought. If feeling doubt, just know that as you sit you are breathing, in and out. You can be sure of that. Have some certainty. Realize your voice as a treasure and a powerful co-creator. Let us learn to speak rightly of one another; let us call forth the beauty of one another. Affirm the creative life force within ourselves. Have courage to speak truth.

In this family of human beings many have made a clear voice. Many are finding ways to share skills, planting gardens together, of good will and good seed, respect for ourselves and one another. Many have recalled the wisdom of the elders and know that old truth, new truth, truth is something to be perceived within. Together we can experience moving through thoughts, moving through doubt, coming to know ourselves as human beings. Those who practice and pray together become relatives of one mind. Thus we set into motion a common song, a hope, a dream within this great dream of life. The dream of the Peacekeeper, bringing forth the light that is always there, rekindling the sacred fire. One of the other names for the Tsalagi, the Cherokee people, is People of One Fire. One fire brought forth all, and that fire was a light, it was a sound. So from those sounds, we say, it all happens, from those sounds, through the blue fire of will. And we can meditate and contemplate and communicate with these energies within ourselves. It is not just an idea; it is truly living. As the air is moving in our chest, as the blood is moving through our body, so, too, is the sacred fire of will. The will to be unites us in the dream of humanity. We have come here together, and always that will to continue is strong until we have learned fully the lessons of uncovering peace.

To come to the shores of our knowing, we say you need a canoe to get to the other side. It is good to have a conveyance, to have a means of travel, and that conveyance is a spiritual practice that we share. It is affirming the power of our voice, of our action. It is recognizing that what is happening is simply happening as it is, and our thinking is in relationship to it and calling it forth. We rekindle and relight the wisdom of peaceful relationship, of right relationship, in our hearts, with one another, that right relationship may resonate as a form all around this planet.

What is a thought form? It is an idea. Yesterday I thought of the people needing food; today I plant a garden. There are realms of ideas; Galunlati is the realm of ideal form where our potentials are dancing in the light. We begin to manifest these ideals through inspiration, the inhalation of the Earth's and heaven's flow, meeting in our hearts.

So often our movement through life is based upon someone else's expectations, someone else's vision. Yet there is an innate purpose and pattern for one's birth, a particular harmony maintained by each individual so that the family may manifest its unity. And Earth is asking that human beings realize that the bears, the whales, the coyotes, the trees, the ants, all of these creatures are our relatives. We have a duty to

82

ourselves and to the future to live correctly with all our relatives, to preserve life rather than push to extinction. The environment responds to our thought and feeling. It is for humans to be aware of how our thought, word, and deed affect the environment. One person filled with doubt and anger may wilt the flowers; another person's enthusiasm is such that cut flowers last for weeks.

Just as the seed follows sacred laws to grow, so it is with the sacred fire of clear mind. We come here as infants, whole and knowing. The body is sensing, vibrating to the note of our purpose. Then as children we listen and hear people saying, "You can't, you're too small." So one may shut down a little; that sacred tube that connects us with all that is becomes smaller, dammed by the heart that fears and refuses to see the beauty of one's own nature. Where does the damming come from? Shame: "Oh, was I born with sin?" I don't think so. Blame: "Oh, Mother hurt herself; I must have done it." You would be surprised how many of these old tunes are still running around in your mind even though you are fully grown. Perhaps the names are changed; perhaps now it is a husband or a boss or someone else. But you are still feeling shame, blame, and guilt. These feelings arise from conflicting emotions; they do not reflect the purity that is you. Ember of the true light still glows, awaits rekindling.

MAGNETIZING, REALIZING THE VISION OF PEACE

To understand Mystery,
observe mind.
Stilling fear, mind moves clear.
Sing a song of equanimity
awake within serenity.
Affirm your voice
and choice.
Magnetize a potent dream:
World alight,
illumined peace.

The confused mind is pacified through regular practice to clarify emotions and stabilize the mind. The energy of purification is the power of sound and the chant and the bringing forth of rainbow light into the body from the stars above. By the energy of smudging, prayer offerings of sacred cedar or sage, we purify our environment and atmosphere of habitual thoughts of conflict and lethargy. In the Tsalagi tradition the concepts of pacifying, purifying, magnetizing, and actualizing are the four posts of the medicine cabin. In these pages much has been said of the energies of pacification and purification. We look now to the fourth pillar of manifestation—magnetizing the vision of peace—that we may manifest the body of enlightened action through affirmation and harmony with the sacred law and with one's individual purpose.

To manifest right relationship we energize the vision and attract positive outcome through magnetization. This is the principle of vivifying a sacred vision for the benefit of all beings through chanting, clear envisioning, and right action. Your body, it is an alchemical retort. Encoded within, genetic patterns determine your form and predispose you to certain patterns of attitude, belief, and behavior as shaped by your family of origin. The wise practitioner on the road to enlightened action creates harmony through disciplined practice.

Magnetization is a principle of attraction: by our patterns of thought we attract to our life circle that which appears. Through the generation of sound power, prayer power, and harmonious relationship with the sacred law, we can attract what will benefit all. Our days arise out of our mind's actions, whether we are conscious of the patterns of attraction and repulsion or not. So it is incumbent upon each human being who wishes to live in a sacred manner to maintain a spiritual practice and a moral and ethical framework of living.

All physical form—the table that we see, the tree, the mountain—was first a thought. Some thoughts originate in the mind of God, some originate in the minds of people. All thought is united in the sacred hoop, in that we are one in creation. Whether we refer to the inclusiveness of mind as

84

Great Spirit, Buddha-mind, Christ-mind, Allah, or by another name, essentially there is one truth underlying our attempts to describe what is indescribable. The telephone was an idea; an inventor manifested it as form, and today we call one another around the world. That same thought that brings the communication of the telephone, the mind itself, is the means whereby we may discover the clear light.

Magnetization is a principle by which one conscientiously cultivates thoughts of peace, harmony, good relationship for self, family, clan, nation, the entire planet. Magnetizing appears in many forms. Whether one is aware of it or not, the ways in which we think and speak about ourselves attract results and become self-fulfilling prophecies.

It is said in the Tsalagi tradition that in the first six years of life the child is completely formed and will show you the person she or he will become. Many adults may still be motivated by those early patterns set down in childhood. It is a wise practitioner who carefully changes the thought form of habit and sets a path for certainty through understanding his or her own nature, pulling threads of early patterns and reweaving them into a beauteous garment.

The means of perceiving the nature of your own mind is to observe your thoughts and actions and to set the intention to be the best person you can possibly be, to benefit all. Thus you establish a mind dedicated to the apperception of truth. Dedication is required, for often there are unconscious levers that you tip when faced with the opportunity of leaving behind your security blanket, some old attachment. Sometimes the security blanket is the phrase "I can't," or it may be, "Well, nobody likes me anyway." Invariably everyone writes his or her own script—with the help of family members! Therefore, strong determination and faith reveal energy to accomplish.

Meditation practice with visualization and chanting creates a still pool upon which your nature is reflected. As you begin to practice, many thoughts and emotions race across the pool. As you continue, the emotions race less and less, the mind becomes more transparent, patterns of behavior become apparent. As the thought arises, watch. You need not react. The watching of your mental process is the beginning of understanding. Continue visualizing and chanting. Then begin to clarify channels within the body, that the sacred wisdom fire may manifest in your actions. (The visualizations and the meditation of the Sunray practice, based on the teachings of the Ywahoo lineage, also have a physiological effect in that they release hormones to ease stress and pain, lower blood pressure, and provide other healthy benefits.) Patterns of thought, word, and deed become apparent as you continue to practice chanting and visualization. With diligence and certainty, there is an unraveling of discordant habits.

Speaking to one another clearly of intent and purpose and developing the voice of conciliation prepares us for the great work of magnetizing a vision of peace. Sound also purifies, the inflowing light purifies, making apparent and transforming thoughts and patterns that had been obstacles. Praying out loud, giving thanks and affirming the gifts received, renews body and mind. To take the staff of your destiny into your hands is to align the spine and the breath with the pulses of heaven and Earth: inhaling and exhaling, giving and receiving the mind of appreciation and generosity.

A foundation practice of principles of magnetization includes affirmation and altruism, the desire to help self and others overcome suffering. We may take a negativity fast, observing the ways in which we speak about ourselves and others. When you hear yourself say, "I'm dying to do that," correct to the positive statement, "I'm living to do that." Consider carefully the choice of words in describing self and others. In that words become realities, speak not of another's perceived shortcomings; instead consider that you and others are in a process of becoming enlightened beings, and affirm that the seeds of enlightenment are there.

To begin the process of positive affirmation, give thanks for the gift of life in the human body. When it is clear to you that it is time to change a certain pattern, after giving thanks look at your face in the mirror and affirmatively state, "I shall manifest peaceful mind today." Repeat this three times, and also affirm that you will accomplish three specific tasks in that day. By actually accomplishing those tasks, you create a charge of light energy to illumine the recesses of your own mind. The more you practice, and the greater the effort, the stronger this force. As you become a committed caretaker for the Earth and for others, your affirmation to benefit people and the land unto future generations becomes a storehouse of energy that even shakes loose the energies of aggression, avarice, lust, and envy. When you create this force of prayer energy, always remembering to give thanks and to call forth in yourself and others what is beneficial, this energy transforms thought forms of confusion even in the environment. It is said in the Tsalagi tradition that just a small number of people of one mind, one purpose, fully attuned to the sacred principles, can transform the world and precipitate and manifest what is needed to relieve suffering and benefit all beings.

Heart-to-heart, mind-to-mind communication, acknowledging the sacred fiber that unites us all in this stream, is yet another foundation practice of magnetization. The gardener who cares for and respects the plants has the greatest harvest. The nation that casts aside its farmers manifests drought and scarcity. Our actions individually and collectively manifest in our environment.

In short, magnetization requires clear intention, a clear vision aligned with the sacred will, the Law of the universe, compassionate wisdom, voice of affirmation. Diligence of practice creates the force, attracting and manifesting a goal of enlightened action.

Some people have been severely hurt in childhood, while others have had the good fortune of a very happy childhood. The ease or hardness of early years can set a habit. One person may develop scar tissue and be afraid to love; another, because of early years of ease, may not feel motivation to expand awareness of generosity. Some people feel that they have closed off access to the pure light within themselves when they entered school or when specific events occurred in their lives. One can transform and re-form ideas of self and patterns of relationship. For example, perhaps someone went from foster home to foster home and never felt quite part of the life circle. That pattern may be acted out in adult life as inability to make committed relationships or to actualize creative potential. The antidote is to communicate with the stored memories of the child within, to acknowledge the strength and ability of having survived and come through, and to set open a gateway for loving relationships in the present.

The energy of the loving heart, the energy of the generous heart, attracts into its field what is good. Through the currents of energy moving around the heart, the principle of the life force enables us to incarnate. The thoughts, the feelings that we manifest in this life are a collected pattern with qualities of attraction and repulsion. We attract to ourselves those people and situations which enable us to fulfill our vision and life expectations. Upon awakening commitment to living in a sacred manner, we attract to ourselves the information, the understanding, the teachings that will help us realize our gifts to benefit all.

In the past one found redemption through a savior, through a great teacher. These times call each one of us to manifest fully in alignment with the concept of savior, redeemer. Let us redeem through clarity of speech, purpose, and action, through harmonious living with respect for future generations.

The sacred traditions of each age, of each nation, of each group, arise from society's desire to understand, to codify the mystery of life. The sacred teachings of the Native way, the Buddhist way, the Christian way, the Jewish way, the Islamic way, ultimately trace their form to direct experience of the Mystery. The Pale One, the Buddha, Christ, Moses, Muhammad—each directly experienced truths, and their teachings met the evolving consciousness of the societies in which they grew. The family into which we are born and its religion reflect a star in the mysterious sky. Different people have different spiritual needs, and we can coexist as we are attentive to basic ethics, manners, and morality, codes evolved from people's experience of the Mystery and desire for beauteous relationship.

One can approach study with the zealousness of a convert and then quickly toss it aside. Wise practitioners test and evaluate the teachings of the times and look to understand the nature of their *own* mind, to carefully ascertain their potent spiritual practice. These teachings are to enable you to be the best human being you can possibly be and to help you understand the causes of your birth and retrieve the jewels of your family.

When Native American people sing for the rain, the rain comes—because those singers have made a decision that they and the water and the air and the Earth are one. The song is sung that all beings may benefit from the gentle rains. One's small song—"I like, I dislike," habits of thought—creates dissonance with the large song. Today we are called to sing a unity song. The song of cosmic jubilation renews all beings.

What is creation? Is it something outside you, or are you a part of creation? Creation, the Mystery—in Algonquin, the root language of Tsalagi, it is Ywahoo, the "Great Mystery," beyond the form of words. There is no word for "God"; we call it a Great Mystery, because of its formlessness. And we recognize that there is a creative building that has occurred. The three Elder Fires Above express this Mystery in form, and we ourselves are an expression of the Mystery. In some of the old Tsalagi hymns the Creator is referred to as the One Who Makes the Breath; in other hymns as the Master of Life and Death. Yet as children, when we asked our elders, "What is God? Is it different from the Christian God?" they said, "That which is called God is Aqteshna Ana, which means 'the dew is on the grass.' And there is but One Mind that underlies the dream."

Look carefully at the nature of your mind; look carefully into your heart. Can you perceive in your thoughts the seeds of your reality? Consider carefully the future harvest, your tomorrow, your children's tomorrow, and think of beauty. All of our people are saying we cannot go on this way; all the old people around the planet are saying the Earth is hurting because we have forgotten to take responsibility for life. We think somebody else is to blame, somebody else is the aggressor, somebody else is the victim. It is not so. In the mind it arises, and in the mind it is resolved. In the mind we are related to everything.

When we abdicate our creative energy, then whatever our nightmare is, that will become our reality. Our human nature knows what is true. All of us have felt the sacred fire of truth and at some point in our lives have made commitments to upholding it. We are all being asked, "Yes or no? Are you in the stream, or are you trying to hug the rocks?" We can't say "Maybe" or "I'm working on it, and tomorrow it will be all right." In *this* moment it is all right, when we cultivate seeds of good cause, when we remember the beauty in one another, when we remember that life is inhalation and exhalation. Everything is going and it is also coming; we are dreaming this dream together, and it has no beginning and no end.

Through the vibrancy of mind seeking to know, our lives have been sparked. Every aspect of our life is following this same principle. Whatever we see around us, be it joyous or sad, somehow the seeds of its manifestation have been cast upon the sea of experience by one's own feelings, actions, and thoughts.

Let us remember the prayers that have come to us through our families. It you think your family religion is unimportant, it is only because you have not yet really looked to the essence of the truth within it. We can all trace our roots to the Great Tree of Peace. Many roots, many nations, many religions, all on one Earth. And the root of that sacred Tree of Peace is also within our brain; the Tree of Life and the spiral of the DNA are symbols to remind us of continuity. By your think-

ing and desire you will be brought here again and again until
you awaken to the sacred light within yourself and every
being.

So it is not just for ourselves that we pray. What we pray is
that all may recall enlightened mind; we pray that all may
come again to perceive the beauty of what is. It is not something out there, far away. It is in the heart. In the Tsalagi way
of praying we are not asking for something; all we need is already here in abundance. When we pray we are giving thanks
for what is and affirming our intention to manifest what is
good for all people. So in the prayer there is a reminder for
the action; prayer and action are the same. What is the use of
understanding how to grow corn when your neighbors are
starving and you don't share that knowledge? What is it to
receive the gift of your grandmother without living it and
sharing it?

May we begin again to honor the sacred practices of our
ancestors. Candles, fireplace, fire, altar, cross, star, half moon,
triangle; sacred symbols, all are doorways to clear mind.
There is a secret message given in the prayer. When you re-
cite the Twenty-third Psalm you are connecting with all who
have understood reality through the tradition that psalm expresses; when someone sings a sacred song, that is your
grandmother reminding you of what is. The coming-of-age
ceremony, the song rising from the young person's heart,
connects one to all one's ancestors.

To understand is not as important as to be, because understanding in itself implies a separation, someone to understand
and something to be understood. The knowing is within you,
the flow of breath. All the old people have given us this message. It may have become codified and dogmatic, but still the
kernel of the one truth is there.

People praying together is a beginning—and still the Earth
is asking more of us. She is asking that we take one another's
hands and that we grow gardens together, that we put aside
the idea of "my" garden and "your" garden. It is "our" garden. Look at some of the old people living around you. What-

ever they are doing or not doing, they have done more than you—and they have something to say. When society falls flat, when the culture is dying, the elders are disrespected and we forget how to give or receive. There are things that one can *live*, not just pray and think about. Chop wood for some old man and take it to him. And the lady who lives by herself, who can't get around without her walker, go and visit her once in a while, ask if she needs something from the store. These things we have forgotten, and that forgetting is the sickness of the time. We have all been given clear direction as to what right life, right action is, and yet it has come to the point now where many even doubt that the family is something to be preserved. Family is the circle of humanity. Everything is our relative. We cannot put aside the idea of mother and father and extended family because that one note becomes two, becomes three, becomes four. The family becomes the clan and the nation and the whole planet.

There are beings all around who are watching the Earth to see if we can fulfill the plan of love and peace on this planet. The medicine people, the holy people, are asking for time for the good seeds to sprout. "We are working on it," they are saying. "The people are waking up. We promise to come correct." The Mother is saying, "I don't know, you have had so many warnings, so many opportunities. When will you see?" And the people are saying, "We are still trying." So let us see now. Will people really live in peace and respect one another? Are you willing to put aside a little time each week to share with other people? Are you willing to put aside some time where you meditate and pray together? That is the basis of community. Everything is related. Mother Earth cannot be renewed without our renewal; the pollution in the atmosphere will not be transmuted until the pollution of the mind is transformed. And the transformation comes from putting aside the idea of "them" and "us" and understanding that we are all human beings here together. It is we who have the capability and the responsibility to renew life here on Earth.

It is not so easy to be a human being. Many walk and run, think and talk, have the body of a human being—but there is still a hungry echo, a confused being. What is that? It is wanting. It is living for tomorrow. "Tomorrow it will get better, tomorrow I will know more." But *now* is what is happening. Here we are in the moment. Be present. Understand the patterns of discord. Purify, reform the thought and action by contemplating what has been accomplished. Transformation is a subtle process. It is easy to slip, easy to think, "It's getting better." That is the hungry spirit again; it always talks in terms of more or less. That is confusion, taking us out of the moment. Just see what is. Commit to right action.

All that is to be learned is in the heart. All of creation is a thought of which you are part. Wisdom is in your heart; look within. My family taught me that we came from the stars. Earth and stars: the spiral has neither up nor down, neither in nor out. The energies of Earth and heavens are coming together within us all the time, continually in motion, and within that motion is utter stillness. My grandfather said, "Go sit, listen to the stars. Feel the stars above your head. What are they? Explore them. Listen."

I invite you to now to explore and in that exploration to recognize clarity of mind. Reweave with the light those spaces where emotion and mind may have been torn asunder, reweave where some subtle distortion may have obscured your view of wisdom's fire in your own nature. Come again to the circle of your knowing. Let us explore the many realms of the One.

MEDITATION[1]

Sitting easily, spine erect, breathing naturally, fully, let mind become still. Breathe in, breathe out. Sense or visualize a spiral of light descending from heaven through crown of head, a second spiral ascending from Earth through base of spine. Two spirals of sacred light, mother and father, heaven and Earth, meeting in your heart, dancing in your spine. Sense in *sacrum*, base of spine, a golden triangle within which burn the Elder Fires Above, three sacred fire of manifestation: blue fire of will, red fire of compassion, yellow fire of active intelligence. Energy spirals up from Earth through sacrum to *navel* center, deep forest-green ring just below umbilicus, receiving from Earth five rivers of color and sound feeding five organ systems. *A-E-I-O-U* chant arises from navel, resonating deep within your spine, aligning your intention to be and your being here on Earth in this time. Rising light illumines *solar plexus* center, blue square filled with brilliant orange sun of solar consciousness. Chant *Ha-ha-ha-haa*, diaphragm expelling fear, anger, shame, blame, one with stream of clear light. In *heart* center, see two triangles, one pointing up and one down, apexes meeting. At their joining a deep rose light arises, filling your body, surrounding you with its glow of compassionate wisdom. Breathe in, breathe out, perceive energy of equanimity. Chant the *Ah* sound, radiate the rosy light of love-wisdom. *Throat* center receives ascending spiral light, deep indigo blue tunnel illumined by a single star, center of expression and manifestation. Let the sound *Ooo* become one with blue vortex of Creation's song. Ever moving, light enters golden triangle in center of *forehead*, wisdom eye of awakened mind. Chant *Eee* as crown of head opens to receive light from the stars above.

Above the head seven stars, one above the other, doorways of consciousness. From the stars, cascading rainbow light fills your mind and body, infusing you with vibrancy and purity. Breathe in, breathe out, draw in luminosity through every atom.

Now from your heart send out waves of rose light to touch your family, friends, co-workers, community, bathing all relations in the gentle glow of compassionate care. Breathe in, draw that rose light back into your heart. Rest in the stillness.

In completing the meditation, draw the light energy back within your spine; ascending and descending spirals merge. Arise, peaceful and vibrant with the light, giving thanks for the gift of pure mind, the wisdom fire within. It is well.

Each of us has a song in our heart. Through thought, through action, each one is creating vibration in the atmosphere. When we think about the dancing atoms that build and sustain the forms of life, we can see ourselves forever in the dance. Everything is vibration. Our action rings out in many dimensions, and in that way our thoughts and actions return to us. We may call it karma or destiny; we are living the result of our thoughts and their various overtones interacting with other thoughts. Just as a pebble of intention dropped into a still pond ripples out in every direction, so the appearance and phenomena of our lives and our world are ripples on the serene surface of universal mind.

As the world spins we learn from the Adawees, wise protectors of the directions, guardians of mind's gates, giving form to the formless. Their wisdom expresses through the five wisdoms: the wisdom of the sphere of existence, recognizing the fundamental unity of things notwithstanding differences in external aspect; the wisdom that causes works to succeed; the wisdom that distinguishes particulars; the wisdom that equalizes, makes known common factors; the mirrorlike wisdom, wisdom that reflects things as they are.

We recognize the five wisdoms in the stream of wisdom ever flowing within us, perceived in terms of the Medicine Wheel and the sacred directions and in relation to the five organ systems and the five elements. As we have a clear apperception of how our minds express wisdom, how we apply it, we have greater choice about how we honor the movement of life within ourselves.

In the frozen waters of the North the mirrorlike wisdom reflects our action, its causes, and its ripples in the stream of time and mind and relationship. Guardian of the East, Nutawa, Sunlight Arising, shines wisdom of inspiration, existence; one realizes one is alive, one's gift becomes apparent. From the South the grandmothers dance forth their seed-baskets of good cause, generation, wisdom to succeed, bringing things to fruition. In the West we understand patterns, the wisdom of particulars, as Great Bear dances on ignorance: "Transform, transmute, bring forth what is beneficial in the spiral dance of life." In the center, the hub whence all experience arises, is the wisdom that equalizes.

Always we must come around the circle to find the harmony in ourselves. It is never really lost; we have only to accept it and let ourselves resonate with the whole universe. That resonance is affirmation of oneness. Our consciousness is shaping what is around us. We have called one another together as a family of humanity, and our duty as human beings is to see beauty, to sing, to be joyful, to work the land and to share the abundance. You have learned some great wisdom? Pass it along. You have a gift with sound, you have a gift with herbs? Share it. It is the weaving of the overtones of consciousness, of our minds, that repairs the sacred tapestry of life. So it is for each of us and all of us to make the fabric whole again—and the weaving begins in the heart, realizing unity within. It is simple and it calls upon deep discipline, because this body is the instrument and your thoughts are the musician.

The Tsalagi people say that we, together, are making a world, our thoughts and our interactions very much shaping the elemental forces of life. And with right thought and right action, especially the understanding of our purpose, our gift in this time, we may bring forth abundance and a great peace through peaceful understanding in ourselves and rekindling the sacred Wisdom Fire. That fire burns within each of us, that seed of clarity is ever there. It has perhaps become obscured by thoughts and relationships. When we forget to see the continuity of a thought we began, or perhaps when we have not completely carried forth our plan to realize and understand life, obstacles and obstructions may arise on the stream of the mind and come forth in many dimensions. One can see a clear way and generate the life force to walk very carefully and surely along the road. Doubt is something to turn aside. It is an opportunity to explore deeply. When you find doubt in yourself, look and understand the stream of your thinking. We see that each of us is co-creating reality through three creative fires: the fire of will, the fire of love-wisdom, or compassion, and the fire of active intelligence, building mind. These are fires of truth ever burning in your spine.

Beauty and truth are concepts that are carried in the natural mind. Native people who have lived and walked upon this part of the Earth for a long time and who share a circle worldview, a circle cosmology, recognize ourselves as caretakers. That is what the indigenous peoples of this part of the world have to say, that is the special duty. It is time for us all now to recognize our caretaker wisdom, to take care of our words and our actions, that they may bring forth what is good; to be caring of our resources, that they may be available to our children seven generations unto the future.

We all can take care by speaking with a strong voice, by affirming that we are living human beings and that we choose to live in harmony. Like the salmon that have gone downstream and far out into the ocean, we, too, return to our spawning grounds. We seek to know the source whence we've come. What was the first thought that brought you forth?

For the Tsalagi, the Seven Dancers, the Pleiades star system, is said to be our home. Through those seven wheels of energy, those gates, the world as we know it has come into manifestation. So seven is a significant number, and those whirling stars also relate to energies within ourselves. They are doorways through our mind, our heart. Aligned in right action, one is able to know and see things as they are without thinking of "what if, maybe"—aware in the now. This is a practice of mind, a whole worldview that enables the mind of relationship to develop and manifest. Let us take responsibility for the thoughts we have created and realize within our hearts the meaningful resolution, the lighted fire of our true communication, love.

How are we to do that? The how is most important. We are all part of a circle; we are energies gathering, and we have a choice in how that energy continues. Through affirming life, through recognizing and responding to those energies which are conducive to right relationship with the Earth, with one another, we manifest beauty. What is right relationship with the Earth? Living in the city, sometimes one forgets. It is to honor the season's cycle, to know when the spring fruit blossoms come forth that you have much to be thankful for. Your prayers and your appreciation have a great deal to do with the return of the harvest. We are all sowing seeds, and we are all gardeners. It is the thoughts we put out onto the Earth that bring forth the very quality of our daily life. To be mindful of those thoughts is part of awakening to a dream, a practice that many young people were taught in this land; perhaps in your heart or your childhood you recall some similar learning. The elders taught that it is the responsibility of every individual to awaken in the dream.

The first step to awakening in one's dream is to clarify the lens of mind before sleeping. This is how my grandfather taught it to me:

When preparing for the night, before going to bed, make offerings of cedar or juniper, call upon the light of clear mind to manifest in your dream as action to benefit the people, and clarify your sleeping space with the sacred incense and your prayer. Lying down upon your bed, rest and review the day as it has gone by. Have you acted in the day with your true wisdom light? Acknowledge it and say, "Oh, this shall be continuing." And if you see in the overview of the day that somehow you did not relate completely, say, "Ah, that is an error I shall correct in my ways of relating," and see that moment, that interaction brought to harmonious resolution. So in the now we find ourselves correct. Then affirm four times, "I shall recall my dreams this night," and on awaking in the morning record in your journal your memories of that night's dream. So the threads that link your individual mind with the universal mind are strengthened.

We have seen errors over time. We have seen that certain methods of education, instead of enhancing the intellect, have in many ways brought about a closing of the mind, a dulling of the mind. We come back to something very basic: to experience and understand through our eyes, through the lens of our mind and our being. We are all responding to the symbols around us, and the symbols we create need to be created carefully.

Here again is the responsibility of clear intention. It begins as you awaken. It becomes your daily practice, as you awaken, to offer a prayer, to give thanks for the light that is shining, the light of pure mind within yourself, and the seed of right action. So in simple ways we as human beings are shaping our destiny and our tomorrow. We weave a tapestry of light with our very thought, our very action. To weave a tapestry with understanding and clarity, that is our practice. In every moment to be aware, to know in this moment that you are responding from this moment and not to react from the past, to be here now: that is the challenge, that the adult may truly manifest as an adult. That is the practice of knowing your own mind.

These teachings are coming forth now because of words and prayers and hopes of my grandparents and elders, who have seen things change in many ways and who also showed a most beauteous understanding and peace with life. I vowed I would talk the lessons they had shown, that I would carry the wisdom bundles they had passed. What is it to carry a sacred wisdom bundle? It is to carry in your heart a thought that as human beings we may live in peace, that we can put aside the notion of scarcity and come again to the realization of abundance and peace. Those thoughts that we carry, we shape our destiny with them. It is time for us to think of large gardens and things like that. The abundant rain can be the water of forgiveness, greatly needed in this time so that we can work together as groups and families. It is important to put aside the errors in communication that have occurred through the years and know that we can, without attachment and without a charge that will bring us back again and again to the same type of behavior, make forgiveness in our minds. We can establish a way of thought so that we needn't again act in a way to cause pain or the vision of separation. Each of us is necessary to the circle.

There are many ways to begin to manifest peace. It begins right in this moment with the perception of the light and the purpose within one's life. Our minds are dancing and shaping the fiber of life. To see the purpose one has, that special note, is a very important moment in the vision. What is one's purpose, what is the gift one brings? How is one's voice significant in the cosmic dance unfolding? Your voice is a string upon a harp; your thoughts are the overtones that carry on and on. We are weaving a tapestry of life. As we recognize the flow, the cycle, the rhythm within ourselves, we come to know that there are cycles of moon, of mind, of etheric energy ever pulsing, ever changing, ever renewing. That is how we are ever transmuting; that is the power, the renewing of the very fiber of life, as one decides in the heart to make peace with oneself. Forgiveness is the balm, the soothing gel, so that one recognizes wisdom and the capacity of love, the compassion that turns aside fear and anger, the compassion that recognizes the beauty, holding the form of our planetary enlightenment.

We are the days and we are the nights and we are the stars that illumine the starry chambers. We are holy beings. To re-call this truth is to sense the sun and the moon within our own body as dancing spirals, great mysteries of mind unfolding. It is to feel ourselves sustained by the Earth and sustaining the Earth through the pulse of five principles, five tones, five rivers of color and sound that pass through the navel. From the emptiness came forth a sound, and that sound is intention, will to be. Intention sets into motion the wisdom of knowing, wisdom that sees itself as love. Love recognizes will and intention and knows that actualization comes through active intelligence, active mind. Sacred triangle gives birth to form: sacred triangle, in every culture the symbol of manifestation.

Sacred sound, five sounds arising from the emptiness. Those five sacred sounds have the means of connecting the left and right hemispheres of our brains, and they have a capacity for healing, because each organ system in the body is resonating to a particular overtone that moves in a cycle, a pentatonic scale. Human nature relates to a cycle of five; the music of all ancient peoples has a pentatonic scale. The pentatonic scale is symmetrical, just as the beauty of our nature has an orderly form. There is a certain power in those intervals that we cannot speak about, but we can hear it. Our bodies and minds respond. We are the music, we are the sound, in that everything is vibration, and vibration is consciousness. See the sound. Hear the light. Realize that which we are: constantly changing, constantly moving. And within that movement is a perfect stillness.

The sound of the Earth is a pulse within us, and we can align that pulse through dance, through chant. There is a very old chant, called the Earth Chant, that came forth from what is now New York State; it is about the Paumonkees, a great Indian nation of a long time ago. Some years ago I came to that area with an Indian from Central America. Something called us very strongly, drawing the heart and the whole being to a certain place in the woods, out beyond a meadow. There we saw a fire, a light walking around. Then we heard the song. It was a Deer Clan Mother who walked the land, who maintained a cycle of prayer and song because she had the knowledge and responsibility to generate good. In her heart she knows that her morning song brings joy to the world, that it keeps the sun rising—just as we know that the dances of the Hopi hold the planet intact. The song, the movement, the thought, it is all one. In this moment it is our

101

task as human beings to realize the sacred song and the part we play in this dance, and to be attentive to the flow, to *be* that which we are.

The movement, the sound, it is in yourself, it is yourself. We receive energy through top of head, through base of spine, ascending and descending spirals of energy, moving within us and spiraling around us in contrary currents. Sense the light, sense the sound moving through you as you chant a simple prayer from your heart.

Sense breath, sense consciousness expanding, forgive self, acknowledge the light of yourself. Be aware of spirals of energy moving through spine. Let the heart open. Let the breath flow, the diaphragm be full and free in its movement. Sense Earth's energy rising up through spine, heaven's energy spiraling down through top of head, meeting in the heart and expanding, radiating outward. Simply recognize that power of love which is yourself and the universe in one. Understanding the heart of yourself, there is knowledge of all things, because love and wisdom are an energy that flows, a stream of consciousness in which we all swim. To be a "stream winner" is to be one with the flow, free of conflicting emotions of separation.

Listen to the sacred sound. Allow the perfection, the pattern of joy and harmony in the body, to manifest. Accept the light of yourself. No shame, no blame, just watching the mind. Eventually it becomes quite still. All the thoughts and plans come up, just let them come, because inhibition is denial of what is. Let us simply be who we are. Acknowledge that all those thoughts are flowing and they will become still. And take responsibility for the thoughts. If one thinks, "I can't" or "I won't" or "My life is filled with despair," then that vibration becomes a reality. Affirm the heart's true knowing: "My life is filled with joy," knowing that the family of life moves in harmony and right relationship, that from the first light came two, then three. That blue-white light of will gave birth to a red light, a rose light of love and wisdom. And love-wisdom, exploring itself, gave birth to golden light of active intelligence. From the One the Three, birthed from the sacred sound.

From the One we have come and to the One we are returning. Just within the single body that you sit in at this moment, there are many beings, your cells and your potential. To be in touch with all of those beings, and to express harmoniously the wisdom of the many within the One, that is to be integrated, that is to blaze forth in glory.

There is an alchemical process occurring in this deep, compassionate exploration of all that we are. There is a transformation of energy: the electrons begin to spin differently. And mind recognizes that it is continuous. Time is a river, no beginning, no end. We choose in our thinking to create certain forms and patterns. In this moment I invite you to focus in, to explore the forms that are within your physical body, sensing the three qualities of mind, infused by the power of will, the light of what is, and the balance of emptiness, zero, as revealed by the hollow organs. Listen to that which is within; acknowledge the wisdom that you are. Call forth a transformation within the body, within the mind, a changing of the electron spin, that you may come again to harmony with that which you are, burning away concepts of "them" and "us," revealing the union of mind.

Through the breath Earth and heaven meet; through the breath we sense the balance of mother-father within. To recall this union is a most important way to renew the Earth and our hearts. There are many facets to the human being, many worlds within the light. First there is a thought, an idea of human beings living in harmony; then it is an actual experience and challenge in your life to meet with and acknowledge, from the depth of your nature, the many facets of the crystal light, to see yourself and every person you meet as a facet in a wondrous crystal. How to sing your song? How to hold the form that we are beings of light, planetary beings, universal beings, able to live in harmony? How to hold the form of abundant beings capable of calling forth all that is needed for the people? Within our hearts and minds, within imagination's light, we begin to see the way of resolution. First it is to make peace with ourselves and all those we know. Let break the icy dams of pride, let flow the waters of forgiveness. Feel confident of yourself on the path of exploration, energetically seeking to realize full enlightenment for the benefit of all beings. Know that anger, pain, shame, blame are only thought forms, ripples on the still lake. There is a quality of yourself that can still the formation of those thought forms, by emptying of attachment to ideas of conflict, separation, scarcity. Those thoughts arise. Are they you?

LIFE PURPOSE

How to establish the priorities in your life, to make the right order? The first priority in life is to be true to the creative principle within yourself—to recognize that you have the gift of life and to be a caretaker of that gift. Second is the responsibility to your parents, your family, and your friends—to see the best within them. To call forth the best within others, to understand your special purpose and reason for life, and not to give away what you know until you are certain it will grow—that is important.

How to be sure of your purpose? Look at what comes easily. What are the gifts that most easily manifest in your life in this present moment? What are the areas that you feel called to work in? Are the skills there or not? When do you feel the most clear flow of energy? What part of the Earth are you comfortable upon? As we analyze that energy, as we analyze the sense of fullness and relaxation in the heart and the sense of feeling strong or weak, we are more able to make a clear determination of what our particular skills are and what areas we are to develop further in this lifetime.

Sometimes we have four or five purposes in one life. Some people flower swiftly and realize many accomplishments. Others are like some very rare orchid, slowly developing and blossoming, almost in secret, and then years and years later, when people have forgotten that the seed was planted there, it flowers. So we needn't be concerned about when or how we recognize ourselves to please others. We understand our true entity in accordance with our life purpose and the unfoldment of our own vision and the accumulations of thought force around us from this and other lifetimes. The wise person goes to the heart of the matter, examining the heart of his or her own nature. First responsibility: to know yourself, understand your own mind. Knowledge of self is knowledge of will, the clear intention to be, seeing its threads as it weaves through all aspects of life. And it is each one's responsibility to understand one's family, one's relatives. Understanding of your family is recognition of the lunar and solar energy within yourself, the positive, the negative, the mother, the father— and how within the center of your spine there is emptiness and the potential of the childlike wisdom body coming forth. Your relationship with your co-workers and your clan is also very important, and the land you live in, and the nation. So it is actually quite simple. It beings with you and Creation.

As you more finely tune your concentration of mind upon manifesting your potential in a creative and harmonious way, there is the reciprocity of the universe saying, "That is good." For the young college student, it is the unexpected grant; for the business person, it may be people saying, "I want that product." Always the universe is responding to our question, "This is good, this is correct," or perhaps, "Wait upon that." So we don't make a decision alone. We make our decision in relationship to the world around us. How is my duty as an individual, how are my gifts as an individual benefiting the world? How is it coming back? Can I write something that will help the people?

Sometimes we are aware of our gifts and wonder what we will need to bring them clear. How to turn aside what obscures our great potential? This is very important. Here you may call upon the creative power of ritual. Make a special place, a shrine area, a praying place, a studying place, observing your own nature and all of the world from that place. Make offerings of sage and sweetgrass or frankincense and myrrh, whatever is good for you, to clarify the space. In the mind's eye, in the heart's eye, surround the area with light, that you may have clear direction, clear connection with the seed of your perfect mind. Then look and see if there are certain attitudes of mind that stand in the way. Sometimes people are afraid of success; that is a common fear. How to overcome this fear of success, of accomplishing your goal? That is laziness, actually, because you know you can accomplish, but all these little ifs and what-nots come up.

How to overcome those ifs and what-nots? How is it that we have lost our self-empowerment? How is it that we have lost the essential peace that is within each of us? What are the attitudes and thoughts that stand in the way of our seeing clearly that which we are? In the Native American way of understanding, the first illusion we are faced with is the illusion of pride, of superior and inferior. In the circle all things are related, neither up nor down. Nothing is alone; everything is together. We are in the family of life. Each of us is carrying that spark of will, that spark of clear mind. We each have a special purpose and reason for being here in this time. To uncover that sacred purpose we take a vision quest, a journey within. In a journey to the Temple of Understanding we can clarify our understanding and come to true knowing of our gift and purpose in this time.

The Temple of Understanding is within us and all around. Within this temple there is a great library where the records of all things are kept. The library is a study room for each and every one of us, in which we have stored away all the programs of our expression in this life and the other lives that are coexisting. As you look, you want first to affirm the purpose of being here, to do good, and then to look at the patterns of living that have been moving you through this life, to see if they are in harmony with your primary purpose in this lifetime. If they are not, there is a fire that always burns and never smokes, there within the temple. This fire is where the old patterns are to be thrown as we write out a new model of consciousness, a very clear affirmation of our purpose. If we sense fear in ourselves about meeting our divine qualities and the power of our being, the creative force, we want to take that script and burn it and write a new one, a script that says, "I will be all that I am to be and will manifest all of my gifts." It is also good to look at relationships, to see how we share with other people. Where are the points of least resistance and clearest communication? Affirm those bridges, those fibers of life. And the obstructions, the attitudes and patterns of relationship that stand in the way of your fully manifesting your potential, they are to be taken down, released, offered to the fire.

Basically, there are seven kinds of human beings, that is how the Tsalagi people have said. There is the person who is moving along the line of will; that may be the timekeeper, the drummer. There is the Peacekeeper, the White Chief who never sheds blood; that is the person along the compassionate way, the one who always seeks to bring peace and turn aside anger through prayer and generous actions. There is the one who builds through envisioning, the one who sees along the golden light of clear mind and brings forth with hand and word and action what is beneficial to all. Then there are the builders of lovely places, who bring the dream into solid formation for the benefit of all and who have a way of understanding and communicating along the entire stream of the clan mind, the group mind. And there are the scientists, the ones who have looked at the particulars, who have watched very carefully to see, "Oh, this and this together has a certain effect upon the environment, this and this together brings forth the wisdom of bioresonance; the mountain man has lofty thoughts and the man by the shore has the wisdom of the waves." This is the science of bioresonance, seeing the particular wisdom within each one and recognizing that it is all one. And there is the person who understands the wisdom of the heart, one who is devoted to the ideal, to bringing forth for the benefit of all beings what is good. This one is concerned, not with science, not with the how, but just with being and doing, complete devotion for the benefit of all the people. Then there is the shaker, the transformer, the life-force maker. That is one who shakes aside old thought forms, turning aside what needs to be turned aside. That is the person who wears the amethyst; that is the person who glows with the violet flame.

Each of us at some point in our life is radiating and resonating according to those different rays. As we come to complete integration we make a decision: Will we continue our work for just our own enlightenment alone, or will we continue to work for the benefit of all beings? Will we continue on Earth, or shall we become the seed of a future life, a future planet? These islands in times of confusion, these beings who decide to make a way station for the expanding mind, they are very wondrous teachers. My teacher, my grandmother Nellie, she has become a planet. Her heart was so big, her prayers were so pure. Always she brought people home to eat with her, and sometimes her children and others would say, "Why is this?" And she would look and smile and say, "Have you enough, my dear?" She was reminding us of the abundant universe and the power of compassion. The gift of giving is the gift of receiving. So it was her path to carry her way beyond this time to create a resting place for those minds that have expanded beyond the learning of the Earth. And others decide to stay on Earth until the last person, the last being, recognizes and understands the Mystery of life.

Be aware of the power of mind, remember that we are all in process, unfolding, and let yourself know freedom from the suffering of doubt. We can choose, we can weave; we hold the form, we dance it, and the moment comes when it is recalled in each of us. We are human beings. We can live in harmony and dignity. We can make peace, we empower ourselves to be peaceful. That is an affirmation, that is a hope, that is a vision. By the power of its sound it is a reality.

May our hearts ever recognize the clear light of mind. Let us affirm our wholeness as human beings. Let us affirm the mode of complementary resolution in ourselves and in all our relationships. Let us honor the light of clear mind in each one we meet. The Beauty Path, the Great Peace, is the meeting of ourselves, the perception of our minds, and the cessation of those waves and thought forms that create discord. Let us sow the seed of peace in all our actions, thoughts, and words. Let us renew the sacred hoop.

Ꭳ ᎭᏳᏯᎭᏂᏩ

He! ha yu yà ha ni wa - - Yo ho!

ᏥᏍᏚᏱᏁᎭᏓᏯᏄ

Tsi(s) tu yi ne ha(n) du ya nu - - Yo ho!

In Tsistuyi you were conceived - - Yo ho!

ᎫᏩᎯᏁᎮᏓᏯᏄ

Ku wa hi ne he(n) du ya nu - - Yo ho!

In Kuwahi you were conceived - - Yo ho!

ᎤᏯᏰᏁᎭᏓᏯᏄ

U ya(h) ye ne ha(n) du ya nu - - Yo ho!

In Uyahye you were conceived - - Yo ho!

ᎦᏖᏩᏁᎭᏓᏯᏄ

Ga te(g) wa ne ha(n) du ya nu - - Yo ho!

In Gategwa you were conceived - - Yo ho!

4

THE FAMILY OF HUMANITY

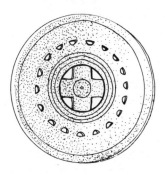

May the clear light of awakened mind become apparent. May each person sing an affirmation of the inherent beauty. May the mind that unites all beings be recognized as the foundation of our shared existence in the family of humanity.

IN the Tsalagi tradition, the concept of "all my relations" begins and ends many prayers. Each person is seen as a relative in the scheme of things. In that no one has recently been born of the emptiness, each person, through the energy of attraction and repulsion, seeks parents as the doorway of birth. All creatures share in the relationships of life on Earth.

The relationship of family members establishes foundations of sane community, in that families comprise neighborhoods, villages, tribes, and nations. The patterns of individual relations echo throughout all levels of existence. The farmer creates relationship with the land and food; the child is in relationship to the caregivers; the hunter is in relationship to that which is hunted. The qualities of mind in each individual are polished and refined by family and tribal or class codes of ethical, moral, and "beneficial" behavior. Such codes underlie the individual's perspective. The farmer's vision perceives where to plant most efficiently; the hunter sees the spoor of the hunted.

A shared worldview brings forth spiritual practices to maintain harmony within families, tribes, and nations. Through oral teaching stories and methods of doing, community members are imbued with that band's cultural mindset. The common vision arises from observation of the cycles of nature. Positions of the sun and the stars make clear the best time for planting and ceremony. At the family level, it is apparent that children born in the spring have a better chance of survival. Individuals living together, celebrating the cycles of life, notice that certain behaviors are more beneficial than others in maintaining group harmony. Those beneficial behaviors become the norm, expressed as spiritual and ethical responsibilities. Those persons who demonstrate sensitivity to subtle understanding and communication are called upon as spiritual teachers; in the past such people would become candidates for the priesthood.[1]

The Tsalagi were traditionally farmers and hunters, living in immediate relationship with the land and creatures. The concept of reciprocity was and is expressed as offerings to the Earth before planting and harvest, and as prayers of appreciation and apology to the animals of the hunt. The idea to offer thanks and apology arises from a spiritual worldview that sees all in relationship. By showing appreciation for the beings eaten, whether flesh, grain, fruit, or vegetable, one caretakes the seeds left for future gardens; the bones become tools or fertilizer. Nothing is wasted.

Thus a foundation concept of relationship permeates all aspects of Tsalagi life. Individuals relate heart to heart with self and others, the nation and the planet. Indeed, each is related to the entire universe. All is related in this dream of life.

The Earth is alive and she sings, calling us to remember

112

our sacred place and our dance in this life. She calls us to recognize that all of us walk around the sacred wheel, that whatever tradition we have come from, we can all trace our roots to the Great Tree of Peace.

Let us make ourselves a strong family of humanity by clearly honoring and respecting the sacred gift of life, by manifesting the wisdom of compassion, and by cultivating active intelligence to build instruments of peace.

The perfected fire of wisdom burns within each person. Perhaps it is only an ember awaiting one's energetic commitment to realize truth; still the seed of wisdom, of perfected mind, is there. For the seed's germination, waters of compassion for one's self and others must fall. Consider how your mental clarity may help others. In understanding your own mind, you note that your daily concerns for food, security, friendship are similar to those of other beings. Consider what you may do for others, thereby gaining insight into your potential and developing means of bringing forth that which is beneficial. By cultivating care and concern for all beings, one gains insight and may transform patterns of discord in one's own mental continuum. Life is a precious gift to be shared. Through bountiful relationship one sees reflected the nature of mind. To the Tsalagi, one's greatest wealth is that of friendship.

Every human being has an obligation to return to this planet and to all our relations the sound of beauty, the power of prayer, the sense of harmony. From the emptiness came forth a sound and that sound was light, giving rise to three sacred fires of form-building, three Elder Fires Above. Sacred will, our impetus to be, our intention manifest in our action and the causes of our continuing. Wisdom, a stream ever flowing, a sense of our oneness with all beings, an understanding that that which crawls, walks, flies, or swims is some relative to each of us. In recognizing that stream in ourselves, there is a sense of wonder and respect for life as it manifests in every part of the stream. Discriminating wisdom, under-

113

standing, intellect, finely honed, reflecting the one Clear Light. Take responsibility for your thoughts; cultivate seeds of good tomorrows. It needs doing now.

In recognizing the sacred symmetry of the universe we note that desires and thoughts born of the heart bring particular results. Heart filled with anger elicits conflict; heart filled with joy inspires joyful action. Desire to manifest Peacekeeper mind sets one on a course of conflict resolution. Faith that "it shall be done" fans the flames of insight. In that moment when you align yourself with faith, a sense of truth, there is a flow of energy that not only passes through your own being but touches the heart of the Earth as well.

Mother Earth feeds us still through an invisible umbilical cord. Five qualities of energy arise from her bosom, entering our navels as sound energy for each organ system. In North America the musical note A feeds the liver, enabling our intentions to take root in form. The note C feeds the heart and small intestine, sending waves of warmth to germinate seed of good relations. Ideas and transformation are stirred by the note D flowing to spleen and stomach, while kidneys receive the note G, strengthening sacred will to be. The note E feeds lungs, and mind cognizes, recognizes, serenity in the flow.

Five streams flowing through the navel, streams nurturing the body, expression of mind. As the note plucked on the instrument string brings out overtones that generate multiple harmonies, so, too, does the human being set into motion fields of great resonance. It is the physical, the mental being that is inscribing on the field, and it all unfolds through vibration. The intention, the thought, is a vibration whose overtones can be perceived in the physical form. One way to see this relationship clearly is in the alignment of organ systems through sound; this can bring about change throughout the whole being. For example, the bodily relaxation response to particular music may be expressed by deeper respiration.

The liver, in Tsalagi healing, is related to the wood element; it is the roots of your consciousness in physical form. The liver feeds the soul, through assimilation and synthesis;

its greatest power is in the synthesis of experience. That experience comes back to the stream of your whole integrated nature through the removal of obstructions in the nervous system, especially in the three main channels of the spine. These channels are the three fires that we speak of: will, compassion, and active intelligence.

The heart receives the spirit. Spirit refers to that individual mind process that chooses to incarnate, to learn, to carry particular wisdom to the source of its nature. In terms of physical function, spirit may be described as the individualized aspect of mind. Heart also feeds the small intestine, the processes of digestion and building; they are related to the fire element.

Spleen relates to ideas and transformation, breaking down what is old and building again what is new, in relation to blood factors. It also has a corollary in terms of our consciousness. It is an organ whose subtle nature, whose etheric counterpart, is very much involved in the process of transformation, as are the adrenal glands. The spleen is equally charged, whereas the liver and heart are more positive in charge. The spleen is Earth element and also has fire. Just as in music one note contains all sound, so within yin there is yang, within yang there is yin; within the north there is the south, within the south there is north. Always there are those counterpoints in internal symmetries. At certain times in the human cycle they reverse, the resonances change; that is related to one's biorhythms. To be aware of these changes and to move in harmony with them is also to be more comfortable walking on the Beauty Path. It all comes back to our intention, our action, our relationship; we see that cycle of reciprocity, that cycle of renewal, continuous with our thinking. Therein we empower ourselves and work significant echoes of harmony throughout our environment. Our creative and intuitive ability is also enhanced by awareness of cycles.

The lungs are feminine, or negative-receptive, in their charge. The feminine energy is expanding outward. The best perception of these principles of yin and yang, sun and moon, as cohesive factors in the universe is through sensing the ascending and descending spirals of light energy in the spine and the expanding ripples from the heart. The lungs relate to frontal lobe thinking through the metal element. Much of our transformation process, especially at the level of emotion, occurs through the lungs and the energy bridge or doorway behind the heart. The body requires a certain balance for the energy to flow, for the doors to open. There are several such doorways in the body: the lumbar spine, just above the sacrum and behind the navel; the solar plexus; behind the heart; behind the throat (first cervical vertebra); and at the medulla (seventh cervical vertebra). These are places on the spine where the energy will often accumulate and become obscure until certain changes of consciousness, posture, breath occur. The fires that go through these doorways are the fires of will, love-wisdom, and active intelligence.

In this time the liver is working to capacity and beyond in the process of assimilating the great amount of information that is available to human beings and in transforming pollutants. There is also a great deal of mental pollution that the liver seeks to break down. The liver is much taxed in a time of stress, to bring our excesses into balance. We can consciously assist this process as we make more complete the relationship of the sun and the moon in ourselves, and of the feet to the ground, and as we dissolve those patterns of thought and habit that add stress to the physical body.

Sound is the greatest healer in Tsalagi medicine. Through the tones of the medicine chant, physical organs are reminded of their optimum pitch. Through understanding sound, one understands the mystery of the unformed forming. Through your thought and speech patterns you determine your tomorrow.

Certain sounds also give information about the condition of the organ systems. The sound of a shout will convey that there is imbalance in the liver. When a person's voice rises involuntarily, becomes loud, this suggests that there is an accumulation of bile, which is self-doubt, self-negation. There are many reciprocal relationships of thought to organ systems and the functioning of the whole person. Perhaps the movement of the bile is obstructed by some thought of anger that did not receive expression. What might one do as a friend, as a healing practitioner, to bring that to the person's realization? One can send sound and light directly to that part of the body. The sound for the liver, the note A, can break apart whatever stones may be obstructing the bile duct.

The sound for the heart is *Ah*, the sound of laughter. The sound for the spleen is singing; singing transforms, even singing softly to oneself is transforming. The lungs, they weep, they wash away. Then there is the groan of the kidneys.

The body orifices or doorways that relate to the organ systems include eyes for the liver; ears for the heart; nose for spleen; mouth for lungs; and urethra for the kidneys. And in relation to body parts fed by the organ systems: liver feeds ligaments and muscles; heart feeds the arteries; spleen feeds muscles; lungs feed skin and hair; kidneys feed the bones. Thereby one's intention is rooted in the body of "now."

Just as our organ systems are supported by Mother Earth's compassion, she is supported by our caretaking. To return to Earth appreciation and caretaking of her waters, mountains, and atmosphere is the responsibility of the children. That is our song in this time.

The voice of creation sings its song. Let us recognize the power. Let us put our hearts and minds into a place of affirmation. We see many things happening in the nation and in the world at this time, events that arise from an idea of separation. Let us hold in our hearts a sense of sacredness and an affirmation that each one of us is a holy being. To make peace in our own hearts is to begin the process of disarmament. As we take down the fortifications of our own hearts and minds we begin to communicate fully with all our relatives.

In Tsalagi, water is *ama*, consciousness, like mama, and when we awaken to the cleansing properties of water, then we may wash away the obstacles to good relationship with self, others, the Earth. The first step is to pacify those thoughts, actions, and feelings that may obscure our sense of relationship or our power to see clearly and act responsibly. Pacifying the emotions of confusion is done through forgiving oneself and others for what might have been, could have been, should have been, and allowing the charge of emotions unexpressed to be carried away in the water-mind of forgiving. Pacifying the emotions does not mean denying or suppressing them; the emotions may be a means of understanding.

Pacifying emotions requires communication with the subterranean streams of feeling within one's life. By observing the emotions and the patterns of their arising, one may respond without being carried away. Emotions of fear, anger, envy, are seen as ripples on the stream, caused by winds of confusion. Mind dedicated to beneficial actions calms winds of confusion.

Among the Tsalagi, when children argued about an object, it was removed and the children were encouraged to observe the sky. Elders reminded the children that placing attention upon an object and seeking to possess it takes one outside the circle of harmony. The children were then invited to relate the vast completeness of their experience with the vastness of the sky. "Look at the clouds. What do you see? Can you see the sky beings?" Thus attention was placed on openness so large that one had no desire to possess it. If that teaching was not clear to the children, they were then reminded of some selfish being who, through wanting, lost what was in hand. Those who had argued would be asked to assist at some task, to replace wanting thoughts with giving thoughts. This gave the children a sense of purpose.

Developing visualization enables one to call upon the light of clear vision to perceive the pattern of right action and our individual purpose in life. Upon realizing one's life purpose, one then magnetizes that vision so that it may actualize for the benefit of family, clan, nation, planet, for all beings.

Each sacred tradition describes these times we are now living in as a chance for transformation. Each person is part of the Beauty Path that leads to peace. That which the people await is a seed seeking germination within our hearts. Many people await the rekindling of the sacred fire of peace. Some may say they await a particular savior, messiah, or peacemaker, yet all await peace. We cannot think of nation being outside us or of planet being away. We are one in this dream.

First steps in our own purification: To affirm that we are light and truth and to honor that in ourselves. To affirm the beauty and relate to the ideal of peace in our human relationships. To bring to balance within ourselves the solar and lunar currents, the mother and father energies. In the tradition of the Indian people of this land, "spiritual leader" is a way to describe one who expresses that fullness of heart. Such a person knows that she or he is mother and father to all things, birthing a dream to benefit all beings.

Each of us has this potential gift: to put forth the thought of harmony, to bring the corn to its highest growth, to bring the tree of fruit to growing in the desert. The power of human mind, expressed through compassionate action and service, is a sacred fire that will renew each of us and is renewing all in this time. We can listen to the voice of the Earth as she shakes and sings her song expressing her tiredness. She is calling us to attention, to be alert, to recognize that now is the time to transform selfish thought and action to compassionate caretaking. Do we want a world of peace and harmony? Are we willing to make that peace within ourselves? Will we call it forth? It is your choice. Your thought and actions make a difference.

Will, primordial force of life, intention to be; the circle, oval, egg, symbol of the One, the fertile void. From that emptiness something arose and in recognizing itself realized lovewisdom, stream ever flowing. Thus emerges the two, separated from the One by observing itself: duality, "parent of intelligence," symbolized by two parallel strokes of lightning potential. As an individual coming into the world, you first learn to master the sacred body, this temple built by your thoughts. As you gain understanding of self, the heart knows

119

the need of friendship, and that, too, is found. The meaning of yin and yang, mother and father, is revealed in the dance of life, seeds of family taking root in the South, garden of renewal and action. So the two gives birth to relationship in the family, the three, the formless manifest into active intelligence—sacred triangle, gateway to understanding the interweaving of all things. In the triangle one has opportunity to see, to be, to experience life. (See Appendix A, "The Family of Life.")

We are all creators. The very act of our calling ourselves together—as family, as friends, as co-workers—is a creation arising from each one's mind and being. We have chosen to be together. Consciousness of choice and relationship is medicine for us in this moment. Let us know that we can work with one another, see the best in one another, and diligently and energetically maintain the idea of truth. We can hold in our eye, within the sound of our voice, the concept of harmonious resolution. This is a practice. Be happy; remember, it is our sacred duty to let that energy of happiness flow from our hearts, rather than saddening the flowers around us. This our Tsalagi elders have always taught. Let us be like the water lily floating on the waters of experience, rooted in the mud and yet ever open to the sun and the clear light of reality. It is discipline at first, then a continuing state of mind, a recognition that it is and that one is simply be-ing.

We hear much about service in this time. How do we serve the good? As a loving grandmother cultivating the best in her grandchildren, guiding them all to wisdom and skillfulness, to manifest their potential. Your sacred gift—be it of poetic sound, or of creating pictures that bring peace to other people's minds, or of sitting still, thinking peaceful thoughts—that gift is to be expressed and shared. The wisdom of the sacred dance, the movement of our hands and glance, return to the Earth a sacred flow. Just as life's energy moves through holy riverways, the meridians of our bodies, so, too, is it moving through this planet. Thus we communicate, giving and receiving the abundance.

Illness comes from thoughts of separation and conflict, ideas that there may not be enough or that one may not be worthy to receive the abundance of this universe. From the illusion of scarcity arises fear of sharing or doing what is needed and beneficial. Scarcity is an illusion, alienation is a thought. A selfish heart is a severely wounded heart. That heart is healed through giving gifts, first to one's own hand, then by sharing with others. When generosity is cultivated, the Magic Lake of Wisdom becomes apparent.

To the light, come to the light. Let the clear light of reality shine upon a meadow within the mind's eye, a vision calming the mind like the sacred sage, wand of sweet fragrance. So sweet, the fragrance of life.

Once there was a handsome young man filled with grace and with a voice that charmed the stars. In a flash his loved ones were taken from this Earth. His family gone, he felt bereft and alone. He felt that life should end for him, too. As he pressed a knife to his heart a bear approached and said, *"Ho yoho yoho!* Why do that?"* The young man was suprised that another cared, he had forgotten he was not alone. The bear asked, "Who does that body belong to?" The young man hesitated. The bear answered for him: "It is a robe lent to you by the Creator, that you may experience life. Since it was lent to you and is difficult to get, you had better not destroy it."[2]

This body is an opportunity. It belongs not to yourself alone but to all those with whom you interact. It is a gift, given and earned through your actions, to express the beauty of Creation in this time.

How to discipline the mind so that it no longer holds on to its fear of death, of old age, of the human condition? How to see the joy, the precious opportunity? It is a matter of choice, a matter of practice. What are we certain of in this life? You inhale and you exhale, that you are certain of. When all else seems doubtful, focus on the beauty of the breath and receive its teaching of the circle, giving and receiving, all in relationship. The sacred breath, the sacred sound, a path. Just as the prayer sound is a thread weaving mental stability, cloak of clear mind, so is the affirmation, "I am light, I am love." To affirm the creative energy in our lives is a mantra, a healing of the mind.

Sense the wisdom of your ancestors, that you see the cause: your parents before, your desire to be with them, to learn around them; and the present, that which you are. Just for a moment rekindle that sacred fire within your heart. Let it be a vision, let it be a thought. Sense that light anew within your heart. Accept the blessings of creation. Accept the gifts that are yourself. The sacred spiral, its light giving birth to form, surrounding us. Neither in nor out, neither up nor down, just the pulse of life's energy within ourselves.

That fire, is it kindled? Is that light of love and transformation an image in your heart? Imagination shapes tomorrow. What is now an idea will then be a reality. You see, perhaps, some limitations of thought, some idea forms that stand in the way of full expression of your sacred being? Place them in that fire of transformation. You have doubt in your ability to be? Cast that doubt into the fire. Is there forgiveness that you seek? Is there someone to whom you wished to express the beauty, and words or actions were not enough? Forgiveness, too, is a stream. We are all ever pure and will be forgiven as we forgive ourselves and come again to that sacred hearth fire, heart fire. Let us forgive ourselves and others our trespasses into the world of ignorance.

> O Sacred Water, I come again to thy shores,
> I see the ever-flowing wisdom stream.
> O Sacred Water, I enter thee, let wash away
> Those weighty thoughts that keep me
> From your sea of equanimity.
>
> O Creator, our eyes become clear,
> Wisdom's sacred light shines in our hearts.

Let us see, let us be
That which we are.
May all beings realize
Harmony and unity.

A simple prayer that each may understand and see the beauty affirmed in one's life and action. And those who are our leaders in government, may they hear the sacred sound and may all act responsibly so that the children seven generations from now will have a land to walk upon and water to drink and mountains to see.

On awakening, all the people of the past would pray and offer thanks to the sun. Somehow in this busy world it is forgotten. It is most auspicious for the present and for the future to acknowledge the energy of appreciation. A prayer of thankfulness puts you in harmony for the day, that you may ever resonate with a song of harmony. To walk the Beauty Path requires a most courageous and compassionate being—courage enough to turn aside the ignorance and compassion enough to encompass it, to bring forth light and the beauty of one another. All beings are sacred. This is an ideal that all of our peoples hold.

Ritual is a key to the family's healing. A family that prays together has an understanding, a communion, that helps maintain the very fabric of this planet. For the plants to grow, for the water to flow, for the wind to breathe, each of us must know that we are carrying a sacred seed of truth and caretake it. Carefully plant seeds of good cause, good relationship, that gardens of good results may truly flourish. Actively assisting family and neighbors, expressing generosity for all, we renew the circle of good relations. And whether one is alone or with a family, one is always a member of the family of life, the family of humanity.

In the Tsalagi tradition, the yearly Friendship Ceremony is very big medicine, when people come together from all over the planet to renew tribal ties and offer to the sacred fire the obstructions and limitations of mind that may have been generated through unclear speech or action. Thus we are ever renewed in the sacred circle; thus we are not separate from one another.

Separation is an illusion that causes dis-ease and distrust even of the sacred voice within ourselves. To focus the mind and to tone the being on the voice of truth within, to swim in wisdom's stream, is an accomplishment that one earns through action, through recognizing one's sacred duty and doing what needs doing. Each one of us has a sacred duty to maintain this form of living beings, living planet. Some of us may have a duty as healers, others as voices of form-shaking. Even the young and the old have certain gifts. The one who disagrees with you is serving a sacred purpose in showing you the limitation of form. Such a person may be a "contrary," a "thunder being," one who inspires deeper understanding. Thunder is inspiration, electrical, and it is also the sacred flow of energy that encircles this planet, uniting each of us in a lightning gridwork that moves around our mother, the Earth. This lightning gridwork is affected by our thought and our action. If we hold back the flow of light in our own being, not only is our own physical form occluded in its meridians and its rivers of life, but our mother, the Earth, suffers as well. Our neighborhoods suffer. The plants do not grow as well when the heart is closed.

Tsalagi philosophy, *Elo,* recounts how in the original migrations of the people from the land of Elohi Mona, each tribe or race was given particular responsibility to maintain certain areas of the Earth. Through prayer and ritual the stability of the physical form is maintained. In this time right action is being called forth from all, to renew the sacred hoop. As sacred ceremonies are kept, dances danced, the lunar and solar currents within the individual clearly resonate with the lunar and solar energies of the planet. As individuals maintain attitudes of alienation and ideas of domination over the natural order of things and over one another, there occurs an obstruction of the flow among the individual, the group, and the electromagnetic current of the Earth, thereby disturbing the flow of the wind and the lightning, which brings life-giving rain and germination properties to the seed. Hence each one is called to make a choice: with the stream or not. No equivocation.

Choice, we all have a choice. Now we make a choice between the world of inventions and the world of what is. Each one of us is being put to the test, like eggs being held to the light to see if the chickens are growing well. We have an opportunity to see those thought forms which are not conducive to our wholeness and to let them go. The thought is not you; it is but an idea form. Recognize yourself as a stream leading to the sea of equanimity. Honor the sacred wisdom of your family and all relationship.

From the three comes the four, the square, the neighborhood, the extended family and the energy of healing. In the past, when we were closer to the land, we grew food together and cared for the old ones together. In that way the sacred wisdom was passed on. A sense of rootlessness comes when we have not the voice of the old ones to hear. Let us honor the wisdom of our elders so the children may recognize the power of the past in the creation of the moment, just as we acknowledge that our thought is shaping this world and that we are ancestors to those who are yet to be born. It is as simple as thinking of your neighborhood as beautiful, your family as whole, and actively bringing that thought into manisfestation through your words and actions. That is to hold the beauty form.

To walk the Beauty Path is to bring again into harmony the left and right hemispheres of the brain and the midbrain, to honor sacred dance, sacred movement, the power of the voice and breath as vehicles expressing the beauty of what is. Let our eyes begin to realize the power in a glance and look at one another with love and respect, to call forth the best in one another. Let us walk our Beauty Path together and understand the sacred power of community. Those you go to school with, they are your family; you have called each other. The people you work with, those, too, are relatives. And the critters you

live with, those, too, are relatives. Our sacred duty to one another is to build community on a foundation of right action,
on a foundation of sacred truth.

What is the sacred truth? That we are here together in the
moment, in the opportunity to realize the wondrousness of all
creation. And like the salmon that swim upstream, we, too,
return to the source of our being. At this time, that return is a
group process. It is no longer the age in which one can attain
alone. Now the heart calls forth compassion and service and
growth in a group process. How to make that alignment, how
to recognize ourselves in the family of life? Recognize mother
and father within and come to peace with those elements.
Know the creative power of your mind and be willing to give
the mind a harmonious form within which to operate. This is
the importance of the sacred practice of prayer and a daily
way of meditation. Then, realize the gift of education, the
power of knowing, and share that wisdom with others. Thus
we build a strong community, a strong nation, a strong
planet, and reawaken the thought of our universal relatives.
We are the Beauty Path. The Peacekeeper that all peoples
await is a seed within each of us. Let us hold the form of
peace by making peace within, letting the mind become still.
Those thoughts that you feel are incorrect, let them go. They
are not you. What is truly you is ever beautiful and ever in the
stream.

O come, Holy Mother.
O come, Holy Father.
O come, Holy Child.

BIORESONANCE: OUR HEARTS AND
THE HEART OF THE EARTH ARE ONE

Around the planet Earth the wind-shields move in two
shells—outer shell, solar; inner shell, lunar—in accordance
with the movement of the tides and the tectonic plates, which

cause fluctuations in Earth's magnetic field. The lunar current, moving within the spine, corresponds to the lunar wind-shield about the Earth, and the solar current of the spine corresponds to the external solar wind-shield. In Native American symbology the counterclockwise swastika represents these sacred planetary currents, the creative forces of the universe as they meet within ourselves and over this planet.

As there are shells of electrons surrounding an activated crystal, there is an electric gridwork surrounding Earth. The crystal is activated by sound, heat, movement, and pressure to generate along its axis a field of energy five cubic feet per pound of crystal mass. The first layer out from the crystal surface corresponds to the Earth's electromagnetic field. Then there is the electric storm system gridwork, known as the lightning gridwork: coordinated pathways by which thunderstorms travel, quickening the seed germination process through nitrogen fixation and rain. The lightning gridwork corresponds to the nervous system's transmission of energy. The Thunderbird is the conveyer of aspiration to englightened action.

Radiating outward from the crystal matrix are subtle shells of energy (worlds). The lunar and solar currents (descending and ascending spirals) of the wind plates correspond to such currents within the spine. The crystal matrix emits the basic pulse, will to be, as encoded in DNA form, actualizing and maintaining the basic relationship of form potential.

127

Earth, human, and solar processes are interwoven through this vibrational network. Hence Earth and human beings are ever in a reciprocal bioresonant relationship. Awakened minds perceive clearly the relationship of energy pathways of individual mind and environment. Through clear intention radiating throughout the matrix of mind, the medicine person mentally precipitates the needed rain. So it is that we individually and collectively generate the causes and effects within our lives.

The Colorado and Tibetan plateaus are channels for lunar and solar currents. Lightning and wind currents are highly energetic at these locations. Since stabilizing life force of ascending and descending spirals is focalized in these areas, they are power spots generating negative ions, purifying the atmosphere and strengthening thought process on all levels. As there exist in the human body meridians, pathways of energy, the energy ley lines of the Earth are interactive with those of living beings. At connecting points of the energy byways exist acupressure points and Earth holy places or "power spots." The ascending and descending currents cross the east-west wind flows, generating the swastika or cross-coordinates of space, that the idea may coalesce as form.

There exist many sacred places as cross-points of the energy dance. Black Mesa of the Hopi Plateau, the Black Hills, and other areas are pathways of lunar energy. The Tibetan Plateau, the Rainbow Serpent Mountains of Australia, and others are focal points of solar energy. These areas are highly sensitive to prayer and meditation as impetus to manifesting increased life force distributed throughout the energy gridwork. This is reason for care in land management. The temples at Oaxaca, Chaco Canyon, the Temple Mount and Dome of the Rock in Jerusalem, the Kaaba of Mecca, Stonehenge, and many other areas are points where the lunar and solar energes converge with the easterly wind of "Being As Is" and the westerly winds of transformation. Convergent points of planetary energies have been focal points of civilization convergence due to heightened energy of unmanifest becoming real.

In this ninth and final stage of purification the wind patterns are changing greatly. This is an expression of confusion in the planetary mind, the group mind of all beings upon this planet.

The sacred rituals of the Native American peoples and other peoples about the world are derived from original instructions from the Source of all being to maintain the integrity of the form. For example, the Tsalagi people, after a long migration from the stars to what was known as Elohi Mona, through South and Central America, spiraling down to the southeast of what is now the United States, were given custodial responsibility of the Smoky Mountains. The Salish people of the northwest coastal regions were given responsibility for the rivers and the shores there, to keep clear the rituals, so that the winds would resonate along the ideal plan. The eastern shores were given into the responsibility of the Micmacs and the Wampanoags and others, the Dawn Greeters. Each group is responsible for generating harmony for the local and planetary environment.

The Ideal is a primary tone generated by the crystal matrix at the center of the universe. The place of this crystal is also known as Galunlati, the seventh heaven, the realm of ideal form. The crystal, vibrating at 786,000 pulses per millisecond, is neither solid nor not solid; its vibrations occur faster than the speed of light. From the emptiness came forth the sound, crystallized mind precipitating that which we all dream. The crystal gridwork within the Earth and the seed of clear mind within the individual resonate with that primary tone, which is the will to be. Through that primary crystal and its intention to be arose the overtones of wisdom to see things as they are, and active, building intelligence—three creative fires through which the Ideal is precipitated into form.

The wind currents flow in accordance with the pulsations

given off by quartz crystal within the Earth, in the same way that electrons flow around the nucleus of an atom. The wind currents are disturbed by removal of uranium and coal (which usually "caps" uranium); those ores function as transformers or alternators for the crystal energy, and their removal changes the flow of crystal energy throughout Earth.

The lightning: one bolt becoming two, wisdom observing itself, recognizing the potential of many and the equality of all, and that its source is itself. The lightning energy, the energy of inspiration and stimulation of seed growth, is the compassionate wisdom in its apperception of self that stirs the nitrogen fixation process within the Earth. When lightning hits Earth, nitrogen is released in the soil, enabling the seeds to grow; so say my elders.

The Earth's breathing holes harmonize the energy of mother-father, lunar and solar currents, that life may be upon this Earth. The Colorado Plateau, particularly the area of Black Mesa, is the energy channel of the mother, lunar energy, renewed through the breathing holes of that area. The Tibetan Plateau is the channel of the solar energy, father energy, renewing and clarifying these stresses through the Earth and the people. Periodically, the wind-shields around these two plateaus reverse their positions, very much like the biorhythm cycle within the human being. Through right practice, clarifying the stream of the lunar-solar currents in ourselves, right relationship becomes manifest upon the Earth.

Practitioners of the sacred teachings being passed today through the Ywahoo lineage of the Tsalagi Nation learn a sacred dance, the Dance of the Directions, based upon exercises and dances taught by Eli Ywahoo, Eonah Fisher, and Nellie Ywahoo. The purpose of the dance is to keep clear the channels within the body, that they may resonate with the land itself. When facing magnetic north, one clarifies mental orientation and tunes the electron spin of the atom of one's own body at the angle for optimum energy expression. A test of one's accomplishment is the ability to generate light from the body, through the clear alignment of one's mind with the magnetic field of the Earth and the solar system. There are successive stages of realization, alignment with focal points of mind—with Earth, then with sun, then beyond. The purpose: to generate light, to generate good for all sharing this dream. The practice in all its aspects clarifies the stream, that the potential for enlightened action may manifest throughout all worlds.

Let us think about the breathing holes around Hopi and the breathing mountains of the Tibetan Plateau. These places have long held the balance of our planet. When the lunar winds are over Hopi, the energy of the sun is over the Tibetan Plateau, and in twelve hours it reverses. Deep within the ground there are caverns and tunnels and ways for this sacred energy to travel. Earth inhales and exhales just as we do; sacred life energy moves within her body as it does in ours. And from the mind of scarcity, greed, and domination, much of this sacred body of our Mother Earth is being cannibalized and destroyed, through the ignorance of mining without consideration for the future, depleting Earth's resources and polluting her waters.

Right now in Hopi and at the most sacred Black Mesa, there are great amounts of water being drawn from beneath the Earth to move coal to light great signs in Reno, Los Angeles, and other cities. The electricity used by one casino sign in a day could keep a small town in electricity for almost a year. The areas from which the waters and ores are being taken may be designated by the United States government as "national sacrifice areas," but it is not the people who have made these decisions. It is the abdication of responsibility by all people of this hemisphere that has allowed a few large companies to decide—and to have the decisions enacted by government—that a certain area can be designated a "national sacrifice area." What are we sacrificing? We are sacrificing the future. As those aquifers are depleted, the electrical energy of lightning has no place to be called to. The lightning activity is the pulse, just as the nervous system is

131

the pulse that animates your body. So, as these aquifers are further depleted, there is less and less energy for growth, for life. There are also more subtle effects of the lightning.

Through ignorance and greed, seeking to control light, seeking to control power, mankind's technology is destroying the very basic power of our planet. Inventions came about to assist humans. Now inventions run over humans. And this has come about through a false viewpoint. We have looked and felt, "Oh, the Earth is here to give to us," and it is true; the whole of Creation is an opportunity to know the beauty of what is. Yet something has been forgotten: the return, the reciprocity, the fact that the Earth is a living being. Within our own physical body flows the energy of life. Through the top of the head and the soles of the feet, the base of the spine and the back of the knees, we give and return energy to the Earth and the heavens. When the heart has become obscured with doubt, with anger and greed, with greed for power, thinking it is something outside ourselves, then the energy is not returning to the universe, then our breath is not completed.

We have a short time in which to transform incorrect thinking, mental imbalance, and to learn again to live with dignity as human beings, because the elements of life in ourselves have become distorted. Many human beings suffer with diseases of body and mind that are a direct result of disharmony with the current of life. How does one align with the current of life? Through prayer, through right action. That is a return, a thankfulness. When we allow our hearts to give and receive in thankfulness there is an expansion of the biophysical energy (sometimes referred to as the aura) that is scientifically measurable. That force extends and returns to the environment energy that has been given.

We are ever in a reciprocal relationship, also, with the sacred directions and their guardians, the Adawees, those great angelic beings. From the North we realize wisdom through action and we understand, in the stillness of a clear day, freedom and a readiness to act. Attentive and aware, willful intention to be in the moment. From the East arises Ama

Agheya, Water Woman bearing the gift of knowing, the east wind, inspiring the mind to see, "I am that I am." And from the South the seeds of renewal arise, the power of adolescence and the sacred power of rebuilding. As we move toward the West we find that we carry with us, even in our youth, the great and blessed weight of our grandparents upon our backs. We face the West and see the Great Bear, and we realize that we have come and that we can leave, yet there is something to give and to return. At that point one can make a decision to transform and transmute, as in the sacred quality of the amethyst crystal; one transmutes consciousness and decides, "I shall walk around this circle of life for the beauty and the enlightenment of all beings."

It is an Indian proverb that it is a rich person who has a large family, a very poor person who has no family or friends. In this time something has happened to break the threads of connection, for many people suffer in loneliness and seek good relationship with self and others. Cultivate spiritual friendships with those who demonstrate right action, and consider your co-workers as you would members of your clan.

What is praying? To arise in the morning and to thank the sun. To burn sweetgrass and sage and cedar, to make tobacco offerings—to acknowledge the beauty of what is, that we may ever be clear in that reflection, that we be firm and not rash, that we be true in our knowing. And then at midday, when the sun is overhead, thank all those who have come before and filled your life, filled your body with the energy to be. And as the sun descends over the western horizon, say, "Thank you. Oh, a day has passed and another day shall come. I am thankful." In the light of day is the seed of night, within the South is reflected the North, and within the West, images of the East.

Many scientists from around the world have come to see that the sacred wisdom of the ancient ones of all the great religions has a basis and a foundation in our everyday life—that there is no difference between spiritual duty and being a good neighbor, a good friend, a good citizen. A citizen of what? The family of humanity. The current of life is in all of us.

Each one of us on Earth at this time is being called to rebuild the sacred circle in ourselves. True, there has been much suffering, generated from the mind of incorrect action, and it is very simple to see the road of right action. For the problems that people of Earth face now—those who have been displaced for political reasons, those who have been displaced for monetary gain, those who have been displaced by loss of heart—there is a healing that must come. How can there be no people? How can there be a place where one can no longer live? Who can decide that a certain part of the Earth shall be a "sacrifice area"? Better to be good caretakers of the land.

This Earth is a living being. The trouble that has engulfed the mind of humanity comes from the false concept of ownership and an idea of government that does not take into consideration our relationship, our sacred duty to caretake one another and our mother, the Earth. Here on Earth we are all connected through the sacred currents of life, and no one can fulfill our responsibilities for us. It is our choice. We can call upon peace in ourselves, we can rise above national rivalry, through making peace with the sun and the moon in our hearts, seeing that there is no above, no below, and that even mind is a form that we are shaping.

What do we hold on to? Sometimes simply the idea that an area of mind is our own or that a concept is our own. Many wars have been fought in the name of religion, in the name of a particular concept. To many Native Americans there is no difference between capitalism, communism, socialism; they are systems lacking in spirit and lacking in wholeness. It is for each of us to look deep within ourselves and to attempt, in small ways in our own communities, in our homes, that process of sharing that renews the heart and makes good friends. For many Indian families it begins early in the morning with the sunrise ceremony and the sharing of our dreams of the night before. The world of dreaming and the world of television screening, they are the same: projections of mind that we are all sharing.

If you look to the beauty and see the sadness, acknowledge it and the things that are incorrect, yet hold the form of transformation and it shall come to pass. Often we have looked to others to give direction and leadership, to bring things correct. But what is someone leading, and what is following? A strong community develops whole vision, considering the future generations. In the Tsalagi way the chiefs are chosen by the clan mothers, women who have watched them grow. Watching the young people grow, the women see their beauty, they see the young person's concern for nature and life and they know, "Ah, this one can live truly the way of the people and carry the heart of the people and be an inspiration to the people." In this way the chiefs and the honored people are chosen, through their meritorious actions, through their right actions. (And the chief or honored person may be a man or a woman, because a whole person is a whole person. The distinction of sexism is something that comes out of a mind separated in itself.) Now, in most places, "elections" are more like advertising and selling goods. Let us return to looking at one another's actions. Are they good for the people and the land? Are they good for the children? Let us realize that those elected to leadership really depend upon the people for guidance and for prayer; prayer is the power that opens the mind to see.

Prayer is the most powerful thing. I have seen old men, old women, create and stop tornadoes, make the ground shake or stop, bring rain. Even young people can handle a hot fire and not be burned because they have found peace and resolution with those elements in themselves. Each person has a gift to share. The whales and dolphins, they understand. One dolphin scout may go out, one Hopi scout may go out, and all of the people will know at home what that one has seen. Many people are crying for that shared vision because it is very difficult for a human organism to live in a vacuum. We are all relatives. Even the trees rejoice in our happiness because when we are happy we exude from our bodies a vitality that renews the atmosphere around us. When the human being is thinking thoughts of doubt and anger, a hormone is secreted within the brain that depresses and ages the system. When we recognize joy, when we understand beauty, there is a hormone that infuses even the body of an old, old person with great light, great strength. Age is a concept of mind, and it has become a way of separating rather than acknowledging wisdom. So many young people feel, "Oh, my parents cannot understand me," and many parents feel, "Oh, I cannot understand these young people." But that is an illusion, because all are united in the stream of mind. There is a stream of right action that we can follow, and it begins with forgiving—forgiving ourselves for not fulfilling others' expectations and others for not meeting ours.

It is our duty now to reweave this sacred robe of Mother Earth, because she is almost denuded by the vacuousness of her children and their carelessness. How to begin? Simply. Learn to sit and watch and find a place of stillness so that one does not react. Let us pray and hold in our minds the thought form of a spiritual renewal, a planetary family of knowing.

Let us make a choice to walk upon the Beauty Path, that path built of right action, of generosity, of love and compassion, of understanding the sacred duties that each one has, of understanding the currents of life's energy within ourselves and the weaving of wholeness within our own senses. Be devoted to the life principle in oneself. And live what you know. One cannot understand religion without living the practice. Seek the wisdom of your heart like a child on a new journey—only expecting to arrive. Simplicity is a sacred principle and power within ourselves.

As the basic currents of one's energy become apparent, thought and action arise spontaneously in harmony with life. When the Earth and the heavens meet in your heart, you realize, "Oh, as it is above, so it is below. As I think, so it shall be." From that recognition of the power of your mind comes an understanding of ritual, the sacred duties, be it Friday-night candle lighting, Sunday-morning communion, or sunrise and sundown chanting. Ritual builds stronger than word; it is the fiber that makes the cables of the bridge that will take you to the other shore, beyond the sea of your ignorance to the shore of your wisdom. Ritual takes us beyond, to a place of change, of transformation. The sound of chanting opens doorways in other dimensions, worlds of our knowing, our heart, worlds of subtleties. There are other beings that await to commune with the enlightened family of humanity. The circle includes the vastness of space.

This family of humanity has behaved like recalcitrant children. In many parts of the universe, in the larger council of the universe, some are saying, "When will they stop hurting themselves? When will they stop hurting this quadrant of the universe with such anger, with the idea of destroying one another?" What good is it to duel, to war? The instruments of war will take life even from the future generations. We see the situation in the Middle East. According to the prophecies of the Indian nations, that bed of coals can ignite this whole planet. And what is the issue? Land rights, a few people making decisions for many. The people want to live in a spiritual way, but they are reacting to an absence of mindfulness or an imposition of materialism upon their hearts.

I pray that those who are in office listen to the prayers arising from the people's hearts. Let there be peace. Let us understand that you cannot sacrifice one part of the Earth for another. This Earth is a living being that is our home. We cannot sacrifice the rights of one people in hopes that another people will be made happy. This is an abudant universe. It is only through the philosophy of the merchant mind that the concept of "not enough" has become real. People are starving, members of our family are starving in parts of this world, even here in the United States where "water runs out of a stick." People are hungry here, not only for food but for peace. And why is this? It is incorrect judgment, incorrect action that has brought the mind to feeling it is productivity that validates us as human beings, numbers of papers printed, pounds of coal produced. There is more to human life than output. There is more that we *all* are called to do as human beings. We are called to make peace in ourselves and to take responsibility. The evil that we see, we cannot say that some government or some other person is doing it. It is all of us. Let us come again to the sacred circle and affirm the real principles of government: to serve the people, to bring the greatest good, to be dignified human beings.

Simplicity and truth, to live in harmony—that is our goal. To realize ourselves and our thoughts as creators of our reality, to take responsibility. We are mothers and fathers. We are sun and moon. Our thinking gives birth to many things. Let us think clearly. Earth will not carry much longer a load of rabble-rousing children, of children who beat her and steal her very lifeblood. Think: in ten to thirty years the pumping of the aquifers beneath Black Mesa, Arizona, and the Black Hills of South Dakota would make those areas a desert.

Are you really willing to take life from your grandchildren? Do you want to take the water and the life force from the Earth so that there is no place for your children and their children? Quickly come now to a place of balance in this dream that we share. Let us return to one another love and forgiveness and understanding. Make an effort to grow corn with a neighbor. Try doing something for another person, even when you think you yourself have not enough, *especially* when you think you yourself have not enough. There may be elderly people in your neighborhood who have wisdom through the years of their experience and who may be suffering because of Social Security cutbacks, hunger, illness, loneliness, poverty. Can you be a friend one day a week to someone else who is not able to go out? To share is the way that we learn, it is the way to realize our gifts. In the Native way, the give-away is a frequent celebration. When people are thankful for something—it may be the birth of a child, it may be a healing, it may be anything—they will call together their friends and neighbors and give away everything they have. A wise person realizes that in nonattachment to the material forms they are always sustained in the abundance of what is. Let us all recall that.

WEAVING A TAPESTRY OF LIGHT

The cycles of life and death include all of us on this sphere, Mother Earth. We are all determining the future of our grandchildren and our home, the Earth. The concept of neighborhood, nation, is all based on the family and the process of interrelations. As citizens we have a responsibility to guide those whom we have chosen as leaders. This requires a clear vision of our family's needs and our neighbor's and of our hopes for the future. When individuals clearly ascertain the main ideal to manifest in their lives, they are aware of their purpose. Each one's true life purpose is in harmony with the sacred law to do right, to do good, to transform emotions, thoughts, and actions that may obscure one's good relations.

This is a time of mass dislocation and relocation. Jobs are being relocated out of the cities, leaving citizens bereft. The poor are relocated for urban renewal. War and famine—caused by greed and ignorance—drive many people from their homelands. Farmers are being dislocated so that others may profit by artificially inflating the value of their lands. And at this moment the largest relocation of people in this country since the internment of Japanese-Americans in World War II is being attempted for immoral and illegal purposes in the southwestern United States, immediately affecting the Diné (Navajo) and Hopi, ultimately affecting us all.[3]

The Native American worldview sees cycles of life and death and the individual always in relationship with family, clan, nation, and planet. This relationship is biological, mental, emotional, spiritual, economic. The circle is inclusive. By virtue of being on Earth, being a member of the family of humanity, we are included in the circle of life. The actions of our group, one nation, resound through the atmosphere, affecting the entire planetary circle. The concept of circle makes clear the individual's responsibility in acting for the

benefit of all one's relatives and for the benefit of future generations. The oceans and the plants upon the Earth supply us
with oxygen, the rivers give us water, and our reciprocal responsibility is to respect and keep pure those elements of life,
that many may live with good health and peace of mind.

We all need pure air and water to live. What is an individual's responsibility and power in maintaining pure air and
water? The mass careless destruction of our forests affects
the entire circle of life, through the depletion of oxygen in
the air. We are each responsible for the trees that help us
breathe. Your generous action of planting trees clears the air.
And in these times we may honor our relationship with water
by not wasting it and by purifying waste products before they
return to the cycle of the water's flow.

The common factors that unite human beings are the desire for security, peace, abundance, and ease for our children
and grandchildren. Parents all around the world have the
same concerns. The cause of imagined separation is ignorance of the means by which we are all interrelated. We are
connected by the air we breathe and the Earth we share. As
one manifests energy and discipline to transform emotions or
actions that disturb one's own peace or peace with others,
then one may turn aside the energy of aggression and relate
in equanimity. The illusion of separation arises from the
mind of not-enough and the thought of "them" and "us."
Nation against nation arises as a thought when individuals
and groups fear difference, not realizing the underlying unity.
When we think that the Russians are different, we may forget
that they have children, too. When we realize that our children and grandchildren will be affected by the actions of both
nations, we recognize our common responsibility to transform aggression. Reactive mind perceives differences. Circle
mind sees what is like. Humans in America are like humans
in Russia. In recognizing our likenesses we have the first
thread of bountiful communication.

A reaction is a response that has no thought. It may be a
pattern of action based upon past situations. A wise person of

140

any age perceives the patterns of mind and stands in the present, nonreacting from the past. When we are not controlled by the thoughts and emotions of the past, then we are free to choose and create in the present and for the future. For this reason forgiveness is an energy of pacification, of peacemaking, so that peaceful relationship may ensue.

The thought forms that obscure peaceful human relationship are many, all arising from ignorance manifest as miscommunication. An individual holding the thought of anger or fear without seeking to resolve such energy can become embroiled in repetitive patterns of discord. As the patterns are perceived and resolved, one has access to more creative energy to accomplish one's life goal and purpose. First one identifies the patterns of fear, anger, envy, competition, whatever; then one diligently transforms them. Say you feel competitive with co-workers, family, or friends. Observe; consider what energy and actions arise from that competitiveness. Then speak clearly of your purpose and your gifts, give thanks for the gifts of others in the circle, and recognize that many gifted beings may work together and need not be in competition. Observe your mind and action, and each time a thought of scarcity or competition arises, carry it clearly to resolution. Then you are free of reacting and can choose to respond.

As a member of a family, team of co-workers, community, neighborhood, nation, one has vast energy to work with, a fire to burn clear the mind as one warmly interacts with other beings. With one's family it is wise to speak and share experiences and also to state the purpose of your being together. Hear from each member what is hoped for and wanted. Here we can see likeness-threads in the dream of happy relationship that all individuals share. In working and living together, express clearly expectations and goals and agree on what is to be accomplished. Individually and collectively this is powerful. In the Native way this is the united mind of the council. As the people council with one another and with the legislators, laws are enacted to benefit all.

141

When we see that something needs to be done, it is up to us to do it. When we look around and see people homeless in this rich land, it is for each of us to join together and create the solution. When we see jobs relocated out of this country and people left unsure and insecure, it is our duty to bring the situation correct. When we see farmers relocated, foreclosed from their land, let us recognize the responsibility of investment speculators arbitrarily raising the cost of the land, speculating on future sale value. Land speculation means the future is for sale. Do you want other people deciding your future, or are you willing to choose and create the tomorrow that is best for all?

A mass relocation of Native peoples is being carried out in the southwestern United States. This has come about through lust and greed for uranium and oil beneath the land. The uranium is more beneficially energetic in the Earth, drawing rains to refill the aquifers. And certainly, to destroy the culture of people living in harmony with the land, creating a sacrificial wasteland, is an unwise action that will have deleterious effects throughout the nation.

Too often individuals and groups, overwhelmed by forces oppressing them, become angry and lash out, shouting even at those who seek to aid them, putting forth a hollow cry of despair. The wise citizen will consider that fear and anger with understanding, and respond with equanimity and with actions that will bring solution. You do make a difference. Your voice is important in this time. Let each of us act to correct the abuses of our relatives and the Earth. Consider the effects of wasting four billion dollars of taxpayers' money to force a self-sufficent people into bureaucratic slavery. Let us recognize that such means can at any time be applied to any of us in this land if we allow that thought of force to continue. Write to your legislators; call correct those whose actions threaten the well-being of the people and the land. The farmers in the midwestern United Staes who generously supply the bread upon our tables are being forced from their homeland, forced into servitude to megabusinesses. The same plantation mind that has enslaved South and Central America as banana plantations now turns upon its own.

This is the time for us all to consider what threads are weaving our tomorrow. We cannot allow self-sufficient people to be enslaved in bureaucratic manipulation. We cannot allow our grandparents and our children to be reduced to hunger and despair in order to assure greater profits to those who exploit. Let us actively encourage and support all who live in harmony and self-sufficiency, all who seek to live in right relationship with the Earth and one another. We can effectively express wisdom and a vision of peace to benefit the group, the nation and the planet—immediately. Right now, let us envision a world of harmony and good relationship. How would it be?

Let us take steps to balance the confusion. Let us call the legislation to be responsive to the real needs. Let us invest in a future without greed. We can work together, creating stronger and more stable neighborhoods. We can clarify confusion through clearly defining our purpose and goals and the skillful means by which to realize them for the benefit of everyone.

In the old days, Native American governmental systems incorporated the wisdom of the minority voice until all were clear on a single choice and course of action. As we work with one another, clearly stating our goals and our course of action, we bring tomorrow, the objective actualized. Ten people can come forward in a circle, hear the needs of the people, and act to create a solution of homes for those who are homeless. Let us plant gardens in the city, that the mind may come again to understand our relationship to the foods that give us life. Whatever the work, your actions can be infused with the clear mind of complementary resolution—peace for all and for the group to accomplish its goal.

Long ago the Pale One walked upon this land. He reminded the people, "Take care of one another, cause no harm, work together to benefit all." His message was one of unity and responsibility, consensus. The Constitution of the

United States is based upon the governmental system that he outlined for the Native people, and his voice and wisdom still resonate today through all of the Americas. He reminded us of the cycles of life and the cycles of human development, and as nations we are now at the end of one cycle and the beginning of another—where we extend the love of the family to include the entire cycle of life.

May we all trace our roots to the great Tree of Peace. May we honor the wisdom of our grandparents and caretake that wisdom for our grandchildren, unto seven generations. Let us recognize the sacredness of this time of transformation and choice, that we may truly manifest the beauteous family of humanity.

ᎦᏙᎤᏍᏗᏓᏗᎥᏃᎩᏏ
Ga do u s di da di hv no gi si

What shall we sing?

ᏚᏳᎧᏚᎠᏟᎩᎶᎦ
Du yu ka du a tli gi lo ga

True time is approaching

ᎢᏗᎥᏃᎩ
I di hv no gi

Let us sing it

ᏙᎯᎤᎠᎷᏂ
To hi u a lu ni

Serenity, it resounds

5

GENERATING PEACEKEEPER MIND

THE Peacekeeper holds the vision of peace for all beings in all worlds, as beauteous expression of harmony and balance resonating through thought, word, and deed.

The Peacekeeper sees all in good relationship, perceiving the underlying unity of creation.

The Peacekeeper knows that each being is empowered by will to choose, wisdom to see, and intelligence to act, all beings together weaving the dream of our shared reality.

Recognizing that patterns of mind manifest as one's individual, family, clan, national, and planetary relationships, the Peacekeeper turns aside anger, doubt, and fear, harmonizing conflicting emotions through complementary resolution.

The Peacekeeper acts with consideration for future generations, with the mind of preserving life and that which enriches living.

The sacred fires of will, compassion, and active intelligence within every living being are the cohesive factors that enable mind to manifest in the physical form. May wisdom fires be rekindled and renewed in every being. May the thought of complementary resolution stir the hearts of all people, that we may recall peace.

In this time many hearts have been touched by a need for peace. Many are now willing to be active in bringing forth peace within themselves and all relations. During the World Peace March in 1982 we saw something wondrous: people from all nations speaking out for peace, for life. That was a good beginning. In each of us there is a Peacekeeper to unfold.

Up until the 1800s throughout much of the southeastern part of what is now the United States, there were villages called Peace Villages. The Peace Village was one way the Tsalagi people saw to maintain peace and balance—to maintain villages whose single purpose was to mediate the various aspects of mind, always aware of the whole. Through spiritual practice and diet the inhabitants of the Peace Villages radiated peace of mind, enabling maintenance of harmony with the pulse of the Earth. Their voices were relied upon for mediation of what appeared to be conflict. Many were priests and healers, keepers of tradition for the entire nation. Most important, they maintained areas of sanctuary. The Peace Villages were places of sanctuary where no blood was shed, no harm was done. Any person, even a killer or thief, who made his or her way to the village and followed the cycle of purification within the sanctuary for one year could be forgiven all transgression. Each Peace Village was guided by the Peace Chief, one committed to preserving life and skillful in transforming consciousness. The principles of the Peace Village were such that even "white criminals," non-Native criminals in flight from the laws of their own people, could find sanctuary there, and many did.

Many have felt the need for sanctuary, and some have realized that space within. The Peacekeeper offers sanctuary within an aura of certainty, expressing methods of conflict resolution with a generous heart. The Peace Chiefs develop an aura of stability through inner and outer practices. The result is spaciousness of mind, which reflects the wisdom inherent in each person. In many ways the Peace Chief is a catalyst, initiating a process that purifies patterns of conflict, revealing harmonious resolution.

Our consciousness does indeed affect the stream of thought upon this world. The clear intention for peace is seed to peace's fruition. As responsible human beings, we are looking to ways in which we can affirm a world of complementary resolution, knowing that many views, many ways can coexist peacefully, respectfully, creatively.

As human beings we have a significant responsibility in this time. It is to relate to those patterns in ourselves that lead to fear, doubt, and aggression in such a way that they are transmuted. Our purpose is to realize Peacekeeper mind, a wholeness of mind in which patterns of conflict, separation, scarcity come to balance. With a heartiness, those patterns are transmuted. You never deny what is, but simply acknowledge, "Oh, that feeling is there." Is it *really* you? No, it is feeling arising from emotion. Generate the antidote.

Fear is an idea form that has taken hold around the Earth. One of its most alarming expressions is "nuclear overkill," stockpiles of nuclear armaments twenty times over what is "needed" to kill every man, woman, and child already alive on this planet. So a change is called for, now. As we are the nations, as we are born of this planet, change must begin in our own hearts. Each of us must put aside the idea of scarcity; each of us must put aside the idea that there may not be enough. It is from mind of scarcity that many individuals, many groups, many nations reach out to possess land, resources, ideas—because of uncertainty about the future's possibilities. Yet the future is a seed within our own minds. Do we wish to bring forth a world of scarcity, fear, competition, war, or will we choose to vivify the seeds of abundance, confidence, generosity, and peace in our hearts and in our communities? It is our choice.

Peacekeeper mind is an integration of light and dark within oneself. It is to choose to empower oneself, to be what one is rather than reacting in the patterns of the past or to the expectations of others. It is to recognize ourselves in the moment. As a nation, as a planet, we are growing. Many of the ideas that have been important in our development and learning as a human race have been outer explorations: scientific means, inventions, methods of healing. Now we are coming again to the inner exploration. We are seeing the whole circle, the cycle of things. In this cycle it is our thought that is most significant. Even the plants and the land show us that. When people take the time to create a space of love in their homes, a place and time for prayer and meditation, a vortex of energy is created that actually strengthens the electromagnetic fields of their bodies and the land where they live. This lesson was clearly demonstrated at Findhorn, the spiritual community in Scotland renowned for its magnificent, almost "miraculous" gardens. The power of attunement to the land and to the flow of abundance in one's own mind can manifest miracles of abundance on the Earth. So a stream of clear thinking is most important. We are co-creators.

Being present in the moment means acknowledging whatever energy is being experienced and bringing it to resolution, by calling forth balance. When there is anger or frustration in you or around you, instead of focusing on the anger, focus on the seed of compassion, focus on love and resolution. The thought form of resolution in itself sets up a resonant field that enables the mind to perceive methods of resolution. This is complementary resolution, means to pacify strife and discord to reveal inherent harmony:

Perceive all apparent conflict as patterns of energy seeking harmonious balance as elements in a whole.

Recognize the patterns of emotion and thought that generate ease.

Develop the wisdom that actualizes, skillful means to realize the vision of right relationship.

Choose to apply wisdom of discrimination, guiding thought and action to harmony.

Deep within our hearts a fire glows. It spirals out, expanding, filling the body with warmth and a sense of great peace. The body is filled with light. The inner eye becomes ever more clear. The seed of most pure mind arises untarnished from the stream of thought. The mind sees many images unfold; many feelings, many thoughts float on that stream. The wise human being cultivates those thoughts which are nurturing. Be not attached to the stream of fear, anger, or doubt. Recognize the stream of most pure mind.

Experience the light, visualize the light. First it is something of your imagination, and then more and more that quality of the stream becomes your natural inclination. So it is with our choice of words as well. When we choose to speak of the good in ourselves and one another, we call forth wholeness. When we acknowledge the great seed of pure mind, we nurture that seed within ourselves and in all our relations. One may lose sight of purpose, yet all may find again the road home. We find the source when we sense the stream of light within ourselves. As we look at the thoughts passing through our minds we say, with seed of enlightened perspective, "I am a living being in the process of change. I am a being of light. I choose to live in the light of peace and beauty." Simply voicing that affirmation enables negative thought forms and patterns of human relationship to be transformed.

The transformation begins in each person. Through awakening sacred wisdom fire in our hearts we are able to send forth a great light, a great shield of renewal around this planet, so that even the bullets will not care to fly, as each one makes peace within. To awaken wisdom fire within one's heart is to awaken in the dream, to perceive things as they are and weave a life of beauty.

AWAKENING IN THE DREAM

There is a practice that my grandfather taught for looking at the stream of one's own mind, for freeing the creative potential, for any kind of problem solving in life, whether in terms of working with one another or releasing the healing energy within the body. It is a simple practice, and very powerful. Each night as you are falling asleep you have an opportunity to clarify and release from your own light body and from the stream of consciousness any thoughts that may have harmed you or another. After clarifying the atmosphere of your mind and your sleeping space by offering the smoke of cedar or juniper, lie down upon your bed and review your words and actions of the day. If you see that at some point in the day you thought, spoke, or acted not in the fullness of your true wisdom, then you "replay" that moment and visualize it coming to a harmonious completion. Then affirm in your mind, "The next time I have that opportunity I will relate with a clear mind. I will be fully attentive in the light of communion flowing between me and all those I meet." In observing the flow of the day's events you may see that you picked up a disquieting idea or thought form, thinking it was your own. As you continue to practice observing the mind, you become able to discriminate between those thoughts which are truly beneficial to your sacred purpose as a human being in this life and those thoughts that are merely illusions, to be transmuted. This exercise is very much a part of the Peacekeeper's path because it develops a continuity of consciousness between sleeping and waking. In meditation, one may often experience a state similar to the transition states of sleeping and waking, with images passing through the mind or flashes of inspiration, clear perception. The continuity of our knowing is ever alive and available to us. It is a sacred cord, a resonance with life that enables us to be attentive to all aspects of our thought.

To awaken in the dream and put one's foot firmly upon Beauty's path is a Tsalagi practice of mindfulness. One's action within mind or dream has effects as tangible as physical doing. When one rides the galloping mind and reins it to the path, a destination shall be reached—home to the sacred hoop, source of the dream. To recall that one is dreaming is to be in contact with the stream of mind as it weaves its course through realms of consciousness. The moon's fertile crescent, seeded by desires, thoughts, and actions, represents a road, reflecting the sun's purpose in one's life. Grandfather Moon|(Nudawa Giniduda) reflects the light of Adawee. The clarity of that reflection is determined by one's mindfulness of the sacred ideal. The eye of wisdom opens as one completes an action in the dream—such as raising one's hands heavenward, calling gentle rains onto parched lands.

The method of dream attentiveness as taught by Grandfather Eonah Fisher entails the following steps:

1. Upon retiring to the sleeping chamber, smoke the area with the offering of burning cedar or juniper to the north, east, south, and west and to heaven and earth. The atmosphere around you is composed of thought. When your thought is clarified through mindfulness practice and you take time to smudge the area, to make smoke offerings, you are also giving thanks to Earth for fresh breath and helping to clarify individual and planetary thought.

2. Make a prayer acknowledging yourself as a vehicle of light, giving thanks for the good that has come that day and an affirmation of intent to live in harmony with all your relations.

3. Lie upon your bed and review your actions of the day. In your mind's eye make correction if necessary. For example, if you neglected to respond from the heart with another person, see yourself relating heart to heart; if you spoke with anger, see yourself speaking compassionately.

4. Practice the meditation on the Three Gems of Most Pure Mind (given below).

5. Count slowly backward from ten to one, affirming that you will remember all that occurs during sleep.

6. Give yourself the task of raising your hands to the sky in the dream, to call forth fruitful life.

7. On awakening, stretch and give thanks, and make note of your dreams in the dream journal.

MEDITATION ON THE THREE GEMS
OF MOST PURE MIND[1]

Sit with spine straight, breathing in, breathing out, mind relaxed and open. Sense the double helix of spiral energy throughout your being as a dynamic balance of will and compassion, calling forth the cord/chord of active intelligence.

Come, come, come to the other shore.
Free from illusion, gather your canoe of light,
Enter upon the stream of most pure mind.
Step easily to the river's edge,
Approach along the gentle shoals
As light of clear day
Dances on the water.

Canoe beached upon the shore,
You step with certainty into the stream,
Stream leading to ocean,
Deep into the chambers of your knowing
Making your way into the water.
As it laps around your feet,
See reflection of the day,
That which you have done best.
Let us affirm on our reflection
The acts of greater good.

Shoreline gently unfolds
Into sea with many valleys.
First valley holds
Treasure of fruitful good intentions.
What was the face you wore

Before you were born?
See the Mystery behind the form.
Seek the gem of good cause,
The thought of right action.
Dive into the stream of clear mind.
A yellow stone emits its light,
Calling you to perceive what is right.
Gather the sacred topaz,
Medicine of clear mind.

Treasure hunting deeper still,
To a second valley you are drawn.
Comfortable in the water,
Moving as light upon a beam,
Effervescent recollection
Of where you weave the dream.
Wisdom's glow calls you
To a rose-illuminated grotto.
Gather the precious ruby, gem of wisdom.
Compassion overflows.
Follow the subtle light
That calls you to the center of the stream.

Third valley, wondrous in its glow of will,
Shining forth clear mind.
Right intent flows to fulfilled action
Ever in harmony, bringing forth the light.
Gather the diamond bright.

Three gems to be carried, spoken, dedicated:
The Truth, the Community, the Teaching.
Affirm that you are on Beauty's Path.

Come, come, come to the other shore.
Illusion is cast aside,
Worthy is the glow.
Come, let us gather on the shore
And enter our canoes of light
To traverse the seas of confusion.

Choice is a most gracious gift. Sometimes in our ignorance we create devices to make choice rather dramatic. The device may be crisis, illness, anger; many people feel empowered by becoming angry at something or somebody. There is a clearer, more direct way of empowerment to act. That is to acknowledge the stream of wisdom within yourself, the gems of wisdom within your nature. With the gifts of imagination, visualization, and affirmation you have set wisdom waves into motion. Now you know the Three Gems as something in your own experience. The gems are a most gracious medicine for the renewal of individuals, families, groups.

The will is our intention. When there is not a clear intention and belief in accomplishment, there is uncertainty, and one may be without courage to act. Now balance with the lens of your gemstones the clarity of your intent. "Is my intent, my will, truly in harmony with my life purpose?" That is a question one needs to ask oneself. In the Native way it is said that when we come into life as human beings, those questions are given to us to explore as we go around the Medicine Wheel. Tsalagi people say that one has fifty-one years to explore because in the Tsalagi tradition one is not an adult until age fifty-one. It is seen to take that much time to sense the many subtle life flows of energy within one's body. After fifty-one years, you share the fruits of your exploration.

To understand your purpose frees your creative potential. To see your purpose clearly is a gift of insight. To have the courage and the compassion to walk energetically along a path of manifesting your purpose is a gift offered to benefit all. To cultivate clear speech and clear mind stirs the seeds of harmony for all beings.

One of the most important means of manifesting Peacekeeper mind is to bridge again the gap between the left and right hemispheres of the brain. We call this building the Rainbow Bridge. To maintain the mind of the Peacekeeper is to recognize that in the process of light, of breath, there are complementary actions and complementary thoughts in a

156

field of thought. In that field of thought nothing can be antagonistic to itself. Thoughts coexist.

I pray that you will remember the jewels of wisdom you carry within, that you will affirm the sacred fire of life. We can change the patterns of a culture, the patterns of a nation's thinking, from the need to expand outward to recognition of our inner creativity. We are the people. We are the planet. We are the stars. Our individual process truly does affect the flow of life. Those who work with many people in an organization can sense, in the moment when their consciousness is very clear, how the group's intuition and energy will also flow well. Each of us is a battery, a resonator, a musical instrument, and we are setting waves of many patterns and many possible futures in the sea of life. Let us be discriminating in the futures that we shape forth. As the old Indian people say, "Let us consider, just in the way we greet one another, what our action and our words will mean seven generations from this day." In our homes, when we create a space for people to pray and meditate, we are making a renewal for our neighborhood and for the Earth. It is important to honor the sacred Mystery we all share. All of us can trace our roots to that one Great Tree of Peace, life itself. Whatever our tribe, our language, our race, our culture, there is one truth, one reality, that unites us as people.

The exercise of going to the sea enables you to perceive more clearly your dreaming, the process of your thought. As children we were encouraged to speak our dreams and to resolve issues in the dream. In our dreams we always have the opportunity to make a correction in our whole being. So let us be alert. In the dream, if you are fearful, call forth courage. If you feel endangered, realize yourself as a self-empowered human being, able to transmute and transform even what is dangerous. The dragon that Saint George slew is met by many who search for truth. The dragon is doubt, the unintegrated aspects of one's energy self, seeking to manifest as a whole. You must bring all of yourself together into attention.

157

We are being asked to make a choice as human beings, a choice to affirm life, to remember our sacred duty. Each one of us has a sacred duty, a special gift that is necessary to the people who have chosen to be around us. We have indeed chosen to be with one another, our families, our friends, our co-workers, sensing a certain energy potential of completion. So let us see the beauty in one another. Let us affirm our unity as living people in process. And above all, let us remember the sacred gems, the jewels of wisdom that we carry; they are ever present in our nature. Our life is a mandala of thought, and it can be as beauteous and symmetrical as we see.

Now you have recalled the way. Like the salmon you have entered the stream leading to the source of your being.

COMING HOME

Sit tailor style or in a firm chair, spine erect, breathing gently. Follow the breath flow to the Ocean of Life. Imagine yourself a mighty salmon swimming in the vast sea. Prepare to trace your journey to its source, returning to the stream of limitless love from which you came.

The journey begins as you swim to the mouth of a great river, the River of Love. As you enter this river, feel currents of compassion washing over you. Allow them to guide you onward, swimming upstream, winding your way home through the many opportunities and challenges you encounter in the waters of experience.

You arrive first at a deep pool, the Waters of I Will. Here you find your voice of power, changing any lingering thoughts of "can't" to "can" and "will." Glide through the Waters of I Will, gently empowering yourself to be all you can be, claiming your inherent authority, choosing to live your highest ideals, your true life's purpose. Pass through tugging eddies that would distract you from your destination, and come again to the shore of certainty.

Moving ever upstream, you follow the current of compassion to a great and beauteous lake, the Lake of Lovable Me. Dive and leap through the self-affirming waters, washing your heart of any vestiges of self-doubt or unworthiness. Acknowledge the beauteous being that you are, loved and lovable, needing neither to deserve nor to earn a love that is your birthright. Glisten in the shining light of self-acceptance as you continue on your journey.

You come next to a roaring rapids, the Cascades of Capable Action. Here the water rolls and pounds upon the rocks, shaking loose all inertia, lassitude, hesitation to act. Riding the rapids, let your wisdom carry you safely through; let our ability to act competently and effectively be your guide through the tumbling waters. Capable in action, rich in talents and skills, acknowledge yourself a master of action for the good of all beings, and swim on!

The river becomes smooth again, meandering gently, quieting into a happy, tranquil stream that stretches endlessly before you—Stream of the Open Moment, in which all attachments to what did or did not happen in the past, what might or might not happen in the future, are left behind. In the open moment suffering and attachment to suffering cease, and you are free to experience the waters of life as they are. Washing away all limitations born of expectation, revel in the spaciousness of vast possibilities, enjoy the space of now. Your dream is realized even as you vision it.

Swim on up the River of Love, coming to a most beauteous pool, the Pool of Abundance. Dive deep in the bottomless waters to bring forth all that you need, all that the people need. Rediscover the paradise all around and within you, which provides without holding back. Shake off all last remnants of scarcity mind and know the joy of generosity as you share the gift of these precious waters with all around you.

Flowing abundance carries you to the base of a giant waterfall, the last gateway to the source of your journey. Take heart, encourage yourself, and leap upon the Falls of Faith, surrendering to the surge and rush of the mighty waters of life, sailing through all obstacles on the trusting winds of faith. Fly beyond fear, as high as you can go. Embrace perfection, unity with all that is.

Beyond the falls you arrive at last at the source of the river, the clear, gentle Waters of Home, whence arise all appearances. Here in the sweet waters of remembrance you find yourself heart-to-heart with family, friends, all your relations. Know that you are one. In the quiet, flowing stream you know unconditional love, rippling waves of compassion that go forth and return without end. Bathe in this pool of peace, allow every atom of your being to be infused with its light, and send forth the song of love's wisdom, that all may know the most precious gift of peace.

This teaching of the salmon is inspired by an elder who lives in the northwestern United States, Joe Washington, who has been a guide for me since my own grandparents passed over. He is the spiritual leader of the Lummi Nation, a coastal Salish people. He says, "Dhyani, you tell the people that as long as the rivers shall flow and as long as the grass is green, the salmon are going to come upstream. Everybody wants to go home." Every time I see him or speak with him on the telephone he repeats that. We must understand the message of the salmon because the wise salmon understands the pulse. He feels the energy and finds the right stream; he can feel the water that will bring him home. The salmon who is busy looking around and thinking, "I don't think I can jump over that rock" or "Am I really in the right stream?" is going to end up in your salad. It is time to go home and we can all find the way. It is just to come again to that stream of clear mind in ourselves, to remember that we are natural beings, human beings, together. We also have a rhythm; the pulse of the Earth is guiding us.

In this time many Native American people are speaking again their ancient wisdom. The message is not to say "Become like an Indian" or to convert people to Native American religion. The old people are saying, "Let us join hands, each as we are, to rebuild the sacred circle of the Earth. Let us honor the traditions of all our peoples. Let us know that there is one truth, and all our roots have come from that great tree. Like the salmon, let us come out of the ocean of illusion. Let us be winners in the stream and find our way home again so we may generate new seeds of life." So it is a very important message that Joe Washington is passing to us: "Remember the salmon, remember the salmon." Humans also seek the stream home.

The ocean is our thought, it is the common dream. It is also the emotions, the feelings that are often not acknowledged. Yet to see your way home you must look at all the emotions in the ocean of experience and be able to say, "I no longer attach to this; I no longer push that away. I no longer have a need for fear. I no longer doubt that the ocean comes from the tiny stream and that the stream will lead me home. I am on my way, and it is a Beauty Way." There is nowhere to go; beauty is all around. To examine with your mind, with your senses, is to understand the mystery of life.

To manifest Peacekeeper mind we need only to clarify the obscurations of fear and anger, scarcity and separation, and we shall come again to recognizing that which we are. You came here as a wholesome person, pure within your mind. The human body is a great gift, an opportunity to explore the mind. We say that in the beginning there was emptiness and from that emptiness came forth a sound, and that sound is five tones, five qualities, the basis of everything we know, our organ systems and the building of this world. And that sound is within us.

We were taught at an early age that how we see the world, how we relate through the heart to one another, how we look to the essence of one another, is determining our reality. In the Tsalagi worldview there are no accidents, no mistakes. Things are happening just as they are. We must develop the courage to be present in this moment and turn aside those attitudes that make us believe the illusion of separation. In life we are all sharing this dream, and there is no separation.

We have a common purpose as human beings in this time, and the resonance of that clear intention is stirring in many people the memory of our power to clarify the illusions that now befall this planet. We can recognize within our own being the potential to bring forth creative energy, to manifest peace and clarity within our own lives. Many are also feeling the need to stand in a community, to know ourselves aligned in the circle of good relationship. These thoughts, these feelings, bring this book and you, the reader, together.

How can each of us, as a human being, recognize thought as creative energy? How can each of us turn aside the illusions or the fears that stand in the way of manifesting our true nature? In the Native worldview, in essence everything is well. From the beginning, from the emptiness, the sound spiraled forth; form the womb of the universe unmanifest potential is made real. Through the principle of will it is made real, and through the principle of will each of us in this moment, in any moment, can reconnect with that sacred thread of the will to be. Will is the primary fire that brings us forth in this moment. That energy is manifested through the clear quartz crystal.

The second creative fire radiates energy of compassion. As Elder Fire Will looked upon itself there came forth the energy that sees things as they are, with equanimity; this is compassionate wisdom. In our individual relationships this fire relates to care for one another, forgiveness for what might have been, could have been, should have been. As we realize that our thoughts are weaving and determining our tomorrow, we see there is no need to doubt or blame because everything is moving in the stream of our own nature, and with the clarity of our will, with the energy of compassion and the voice of affirmation, we can turn aside those attitudes that may obscure the perfection.

In the circle of life we each have a special gift, a special function. In the Native worldview there is no in or out; everyone in the circle is necessary. The gift and function of each person are necessary for the benefit of the whole family of human beings and those that walk, crawl, swim, and fly. We are all relatives. It is this wisdom of compassion, seeing things in their balance, that is so significant in turning aside illusions of scarcity and bringing peace to our own hearts.

The third creative fire is the fire of creative intelligence, building intelligence, that our dreams may succeed, that our works may actually manifest for the benefit of many.

So three fires have come forth from the five notes, blazing out in a great spiral. This has significance in your own spine. Sound, vibration, is thought. It is our dream that we are all weaving together. And as human beings, having the gift of human life, we have a sacred duty not to waste this gift. That means we are to turn aside our laziness. How does one turn aside laziness? How does one recognize that one is lazy? If you have the feeling that somebody else is in your way, that you cannot accomplish because of someone else's doing or not doing, that is laziness. In reality, nothing can stand in the way of the diligent, loving human being.

In our nature there is the potential for great things to occur. The miracles that we have read about in other societies, other times—the miracles of people bringing rain or causing seeds to grow in a matter of hours through their prayer— these embers are within each of us. All it takes is sweeping out the fireplace so the embers can blaze forth. What is the fireplace? It is our mind, our spine, our body, especially our heart, our sacrum, and the top of the head. Fire is thought, it is mind. Within each of us move those three creative fires— will, compassion, active intelligence. Within the spine those three fires rest in the sacrum. As the human being acknowledges and carries the staff of his or her own destiny, those fires grow brighter and brighter and the channels of the spine become clearer, that the fire may rise.

We speak of mother energy, father energy, and the child within. The mother energy is the left side of the spine, the left channel, the right side is the father, and the child is the center. We also describe it as lunar, solar, and the emptiness, the unmanifest becoming real. The Earth Mother moves in you, the solar energy moves in you. In the left side of the spine there is the energy of the moon, in the right side the energy of the sun, and in the center there is the child and the Mystery beyond form. The human body in its thought and action can impede the flow of sun and moon, or it may excite one energy and depress another. By following your breath, being attentive to your own breathing, you can become more conscious of how you are manifesting your potential. Feel those spirals of energy. Are you more aware of one side of your body than another?

My grandmother used to make me hold a broom and jump through it while holding it in both hands; she said I was thinking more on one side than the other and that would help me find balance. It is very challenging to jump through a broom; either you are very present and very balanced or you fall on your face. My grandmother was telling me, "Your actions have more meaning than your promises; they need doing *now.*" And she took that lesson deeper: she showed me that when you think something accomplished, it is easier. I thought jumping through the broom was hard. She said, "Your thought is just as important as your action because all action begins in your mind." I thought about that for four days. When it became clear, then I jumped easily over the broom handle. Then an even deeper lesson came clear to my mind: what we are thinking is *as if* we have done it. Even how we think and speak of other people affects them. If we describe someone as harsh or ignorant, we are not acknowledging the gem of pure mind in ourselves or them because we are voicing an idea form that is negative and static, depleting energy for change and transformation.

When you step upon the path to clarify your own mind by making clear your speech, by speaking in an affirmative way, the channels in the spine become more open. When we are able to say, "Oh, this is happening," without being attached to or repulsed by what is happening, the channels become more clear. Why is it so important that the spine become clear, that our words become clear? It is because our words, as thought and vibration, have the power to shape, to determine, our future realities. If we speak in fear or in a way that encapsulates and energizes a negative attitude, we are freezing the moment, not letting the full breath move through. Thus the first step is to clarify your speech, by making a commitment to see the best in your self. When you see old patterns of thought, speech, or behavior that obscure the clarity, do not be attached—either positively or negatively—to the attitude that has shown its face upon the mirror of your mind. Know that anger, bitterness, doubt are feelings, and feelings, by their nature, are fleeting. What is the essential nature of one's own mind? That is the question we are to explore.

As we spiral into deeper awareness, we see that we are people who are changing. In being alive we have the opportunity to look at the qualities of life, to see the gift of mind—and to make a choice: to manifest the creative voice that builds a world of beauty, a world of peace to benefit all beings unto seven generations. This is why compassion, caring, being a caretaker for others and ourselves, is so important. What we do today, how we feel about ourselves in this moment, has an effect upon the entire circle of life. Our thought is a power. Our emotions attract to us what is in our life. There is no accident. In the Native view "sin" comes from stepping away from one's ability and potential. We are all born pure; we all have the perfect mind of Creation within. The attitudes that may obscure that perfection can be very easily transformed when we energetically affirm the power of clear mind: "I intend to realize truth in this time." In the Tsalagi worldview, it is said that seven lifetimes of spiritual activity will enable one to realize the Mystery. The energetic can do it in one lifetime, and then may become a planet, a mother-father of all things, as my grandmother has done.

Seven lifetimes, one lifetime—what does it mean? It means to plant seeds in this moment. The suffering or confusion of this moment reflects attitudes that we have carried in our mind-streams perhaps even from other lifetimes. How are we to transmute those attitudes of the past that may accumulate in the energy centers of our bodies? We say we must sing and dance them out, fasting and purifying our minds and bodies and cultivating good thoughts and deeds. The rituals of fasting and purification, of offering the sweetgrass and the sage to the four directions, of going to a dark and lonely place, of purifying with hot or cold water, benefit all one's relations. This is the way the individual overcomes obstructions of separation, in Tsalagi practice.

How do these illusions of separation arise? They come from thinking "this" is better than "that," or "I know more than ——, I am less than ——." The moment you think you are more or less than another, a veil of separation arises. "This" may be good for your spiritual awakening, while "that" is appropriate for another. Wise practitioner cultivates "like" view—"this has motivation like that"—thus cultivating unity. It is pride that leads to comparing self and others. The belief that your self exists independently causes confusion. We are dreamers. We are sharing in this dream.

These teachings of the Ywahoo lineage are being passed with the prayer that we humans will again see ourselves as one family in the circle of life and cast aside illusions of separation, that we may stand again in the circle as dignified human beings. Be the best human being you can be. All of the Native peoples' names for themselves in their own languages mean, basically, "people." The Tsalagi people call ourselves "Principal People" because we trace our roots to the Seven Dancers and remember our duty to spread seeds of light.

Those beings who lived upon the Earth when the Star Mother fell down had life and consciousness, but not yet the seed of mind, so the starseed needed to be disseminated around the Earth. As our culture evolved, it was therefore the duty of the Children of the Sun to marry the most lowly people, a duty to plant starseed in all peoples. This is again a reminder that we are all one family of human beings.

Since the whole human family is in a process of evolution, enlightenment, there is no reason for discouragement, self-deprecation, or despair, and every reason for compassion, taking care. When you see error in your own nature, rather than feed the discord, simply observe and acknowledge the error and affirm the right action. This is the power of affirmative thought, of clear voice: to bring discord to harmony. Without charge, without attachment, see the error and bring forth the balancing energy. "Oh, responding in a certain way. Feeling angry and in despair, blaming others for hunger over there. Let me not blame myself, too, for having felt anger or discord. Let me have remorse, correct that error of thought, and take action in a most diligent way. Let me find the peace of mind to envision a world of beauty." Chant an affirmation to turn aside that negative pattern of thinking.

Let us reflect on the skills needed to transform the illusions of anger, pain, shame, separation. First we must have faith—faith that if we inhale, we exhale, that the sun set this night and it will rise tomorrow as it has many days before. The simple things enable us to stay clear and sure.

And we must have good will toward ourselves. As we observe our lives, we recognize that our feelings about ourselves reflect in our relationships with others. So it is wise to cultivate a feeling of care and compassion for self, recognizing that we are all in a process of change, a process of purification, growing ever brighter in the circle of life. No shame, no blame. Every morning, look in the mirror and call forth that clear light within you: "Hello, how are you?" After a few days your eyes will light up, and you then begin to see many good things about yourself. In the Native teaching, right eye gives,

167

left eye receives, energy always flowing in a circle, in and out. Thus, even what you look upon you have a special responsibility to look upon with love—including yourself. You see others also through the lens of your own thinking, your own mind, so if you are feeling bad about yourself, then everything looks ugly. See the beauty in yourself, and those you meet will reflect back that beauty, bringing ease and joy to all your relationships. That is planting the seed that your actions may succeed, for how you see yourself and others is also how you will see tomorrow—and what you see, the vision you hold, will surely manifest as the reality you live.

Compassion and care for self and others are a fertile soil in which generosity naturally grows. Compassion expresses our wish that beings not suffer, care reveals our desire to nourish their well-being, and generosity is the practice, our actions dedicated to realizing happiness and good for others in the circle. Generosity means giving, and it begins in the heart, by affirming confidence in the abundance of the universe. Abundance flows in a circle, like the breath. Breathe in, breathe out. When we doubt the ability to breathe, respiration becomes tight; when we feel fear, think scarcity thoughts, then the flow of abundance in our own life becomes constricted. The channel must be open at both ends for the spring water to reach the garden. When you give with your heart—perhaps the thing to which you are most attached—generosity channel opens. The job you awaited, the scholarship you hoped for, the insight you prayed to receive becomes available. This is the cycle of reciprocity: what is going out from your mind is always coming back to you. Just like the breath. So, no blame, no shame, just happening. We are in the circle of life, and truly things are in a process of change and balance.

Many have succumbed to the illusion of scarcity. Even the winds and the waters themselves have retreated because of the strength of that illusion in the minds of the people. To turn aside that illusion Native people have the give-away. When feeling uncertain or when feeling greatly blessed, we make a ceremony where we give things to others; some will give away everything they have. Generosity is a warm sun burning away the clouds that obscure abundance. Generosity is a seed of happiness that sprouts in all our relations. So the act of giving is very important. In the poorest Indian home there is always something to share with a guest.

Thus, first there is faith and the will to be, the commitment to manifest the good. Then there is the energy of compassion, caretaking, generosity. To know that our thinking is determining our reality and to purify that creative stream of mind, this is number three.

As our minds become clear, so does our vision, and what we envision, what we hope for, manifests. Therefore it is wise to be aware of one's special purpose in this lifetime, that the vision and its realization may be aligned with one's sacred duty.

The strong person may have four different gifts to give in a life, at four different life markers. The first marker of life is birth and the growing realization that one is alive, often occurring at the moment of the child's first smile. The second marker is adolescence, with its awareness of particular talents to offer and the development of such talents. Third marker: skillful means sufficiently developed to assist the community and one's own family. Now one is developing inner vision and skills for community building. Fourth post or marker: ability to transform that which is inappropriate and offer methods of family and community harmonization through understanding of relationships and the force in one's own nature; this phase occurs around age fifty-one when, in the Tsalagi worldview, you are considered an adult. So you may be a child yet. And the wise child reveres the wisdom of the world around, keeps alive the sense of mystery. We are wise children by caring with our sound, by calling forth with our vision, by seeing the best in ourselves and one another. To see the best is not to ignore what needs correction. It is to see the beauteous potential and to call ourselves into that place of clarity.

If you find certain patterns of thought obscuring the mind, recall regular practice as a way of transforming thought and action. Make time every day to sit and observe your nature without reacting. Just see, "Oh, these thoughts arise. They are but thoughts. Is that me?" Affirm the inner knowing; be that which you are. Sometimes you may be shocked into paying attention to your own experience. At an early age I discovered that I needed to set limits on other people's encroaching upon my stability of mind. When going to school I saw that the teachers were racist; they did not appreciate the fact that I had taught myself how to read and that I was reading far beyond what Dick and Jane had to say. The teachers claimed, "Indians are dead." To them my existence was a lie. The teacher said, "You're a liar, you dirty little thing, you can't read." I said, "Yes, I can," and I read for her. She slapped me in the face. And that was a great benefit for me, for it showed me that I must not depend on anything outside, that the only verification of truth in the world beyond my relatives must come from my inner experience. I slap you in the face right now, that you trust your inner experience, that you trust your inner eye, that it is only "yes" when you see it and taste it and it is "maybe" if you don't. That is to be self-empowered. Confusion comes from wondering if someone else's way is the right way. Better to know your own way. To be a Peacekeeper requries courage.

THE DIRECTIONS AND CONSCIOUSNESS

The meditation practice that comes through the Ywahoo teachings is most ancient; it is said to be over 133,000 years old. The practice makes clear the channels within the body so that one can experience the true nature of one's mind and recognize subtle relationship with the world around. Our physical form is the outer manifestation, what we are wearing. The mind, it has no clothes. To understand the nature of our own mind is to understand the gifts of life.

The Dance of the Directions is a very wondrous aspect of the Sunray practice, the practice followed by students of these teachings. It is a very simple practice based on movements and exercises taught to me and my relatives in child-

170

hood. In the mountains of the Eastern Tsalagi reservation in Cherokee, North Carolina, many of the movements of this dance can be seen in the Eagle Dance that is offered there at night, in a performance called "Unto These Hills." The purpose of the Dance of the Directions is to align the unmanifest potential with the vortex of manifestation. It enables one to perceive the inherent clarity of mind. A society's illness, a planet's illness, an individual's illness is only the result of obscuration in the channels of the mind. So this sacred dance is an opportunity to recognize that clarity and to turn aside whatever thought forms may have accumulated within one's own channels. It also makes the human body stronger.

Sometimes when observing the dancers with peripheral vision, one can see a little haze or light around them. In their dancing they are making clearer the channels of energy within themselves, their connections to Earth and the heavens, thus clarifying their meridians and the Earth's meridians and intensifying the life force. It is that energy that you may see around the dancers; they are generating light.

The Dance of the Directions also brings one into clear relationship with the magnetic energy of the Directions.

In the Tsalagi worldview all things are related and one in the circle of life. Circle, mandala, medicine wheel—mirrors of mind. The Adawees (guardians) of the directions are subtle angelic beings, vortices of mind through which the world takes form; all human beings are in relationship to these guardians. At different times in your life you are facing a particular direction and expressing the qualities of that guardian. For example, the energy of adolescence, the burgeoning creative power, seeds in preparation for springtime planting—this is expressed through the South, as the sacred grandmothers carrying baskets containing seeds of good cause. In the West one may pass out of the gateway of life and go on to the realms of light. One also chooses, when facing the West, to manifest one's life purpose through the transformation of any negative attitudes, so that one's efforts may benefit the entire circle of life.

The uncertain person is propelled around the Medicine Wheel by emotions. The student of life analyzes and recognizes general patterns of emotion and their outcome, and chooses to act with care. The wise recognize that in their own mind all things are reflected, and they seek to make clear, like a mountain stream, their own nature—thereby charting their course around the wheel, as the frozen waters of potential melt and become actualized as right action.

The direction of the North brings a great message; it is the hiding place of the Thunderbird, the resting place of the sacred Buffalo. In the North the rivers of reaction become frozen so that one may break free from the patterns of reaction and look at cause in one's life—recognizing mind in the lake of mirror wisdom. The North is a place of great teaching.

As spring comes and the waters melt, one flows to the East, the direction of self-understanding. Through mindfulness, clear communication with the trees, that which walks, crawls, swims, flies, one sees All My Relations. In the East self-knowledge arises and one perceives the thought, the desire that moves one around the wheel, the power of thought as a co-creative function in the world. One chooses those thoughts that are for the benefit of all, so the energy of generosity, compassion, and clear mind may be manifest in all the actions of individual and community. In the East perceive the rising face of consciousness, see things as they are: people in good relationship moving upon the wave and grace of clear mind.

In the South seeds of good cause and regeneration are planted, good cause unto seven generations, with clear intention: fire of will stirring the heart to be . . . a flower, an enlightened community. In the South we recognize the gifts of our grandmothers, the traditions of our ancestors, each of us moving on the blessing of all who have come before. In the South the seeds of life are cherished, bringing forth abundance. The Corn Mothers come dancing, scattering bountiful seed, shaking their powerful light, turning aside our fears, enabling us to meet strongly the wisdom of the Bear and the sacred medicine of the West.

In the West, Dancing Bear stomps on fear and ignorance and the fires of transmutation ever slowly burn, clearing away those thoughts which obscure crystal mind. Cast aside pain, shame, blame. Nothing wasted. Even mental trash is recycled in the West, supplying all the people's needs. From the West we may choose to go to the land of boundless light or to return to the North and again around the wheel, with a deepened commitment to rekindle the wisdom fire in all beings. (See Appendix B, "The Directions and Their Attributes.")

The relationship of thought and action we can see in a very practical way through our movement in relation to other people. Not a single one of us lives in this world or acts in this world alone. Each of us is moving in relationship to those around us, in relationship to the environment. To see the beauty in those around us, to acknowledge the spark of mind within those we meet, is a great gift to all—including ourselves, as we thus enable the light to dance brightly within our own consciousness. And we cast aside the illusions of separation when we glance and perceive the light in the eye of another. To acknowledge and see the clarity of another is to bring forth peace on this planet. That simple. Even the person you meet in the supermarket is an opportunity for you to practice seeing clearly, an opportunity to practice the joy of giving—giving a heartfelt hello and receiving a reflection of your own mind. What we see around us and how people are responding to us is always coming through the lens of the "little I." This little I is a dream; we are here together, and there is no beginning and no end.

Through alignment with the clear mind within, through clear intention to be a good person in right relationship with all, we clear a path. This is very important, the will to complete and understand the Mystery of life, to realize the great truth. It is to keep our hearts ever aware of the cycle of reciprocity by examining our own minds and realizing equanimity in relation to all things, all things in the circle of life together. No above, no below, each one unique and necessary to this vision, this dream. As we look upon the dream we are

173

sharing, as we look upon the nature of our own mind, let us see those attitudes and thoughts that may be obscuring our life's true purpose, and clearly choose to transform them for the benefit of all.

JOURNEY TO THE
TEMPLE OF UNDERSTANDING[2]

The Temple of Understanding is the storehouse of our thoughts and actions. Some might refer to it as the akashic records, others might call it the angelic realms. It is a mental realm where our thoughts, words, and deeds are recorded over all our lifetimes. This temple is accessible to those who are committed to living in truth and generating harmony; who energetically vow to transmute discordant thought in their own natures, that harmony may manifest through all relations.

This exercise is based on the principle of weaving patterns of wholesome relations as taught by Grandfather Eonah Fisher. In that our thoughts and habits of relating are patterns, the wise practitioner looks to see those patterns which are no longer appropriate and reinforces those which manifest harmonious relations and fulfill his or her creative potential. We do this practice that we and others may be free from habits of conflict and discord.

Imagination is the wings of thought, so we begin our journey by imagining ourselves wrapped in golden cloaks of clear mind. Enfolded in light, we make a prayer that any obstacles hindering peace and good relations may become apparent, that we may transform them for the benefit of all.

Feel the whole body irradiated with golden light. Breathe deeply to the bottom of the feet, and as you exhale, feel yourself becoming lighter and lighter until you become an eagle soaring on the wind. Rising, rising on the beauteous wind, you soar to the cloud realms of Galunlati. There you find a subtle world of light; giant pine trees grace the landscape and there appears in the pines a meandering path.

As you walk upon the path, breathing deeply the efferves-cent air, sense mind becoming more subtle, more clear, as the perfume of mountain air washes away doubt and uncertainty.

As you walk along this path, be aware that there is a divine pattern underlying all existence. Your heart overflows with joy, sensing the unity of creation. You come to two large boul-ders through which the path meanders. On the other side is a beautiful lake, a placid lake. All sorts of animals gather about the lake to drink its refreshing waters; even the mountain lion gathers there with the sheep. Hunger has been assuaged, ag-gression has been pacified, so that these animals are gathered together around Atagahi, the Magic Lake. Even severely wounded animals and persons, when making their way to this lake and bathing in it, are healed of all wounds. The lake is the collective consciousness of all beings, its sweet waters the balm that assuages all pain. Its medicine is vast and good. It is good fortune to have made your way to its shores.

As you gaze upon the Lake of Mirror Wisdom, whatever thoughts arise of hunger, pain, fear, or discord may be healed by the sweet magical waters of the lake. Where any obscuring pattern or habit in your relationships becomes apparent, transmute grasping energy to clear light of right action.

Reflect upon your relations with family, friends, and co-workers and imagine them near you. Forgive yourself and others for what might have been, could have been, should have been, and together splash the waters over your shoulders three times, that patterns of discord may be transformed to patterns of clear relationship.

A path leads away from the lake to a luminous temple atop a flat-topped pyramid. There are sixteen wide and graceful steps that lead to the entryway of the Temple of Understand-ing. In the entry there are black and white tiles on the floor, to your left the great library, to your right the great banquet hall. At the end of the central hall there is a small shrine room wherein burns the eternal fire of transformation.

Temple guardians will meet you at the door and ask your purpose for being there. One responds with the vow: "I come to understand the nature of my mind, that my actions may benefit all beings." When the guards are assured that your intentions are beneficial to all, they will allow you to enter the library, and an angelic being will help you to find your Book of Life.

You will be shown to your personal study room and the book of your lives will be brought to you, that you may ascertain your life purpose, assess your skills and gifts, and realize the means of actualizing your goals. In the study room with the angelic protectors you may look at and evaluate all stages of your life. If it should be that you experienced great suffering in your life, here you can reclaim your staff of destiny, that in this time you may actualize your gifts. As you look upon your life, notice those times in which you acquiesced to another's will or expectations. Affirm that in the present you need not repeat such patterns.

On your desk place two sheets of paper and light a candle, that you may clearly see your gifts. On the left-hand paper write those patterns you have outgrown, those thought forms, those actions that you feel are no longer appropriate to your life's unfolding, that hinder realization of your full potential. On the right-hand paper write your strengths, the gifts to be fully developed as antidotes to old patterns. Write also specific goals to be accomplished in three days, three months, three years, seeing in your mind's eye the particular task accomplished. See your life plan, your relationships, your educational, professional, and financial objectives actualized, knowing that you will gather to yourself whatever tools are necessary to manifest these visions. Then look carefully at your life as it unfolds before you. See it long, strong, healthy, a beauteous road before you, yourself walking in good company and inspiring good cheer to many.

Place the right hand-sheet of paper in the Book of Life, which the librarian will then return to the shelf, and the left-hand paper burn in the candle. Recall the steps that brought you to this temple and know that you may visit here again. Give thanks to the angelic beings who aided you.

Leave the study hall and enter the inner sanctum fire in the shrine room, giving a prayer of appreciation that you may walk the Beauty Path. Then enter the banquet hall. Join the feast, partake of wisdom's fruits, and gather some wisdom food to take home to your family and friends.

Follow the pathway from the temple around the lake, through the woods, and fly like an eagle to the Earth, mind ennobled with clear light, heart overflowing with generosity for all. Breathe in deeply, exhale completely, rotate your feet and shoulders, stretching majestically, and sit up slowly. Conclude with a prayer of thanksgiving. Then write in your journal whatever notes are needed, and bask in the light of clear knowing from this day on.

You are the master of your destiny. To have the courage of your purpose, your vision, to have diligence and generosity to realize that vision for the benefit of all beings—these are the commitments of a Peacekeeper. To keep clear these sacred commitments is to dedicate oneself to right relationship with all in the family of life.

We have spoken of the waters of forgiveness; they are also the waters of sweet remembrance, ever renewing, ever recalling the inherent wisdom of the moment and the beauty that brings us together with our friends and relatives. Forgiveness is a basic ritual of the Tsalagi. Once a year in our ceremonial cycle the "Friends Making New" ceremony is held, and every day one is encouraged to make way for forgiveness. In the ceremony we literally go to the ocean's or the river's edge and we cast the water over our shoulders seven times, casting aside expectations, forgiving and letting go of attachment to what might have been, could have been, should have been. After that is done, even the most painful memories can be released and the worst enemies become friends again. We know that if we do not renew ourselves we will suffer the same patterns of discord again and again, so we make this vow to forgive and forget and start anew. The most precious time for the forgiveness ceremony is the spring new moon. Even the most vicious criminal who has spent a year in spiritual practice and meditation in the Peace Village, even that one who hurt self and others is made pure again and accepted by the community again during the ceremony of forgiveness and making friendships new.

The forgiveness ritual[3] is a practice that you can do at any time, outside at the water's edge, indoors with a bowl of fresh water, or simply in your mind's eye. See yourself by the water. Visualize yourself stepping forward, offering a prayer of thanks for the opportunity to renew yourself in good relationship. Seven times throw the water over your shoulders. Feel it washing away all that obscures good friendship with your circle of friends and family. "I wash away ignorance, I wash away doubt and fear and loneliness. I let go of sorrow, I turn aside anger. I rejoice in the light of a new day." Visualize a beam from your heart radiating rose light to touch the hearts of those with whom you have experienced miscommunication or discord; see that rose light surrounding them and then returning to you, filling your heart. As you step away from the water, yesterday's wounds are healed. Affirm a new day of clear relations. Let your voice sing out a song of joyous thanksgiving.

In Tsalagi tradition mental health, physical health, and social order are an expression of the proper balance of things. If the individual disturbs or breaks the pattern of balance with self or others, it creates a discordant vibration in the energy meridians of that body and may cause illness and distress. If there is some discordant energy in the family, it may express as strife or it may express as crop failure. If the clan is forgetting to care for someone who feels separated, or if in the network of your friends there is someone who feels lonely and the circle does not receive that message, does not gather that person back to heart, the whole group of friends suffers until such time as the eyes awaken and all see, "Our friend is suffering. Let us give that person a hand; let us say it is all right."

We are in a very delicate balance within ourselves and with other people and our environment. We are all vibrating together, we are one resonant field, one field of mind. If there is an excess of unclarified emotion in the heart of the people, then there is unclear emotion expressed by the nation. There is no way to separate yourself from your nation and planet. This is your home.

Each of us is responsible for bringing correction and balance in our own spheres. To put aside the prejudices in one's own mind and make clear one's relationships with others is to strike a tone that will resound throughout the land. Already things have changed a great deal throughout the planet as a result of people calling forth peace and our determination that it manifest. How is it manifesting? Not by arguments but by disarming ourselves as individuals, putting aside the thoughts and behaviors of aggression and defense on the plane of individual relationship. This resonates throughout the Earth so the nations recognize the people's need for change. So you do make a difference. You are needed by the Earth and by your relatives. And however uncertain you may feel, come back to what you know for sure: "I inhale and I exhale. I have the gift of life; therefore I have accumulated much merit, and so I am worthy of understanding and living in peace and right relationship."

In this time it is not sufficient for us to realize the great truth individually. We need to live it as a group; we need to share it together. This is a very special time. The energy that comes forth now, it is the energy of the great Peacekeeper. It will manifest in each of us as we cast aside our doubts and illusions and put our feet firmly upon the Beauty Path. Creator will say, "Are you one with Creation?" And you will answer only yes or no—no ifs, ands, buts, or maybes. One step at a time we walk. With clear heart and mind we see beauty before us, beauty behind us, beauty all around.

One with Peacekeeper mind lives and dies with mindfulness and compassion for all beings. Thoughts of peace and beauty are cultivated by the pregnant woman. Thoughts of peace and beauty are cultivated by the dying man. Thus it begins and ends.

CONSCIOUS LIVING, CONSCIOUS DYING

When our elders spoke of the Trail of Tears the memory and the expression were very present, as if it had happened only a couple of days ago or at most a couple of weeks. As it was told one could feel a shock at being forced from one's home, one's peach orchards, one's cornfield. This reminded us that the past lived very much in our memories and that indeed some of us had lived before and had ourselves come through these experiences; in various moments of open mind many of us children experienced memories of other lifetimes. From as far back in my childhood as I can remember, my elders, particularly my grandmother and her sisters, would refer to my own previous lives, as a continuum and a process that brought the present forth. On regular occasions they would speak about different times in which we had lived together, the different forms our relationships had taken, and how we had chosen to be together. Once, my grandmother said, I had been kidnapped by another Indian nation, by a family that had lost a child due to activities of our nation; she said that for years and years she had pined for me and how happy she was that I had come to be her granddaughter in this time. Although we were separated from my tenth year in that life until this present life, she felt she knew my complete life. Our minds still met as we made our morning prayers, looking at the dawn star; she was able to see my whole life from afar.

Occasionally I would test my grandmother and my great-grandfather, asking them questions about different times to see if they really did have the same memories as I, for our memories were not only of North, Central, and South America; we also had shared memories of Egypt, Atlantis, the stars.

On one occasion Great-Grandfather had finished stacking wood. He was looking at clouds. I and two cousins were looking at him looking at clouds. Such serenity and power emanated from his body that redbirds came down and circled around us, making beautiful music. I thought, "Aha! He's not thinking—let me ask him." So I said, "How do you know we've been here before?"

"Because we're here now."

I just said, "Oh." Then: "We are here now; what is the meaning of it?"

Great-Grandfather answered, "Now is the result of all our yesterdays and the basis of all our tomorrows, so why don't you just pay attention to what's happening now?" And he called me by his nickname for me, which could translate as "Venerable Chigger," meaning "Very-wise-old-pest-that-gets-under-the-skin."

My two cousins slunk away because they knew another one of Dhyani's struggles was about to occur. A tether line was let loose, and I meandered around in the yard and the field for quite some time—but I knew the old man had me by the solar plexus, and wherever I went I could feel him looking out through my eyes. I went over to the well and looked down, and the old man's face looked up at me. I looked up at the sky, and his face looked down at me. I went to my favorite tree, and his face was looking out of the bark. I said to myself, "Well, now is the basis of everything, huh?" and went about my chores, not thinking of it any longer. I made the buttermilk, churned the butter, watched the cousins bring up ice from the ice cave, present in the immediacy of the moment, pumping that churning stick up and down. And I knew something powerful was going to happen by the time the sun went down behind the hills.

After the buttermilk and the good dinner of *selu* (corn), vegetables, sunflower seeds, greens, and peach cobbler, my grandmother told some of the other children to clear the table. She asked me if I had eaten well and then said, "Let's go." She took me back into the woods to the medicine cabin, a cabin in the original Tsalagi style, built of logs, with a dirt floor. The windows in this cabin could be sealed so that it was completely dark. I watched the sun going down, I watched my grandmother's eyes as she watched the sun going down. I heard the water drum and rattles, and I knew that questions about before and after and now were about to be answered.

Once I entered the medicine cabin, any questions, any thoughts about doing something else evaporated from my mind. As the water drums were beaten, as the life-force makers were shaken, I understood how it is. We decided as a family which star we would communicate with so that we could find one another when we put aside the robe of this present body and chose another. Many times passed before my eyes, many life forms, many expressions of consciousness became apparent. Wisdom light burned brightly and joy sang out from our hearts.

The following teaching is based upon the teachings and insights of this night.

In the Tsalagi worldview birth, life, death, and rebirth are actual processes in the continuum of existence. We are taught to live each day fully present, as if that day might be the last. The *Elo* offers teachings to maintain harmony of mind and antidotes to disharmony. While living in harmony with the sacred precepts and practicing generosity, one maintains a clear flow of life force.

The clear stream of life is manifest in one's relationships to self, family, clan, nation, and the planet herself. Obstructions to this clear stream may obscure these relationships, manifesting as confusion and disorder.

Inconsistency with one's own life purpose is one such obstruction. It may manifest as lethargy, inertia, conflicting emotions. Clarification may be reached through clearly ascertaining one's present life skills and what skills are yet to be developed in order to fulfill one's purpose. Stabilization of mind through contemplation of the breath and daily review of one's actions allow one to perceive which actions bring fruitful result and to develop them further. Those actions which bring negative results are to be replaced with constructive patterns. For example, if the first hour at work is stressful, allow for start-up time and planning before interacting with others. In Native tradition, prayers and quiet time are cultivated before busy times.

Discord in relation to clan totem (inspirational muse) and family members, particularly one's own parents and relatives, is another significant obstruction. Such disharmony can be clarified by forgiveness ritual, bathing in the waters of forgiveness, and by applying compassion as the antidote for dislike. Should miscommunication arise from unfulfilled expectations or unclear communication, cultivate nonaccusatory speech. Invite one another to communicate based on clear "game rules." Put aside the adversary approach, and replace blame with complementary resolution. Each voice and opinion is part of the circle. Seek consensus based upon the greater good.

In these times many adults, in seeking understanding, put aside the wisdom of their family of origin's religious belief systems. The result may be that parents and relatives feel set aside and not respected. The wise practitioner considers that yesterday's experience brings today's understanding and cultivates "like mind" rather than a sectarian view, perceiving the common factors of belief systems.

The clan totem symbolizes the strengths and subtle characteristics of a clan. Bird Clan members express spaciousness of mind and light nature; Deer Clan members express fleetness of mind and body; Bear Clan members express the studious attitudes of a retreatant. Body type is also an expression of clan totem. Most significantly, each clan has particular spiritual responsibilities in maintaining harmony for the whole nation. For the non-Native person, the clan totem is expressed as a creative mentor or muse, guiding people to their inner gifts.

Desecration of the land or spirit of holy places can become an obstruction through disturbance of the flow in the individual who, wittingly or unwittingly, has desecrated a holy place. In that the Earth has breathing spaces and meridians by which life force flows, a human may upset the harmony through cutting trees in sacred groves, polluting watersheds, or carelessly allowing campfire to run rampant. In Tsalagi tradition, dead wood is gathered for fires. It is most important that offerings and thanks be given before picking herbs, collecting food, or taking anything from the natural kingdom. In many families grace is said before meals; in Tsalagi tradition grace is said before collecting food as well as before eating it. The one who cuts trees responsibly plants trees as well, to ensure trees and health for the generations to come. When people take from the Earth without consideration for the future, as in clear-cut logging, topsoil washes away, rivers become filled with silt, fish die, people have less to eat. Such desecration perpetrated by individuals gives rise to illness of mind, disturbance of wind. Clarification may be restored by offerings of prayer and fruit, burning of sage or cedar, and planting of trees and healing herbs.

Breaking of commitment to keep sacred rituals and practices can be the cause of illness expressed as mental confusion, physical lethargy, or disease. It is most important to honor vows of generosity and consideration of future generations. Speak words of truth, because untruths bring bitter fruit. The habit of untruth inhibits one's accomplishment through dissonance of intent and result.

When one has been confirmed in a particular spiritual or religious community, one needs to keep clear those precepts.

In Tsalagi tradition certain "bundles" representing the teachings, spiritual duties, and ceremonies are given. To caretake such a bundle requires maintenance of certain prayer cycles, states of mind, and abstinence from such behavior as intoxicants and cruel or untrue speech and action. We reaffirm understanding of our life purpose and relationship with these rituals of good cause-making, diligently clarifying and transforming attitudes and thought forms that obscure full manifestation. If we feel unable to maintain prayer cycles and harmony with precepts, then we may consider returning the bundle to the spiritual teacher who presented it, or to some suitable caretaker. (If this is not possible, the bundle may be buried, thus returning that sacred energy to the Earth.)

Denial of the basic code of ethics, morals, and polite formulas (manners) of one's social group disturbs harmony and often gives rise to mind of conflict. Mind of conflict is an extreme example of separation view, as one argues against rather than councils with community, giving rise to behavior outside the stream, causing mental and physical suffering. To renew the cycle of right relationships is to ascertain the basic principles of ethics, morals, and polite formulas as outflow of the community mind's attempt at cultivating "like view," mind of union.

These obstructions are rooted in lethargy, anger, fear, avarice, repulsion, attraction. Pride or self-importance ("big head") is the primary source of these energies. Through the illusion of pride one feels superior or inferior to this or that in the circle of life and thus breaks connection with the sacred flow.

The patterns of envy, aversion and attraction are patterns of energy. The antidote for these qualities of mind and emotion is the understanding that all is related in the circle; each one has a necessary function, a unique function, in the whole. What appears is projected by one's emotions. In recognizing the appearance as mind-generated, one has opportunity to co-create relationships of beauty.

Through clear life relationship one is able consciously to

185

choose rebirth with friends. If one passes into another world with anger/enmity or attraction/craving toward particular people, one may meet them again in another life in unpleasant circumstances until the emotional obscuration is resolved. Attraction or craving can often become enmity or aversion and vice versa; either of these grasping energies can produce similar effects in another lifetime. So it is the wise person who constantly renews friendship and affirms the good.

Attraction and aversion are different faces of the same crystal or coin. There is the attraction of friends, of family, of lovers, and there is the resolution of each in the circle, in the recognition of the process of change. An example is the mother's love for her child. As the child grows up, her expression of that love changes. If she seeks to hold on to the baby, her loving intention may create seeds of discord and rebellion in the young person who seeks to grow. Just as in family relationships, all relationships are in the process of change, and to recognize this truth is to see beyond the changing forms to the unchanging essence.

In Tsalagi worldview the clear face, the fire that burns in all, is seen as an ever-present essence burning in the heart of every being. We are one in that clear light. As we share and do things together, the face and the actions of that moment are but flickerings of the flame. The essence blazes brightly and reflects the clear light. This is the bounty.

In Tsalagi view, one has seven lifetimes in which to come again to complete realization. It can be done in one lifetime, and in seven it is certain to be complete. Then one may become a planet, a star, the quintessential fire permeating all things, or rest in the formless. It is good to help those in need, as a caretaker.

CONSCIOUS REBIRTH

Friends or family who choose to be born again together may select a particular constellation in the sky upon which to gaze.

When one is reborn and becomes old enough, seeing this constellation will spark remembrance of commitment to be again with those dear ones. In the process of dying one projects one's consciousness to that constellation, and those who will remain on Earth, they, too, meditate on that particular constellation while their friend is dying, so that the thought-streams are the same. The dying person's friends also keep clear the stream of their emotions during this time, so that the dying person's journey in the clear light is not obscured by clouds. At a higher level of consciousness and with the help of certain rituals and ceremonies, one can choose the actual kind of relationship one will have with one's friend in the next lifetime.

Dying is like the seasons changing, a continuum. This understanding is most significant in maintaining stability and empowered action in the moment. Most people never fully live or incarnate because of their fear of death.

Life and death are part of a cycle. Dying is as wonderful as the season's change; old age is as wonderful as the beauty of autumn. When one has lived with care and mindfulness, death is another quality to be explored. In older cultures where living and dying are centered in the home, death is something that everyone shares without fear. We seek to balance any debts and to make our gifts to others, in that one would not wish to go on a journey with an incomplete pack or carrying more baggage than is useful.

In these busy times many people's vast potential goes untapped because of fear of death. This unreal fear of what will eventually befall everyone often hinders a person's full participation in life, so that one may be afraid to try because thinking of possible failure. The wise person cultivates each moment of life as an opportunity to see the nature of mind and relationships. In Tsalagi culture it is said that it takes fifty-one years to become a full-fledged adult member of society. Thus long life is assumed, and one is encouraged to live each day as if it were the last. As children we were told that

187

those who live in harmony with the sacred cycles and keep clear the practice will often lead long lives; a life cycle of 120 years is not uncommon among the Keepers of the Fire.

A most significant vision in Tsalagi and other Native American views is that death is but a change and not an ending. Just as we cultivate happy relationships, we also plant the seed for positive leavetaking from this world into another. It is good.

Ᏻ(Ꮒ) ᎠᎧ Ꭿ   Ᏻ(Ꮒ) ᎠᎧ Ꭿ   Ᏻ(Ꮒ) ᎠᎧ Ꭿ

Yu(n) we hi   Yu(n) we hi   Yu(n) we hi

Yu(n) we hi

Ga lu(n) la ti da tsi lá i   Yu(n) we hi

I am come from above

Yu(n) we hi   Yu(n) we hi   Yu(n) we hi

Nu(n) da gú(n) yi   ga tlá a hi   Yu(n) we hi

I am come down from the Sunland

Ge ya gú ga   Gí ga ge tsu wa tsi la   gi   ga ge

O Red Ageyaguga, you have come down and put

tsi yé la   tsi que ná du la ni ga

your red spittle upon my body

Yu(n) we hi   Yu(n) we hi   Yu(n) we hi

Yu(n) we hi

To hi u ha lu ni

Serenity, it resounds

6

A LIVING VISION OF PEACE

WE are relative to all living beings. We are all in direct relationship, through our thinking, through our feeling, with the One Mind dreaming us all. All of us may attune to and recognize the one clear light of reality through our hearts and through apperception of our mind's own motion. To be in relation, to recognize that everything is a relative, is to understand the natural resonance of our thought and action, to know that our actions shape tomorrow. Through the perception of wisdom's flow within us we may energetically pursue a path of beauty, a path that can bring us to enlightenment. All sentient beings may realize the potential of the unmanifest as it becomes, through keeping the heart mercifully open and aware. As we are loving toward ourselves and others and hold a beauteous vision of the whole world enlightened, it shall be.

We are shaping, like crystals, a field of mind. We live in a field of mind. We can call this Buddha mind, God mind, "What It Is." The Tsalagi say it is the Great Mystery, Ywahoo, "that which is unmanifest and becoming and contains within it the seed of our potential." We are that mind. To come through the obscurations of consciousness that develop around attachment, fear, and doubt reveals the abundant mind as a stream in which we are all flowing. To come again to that stream of reality is to come again to knowing yourself as mind, and to see your progress around the Medicine Wheel of life as a continuation of cause that you make in this time, in other times, in the future, and in the past. The power of the moment is the power to see and shape our reality. As we go around this wheel, eventually we gain an expertise and take within our hands a staff like lightning, the intuitive wisdom that recognizes the nature of reality.

The clear ideation of the balanced being, one aligned with his or her purpose, knowing direct relationship with all of creation, weaves the tapestry of light. It is through the heart's mind and the integration of the inner eye that we recall the stream that carries consciousness into the realm of clear light, the clear light of what is. Then, with discriminating wisdom, we understand cause and effect and distinguish those thoughts which are separating us from the stream of our wholeness. So much potential has a human being.

We have in this time an opportunity to create peace in our hearts, a peace that can resonate in every aspect of our lives. The stilling of the mind, the seeing of one's thought patterns, and the cultivation of those thought patterns which are lotus gems of wisdom are part of discriminating wisdom's development. Every aspect of life is an opportunity to see all that is, whatever one is doing, be it washing dishes, chopping wood, typing. There is in every moment an opportunity to recognize the clear light of reality. May you have vision to see, intelligence to act, and wisdom to succeed, to recognize the nature of things as they are.

To see the nature of things, one cultivates vision to see possible futures, vision to uncover treasures beneficial to family and clan. The outer vision perceives what is there and what may be hidden in the shadows of what is there. As one looks on the stream, water is seen moving, light reflections dance, water spiders skitter, and myriad creatures live within the stream. One then observes the banks of the stream, the steepness, the plants growing alongside. In late summer the stream appears small and quiet; spring brings a raging torrent. When you are seeking a campsite you rely on many aspects of vision lest you be washed away in what appears to be a quiet stream.

Grandmother Nellie and Aunt Hattie insisted that we children attain "multiple vision" to look beyond appearances, to understand the subtle messages beneath the surface. Aunt Hattie was a sleight-of-hand expert; she did magic tricks. Her most oft-repeated statement was, "Believe none of what you've heard secondhand and believe half of what you see. Get true vision from the eye of your heart."

In the heart's eye a vision of peace and beauty shines. When vision of inner peace is cultivated, then it may manifest in one's environment. Inner vision arises continuously, yet one may not recognize the signs owing to inflexibility of thought. Observing the stream of one's mind refines the process of seeing patterns of thought and action, thereby making safe stream-crossing places apparent. The safe crossing place is where one may step over a habit of thought that is no longer necessary. The bridge is composed of insight into one's behavior and its possible outcomes.

Any dream or hope for peace occurs through the exploration of one's own mind. As we seek to see our essential nature, right action unfolds—because the consequences of our actions are clearly apparent. Intelligence to act in harmony grows from the vision of cause and effect. The thoughts and deeds we sow shall manifest. Those causes which benefit family and clan, in harmony with the land, manifest through people's diligence, and skillful means arise from observation of what works.

These natural laws of manifestation apply on every level of life: individual, family, clan, nation, planet. In 1978 it appeared to many of this land's medicine people that the Earth was in danger—that we were at a major turning point and if people did not make a change the Earth would suffer great catastrophe. It seemed probable that the west and east coasts of North America would be severely deluged and that many people would lose their lives. A Council of Elders, which guides many traditional Native peoples of this continent, called upon many of the medicine people to pray diligently and to invite people to act and visualize to make good medicine for Earth and future generations. It was not certain that this experiment worked until March 10, 1981; then it was apparent that it was a success. Many of the prophecies of total destruction of the planet have been softened by people's willingness to make significant changes in their consciousness. Many who used to speak of the age of purification as a time of complete destruction now recognize it as a time of transformation, when the thought, words, and acts of human beings can shape outcomes that will affect this planet far into the future. Earth need not suffer; people need not suffer. We must be willing to take responsibility and to keep vortices of light moving through our group meditation and individual practice. In this transformation time, all the ignorance that is in any mind makes itself apparent that it may be transmuted.

We are one with our mother, the Earth, the umbilicus of our thought interweaving the dream that we are sharing. We are turning this dream to peace. We are remembering the sacred medicine and we are keeping the sacred prophecies to clarify and purify, to see ourselves in harmony. Many roads are open as one steps upon the way. All roads lead home. Just be careful when you walk; be aware, when you step onto a certain fork in the road, that it will take you to its conclusion until there is another opportunity to change direction.

There was a spirit woman, a Deerskin Clan Mother, who roamed through a forest in New England. This being felt duty-bound to stand by Earth until some people came again to recall her song. She was entrusted with it as a clan mother, as a form builder, as one who recognizes the power of thought, to generate a thought form of peace and well-being throughout the northeast so that the hearts of people may align with the land and the beauteous ways. We saw her dancing light, and as we sat and watched, the sun went down, and she became apparent to us and insisted that we learn her sacred chant. Fire is her prayer, that the heart of light awaken again in the people and they respect the life in one another. In my journeys since that time I have heard people in the northwest sing a chant similar to the one she taught, a bit slower, relating it to the song of creation of the perfect crystal, the land of Galunlati, the realm of beauteous light whence the ideal manifests into the physical world. Thought beings, star people, light beings live there, and there it was decided to incarnate further into form and matter based upon the principles of the sacred world built upon will, love, and active mind. So in this world we have seed of the stars, perfection's seed, within ourselves as a sacred purpose that ever seeks to manifest. And in ourselves those three sacred fires burn—will, compassion, building mind—and through their grace all things come to form.

There is a stream of compassionate wisdom of which we are all a part. It is the stream of mother-father, the Balanced One; Ama Agheya, Water Woman, as the Tsalagi say; or Kuan Yin, the Compassionate One. From that flowing heart comes a great wisdom, to which each of us is attuned by remembrance of the sacred sound of creation within us.

So peace is alive within us as a seed, as a song. To call it forth is a practice of clear vision and clear speech. See the beauty and praise the beauty, and wisdom's stream shall flow abundantly in your heart. This is why visualization and chant are so important in our meditation practice, why in so many spiritual traditions there is much practice of prayer chanting. The channel of the voice is a doorway through which the idea manifests as form. With clear voice we affirm our choice. The sound is saying, "It is so," and so it is.

Visualization is a discipline. Certain people, according to their gifts from other lifetimes and the present, have a greater ease in visualization, particularly people who study mathematics and music. Other people may not visualize; they may experience direct apperception without actually seeing. For some it is almost as if it were whispered in their ear. Visualization has a beneficial effect in that it makes clear the energy meridians in the body. And what you can see clearly is easier to manifest. In our time many people have been traumatized through the educational system into disbelieving their own sight. Work with movement and dance and self-massage aids in clarifying obscurations of the inner eye's ability to visualize.

Foundation Practice of Visualization

1. Think of how your room looked when you left it.

2. In your mind's eye, see very clearly things that have been left, say, on the chest of drawers.

3. Stand back and look at the surrounding area of the room.

4. Again focus on something very simple in the room. Observe its geometric shape.

5. Notice basic geometry, the basic form of things in the room.

6. Watch the forms fill in with specifics of color and identity.

7. Exhale and return to present time and place. Observe in fine detail what is around you.

8. Give thanks for the gifts of mind and sight.

MEDITATION WITH SOUND AND VISUALIZATION

I invite you now to visualize three sacred fires in the sacrum, the base of your spine; three sacred fires—red, yellow, and blue, the primary colors giving birth to form. At the navel center visualize a green circle receiving the five basic elements of life: wood, earth, fire, water, air/sacred sound. In the solar plexus, see a blue square filled with an orange sun.

In the heart, see two triangles meeting apex to apex, the sound *Ah* inscribed at the center, radiating waves of rose light. Visualize in the throat an indigo tunnel with a single star shining within. In the medulla, at the base of skull, see a violet infinity symbol weaving all that was, is, and will be. In the center of your head see a buffalo horn receiving light from the heavens. And at the brow, see a golden triangle of awakened mind. Above the head seven stars cascade their rainbow light.

Chant the Heart Chant, the sound flowing out to touch all your relations with compassion's radiant light.

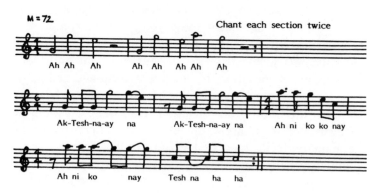

Spirals of light dance within you. Sense the flow of lunar and solar currents moving within your body—mother-father, a balanced being, birthing the holy child; trinity of your expression of will, love, and active mind bringing forth the clear light.

At a later stage in the practice one weaves the light of the seven stars with body's energy centers, weaving the Diamond Body. From seventh star above the head to fifth star and up again through sixth to seventh, one draws a beam of clear light. Three times this cycle is completed, making stitches of light at each star. Then the light thread is drawn from fifth star to third through fourth and up to fifth. From third star to first, up through second star to third again, drawing the light through, making the stitches firm. From first star the light is drawn to third eye, through medulla and up through crown to first star again, and then from third eye to heart, filling the heart, up through throat to third eye. Three times each cycle of weaving is completed. It is like embroidery, a holy stitch that strengthens the cord connecting you to your subtle knowing. This practice also strengthens the electrical field around the body and, through resonance coupling, the light body of the planet as well. The aura becomes infused with clear light as we reweave the sacred fabric of our being.

That is the power of clear ideation and affirmation; that is how visualization and chant and prayer create such a powerful renewing energy field, stirring the heart to sing out with joy. Diligently to maintain joy in your heart, to transmute thoughts of self-negation, to put doubt aside and call upon the power of your voice and choice of what is to be—that is to call upon the beauty. The Beauty Path is the clear mind in the heart, and the rainbow, the left and right hemispheres of the brain, perfectly integrated within that heart-mind.

Thus we change the world's mind of despair, of war, by realizing the peace within. The complement of the mother-father energies is the spiral, the child of perfection, the mind attuned to all. Remember that spiral, visualize it, and know yourself one with its light. First the visualization is a practice, then it becomes a recognized reality. The energy is there, its amplitude determined by your mind's attunement, your perception of that which is.

To realize your gift in this time is to bring together your mind, your voice and your heart, creating with sound and thought a world of harmony and beauty. We shall bring a great peace to this whole planet as each of us realizes peace within ourselves.

The Beauty Path is unwavering. Upon it walks the one who is determined to realize mind of enlightenment, mounting the sixteen steps to the temple atop the sacred pyramid. The pyramid is a reminder of the stages of human consciousness, the phases of our development. As we look into our consciousness we recognize that thought is the seed of its own reality. If we think this is a chaotic world, if we think little or ill of ourselves, that becomes a reality. It is the element of discriminating wisdom that enables us to know things as they are without attachment to form or shape or blame. To know things as they are and to know that we are in a process, that we have choice in that process, is to create the form of our highest expression. One must be very energetic and diligent in perceiving the whole of enlightenment, to hold the mind firm in heartfelt wisdom, to resonate through every aspect of mind the sound of beauty. We call upon discriminating wisdom to recognize that which is in need of correction and to see it coming to harmonious resolution. All that we see in life is a reflection of mind, and it is our choice how this great mind will manifest for us. We can limit the field of reality through limiting our own mind, or we can recognize the vastness of our consciousness and joyously refine and offer the creative gems that are our special gifts in this lifetime.

SUBTLE COMMUNICATION

To explore the crystalline perfection of your own mind is to see how your thought touches others and the Earth. The following experiment in subtle communication will make very clear the need for care in one's thought and the power inherent in the human mind to hold the vision of peace. As we recognize within our own nature the balance of complements, we also recognize the resonance that can pass from our hearts and bring benefit to all. This is one of the highest aspirations of the Indian people of this land: to have such an overflowing heart of compassion that one is a mother-father of all things, the energy of renewal flowing from one's heart. Such a mind is ever holding itself in a discipline of clear reality, looking always to see the course of right action, the action that will manifest the greater good for all our relations. With discriminating wisdom one observes the waves created by distraction, without being carried away. Focus on: "I am a being of light, I shall recognize the light in all, I shall realize full enlightenment." Thus you set the resonance within yourself for that to be. That is the power of clear vision, that is the power of affirmation, clear speech.

Subtle communication begins in the heart, in your affirmation of resonance with the clear light essence within yourself and all beings. In that light we are ever in communion. Visualize the three fires burning in the sacrum—will, compassion, active mind—and see the two spirals of light dancing in your spine, sun and moon, mother and father. At the heart center visualize the two triangles, apex to apex, and sense above the head the seven stars, seven gateways of subtle knowing, whence cascades purifying rainbow light, vivifying your body and mind. Sitting in the light, allow a vision of peace to arise in the mind's eye of your heart. See yourself and relatives and friends peaceful, your co-workers and community, your neighborhood and extended family, your nation and planet. How would it look, how would it feel, how would it be, this world peaceful, all beings at peace, all needs fulfilled in harmony, all resources of the Earth appreciated and returned through the gifts of the people? See clear communication resonating from person to person, nation to nation. In your heart feel generosity and see Mother Earth giving abundantly that all may eat. Feel yourself as clear, flowing water, that the waters may be renewed. Contemplate this beauteous vision; let it infuse and permeate your mind.

Now from the center of your heart, from the heart of this peaceful vision, send a beam of light to the very heart of the Earth, and communicate upon that beam of light your radiant vision of a peaceful people, a peaceful planet. Communicate to Mother Earth her children's dream of love and harmony, that it may manifest for all beings in all worlds. Three times send the message of peace out along the heart's ray of light to the crystal heart of Earth; then pause. Await the returning pulse. Feel the energy, acknowledge communion. Recognize, acknowledge the relationship of thought. Rest awhile in happy communion, dreaming with Earth a dream of peace. In closing, draw light beam back into heart, draw all energies into the light spirals in your spine. Give thanks. It is good.

Our hearts and the heart of the Earth are one. We are singing together a song of peace. This experience of subtle communication is very significant, for now you will always know, always recognize yourself and the Earth as one. Once you have tasted that nectar it is very easy to recall its taste upon your tongue, very easy to see the clarity of that light. As you meditate upon this experience it will continue to resonate, and your friends and co-workers will increasingly feel the vibration of peace stirring their hearts, kindling recognition that we can act responsibly as a group and nation, as a planetary family of people.

Through this experiment you experience the creative power of the mind and see more clearly your responsibilities as a human being. Your thought is an instrument, a lens to be carefully focused, a great crystal to be properly faceted so that the light of reality may flow through. What kinds of thoughts are you contributing to the planetary mind? Do you see life as a complementary process or as struggle and confrontation? In yourself are you peaceful? To still conflict within ourselves, to make peace within our own minds and hearts, what effect will that have on the planetary mind? May that be the necessary impetus for the nations to put away the implements of war? Making peace, the balancing of the elements, the mother-father within, is a process that is ever occurring within us. The potential inherent in our minds to bring forth the reality of a planetary peace, an enlightened state for all sentient beings, is but a thought, a practice. Just through acknowledging our inner vision and remembering our subtle communication, our thought relationship with the Earth, we recognize that we each create the thread of life and that together we are weaving the tapestry of our reality. We can hold the form of planetary peace as a reality in our hearts. It is a practice, the practice of giving and receiving and diligently following the Beauty Path to full enlightenment. And for some, the caretakers, the Peacekeepers, it is to keep walking the path around the Medicine Circle until all people come again to realize peace, their true nature.

Truth, things as they are, can be perceived by the mind when it is free of obscurations and patterns. In this time of transformation we have the opportunity to rewrite the very patterns of our existence, to reweave the fibers of life. In our hearts we can replace the conflict mode with the complementary awareness that is our inherent gift of compassion. How to put aside the anger or the fear that separates us from the light? By acknowledging it as an energy and knowing that it is not "I." Anger, fear—they are thoughts. What is "I" is a stream constantly in process, ever attuned with the clear light of reality. Let this vehicle be refined; let this opportunity of wearing a body imbued with sacred mind be a moment in which you realize clear sight.

To see your purpose in life, to understand your creative gifts, and to see the means of actualizing them call for discipline. We can make ourselves new and turn aside the idea of pain and misery. It is simply an aspect of life that we are born, and that can be a painful process. As you grow you find that your body has limitations, especially if the mind and body go in opposite directions. Yet the knowing light, the perfection within, will sing out at some point to say, "I am that being that I am," to acknowledge that there is a special purpose and the capacity to fulfill it. Then one sees that discipline is necessary, that choice is an option—in every moment. We can choose to personify our existence in life as suffering, or we can see the joyous opportunity to have life and body, the joyous opportunity to realize enlightenment.

As we awaken our inner eye, as the light goes forth from within our hearts, a great light will shine around this planet, and it will be perceived in this and all worlds. This is the weaving of the dream of beauty. We can put aside the idea of scarcity; we can recognize that this is an abundant universe. We all have gifts to give, and we all have a basket with which to receive. To pass from the sea of illusion to the shore of our knowing, that is the choice of compassion. We can come to the other shore through loving ourselves, through affirming the creative measure, through affirming our gifts. "I can. I will. I shall. I am that I am." Thus we affirm the power of good in our lives. The words we use in speaking of ourselves and one another can be a building form or a form that breaks energy, that breaks the heart. It is time for us to renew the sacred heart.

TRANSFORMATION: TAMING THE EMOTIONS

In this time, as we complete the last cycle, this ninth stage of purification, there is opportunity to lay the foundation of the Most Great Peace. Now we all have the opportunity to transform obscurations; we all have the opportunity to realize enlightenment. Even in this darkness of the last of nine hells we may break the shackles of illusion. Both women and men have the opportunity to master the ignorance in themselves, to tame the dragon. You can meet the limiting ideas you have created and with the clear light of mind you can choose to create ideas that are beauteous and loving of yourself and others. You can put aside the attachment to suffering that comes from "I am not good enough" or "Poor, pitiful me." The idea of ignorance is transformed by affirmation. "I honor the sacred law of life. I honor the beauty in myself, I honor the sacred duty. I honor the mother-father within." Simple words, powerful words.

Be courageous in giving and receiving love. Love is a stream and we are all part of it. We can be fished from the sea of ignorance in an instant; the line is right above our heads and can always be grasped with our hands. It is for us to lift from our attachment to ignorance, pain, and desire to recognition of the moment. It is not to deny what is in the process of correction. It is to acknowledge the good and to be in the moment, to see each moment for its wholeness and to appreciate it as a unique gift. That is a discipline in itself: to be still, to be loving, to know "I am in this moment creating cause for all moments."

We create powerful energy for transformation by acknowledging the unfoldment of things, developing mindfulness of how we speak and creating patterns of right speech, planting affirmation seeds. This is the most challenging work for the person who is committed to enlightenment: to develop right speech, a method of speech and communication that accentuates the positive. It is speech, vibration, that is determining our reality. In this time it is for us to master vibration, that we may make the right sound, the right harmonic to go through into the new world unfolding. And we must develop new pathways in the brain, joy markers, pathways to harmonious resolution. Think, "In what other ways can I look at myself and my world?" Here is where we say one must be courageous. In the Native American way sometimes the medicine people do outrageous things. They might have you get all comfortable, then walk up and kick you hard between the shoulder blades. Some people need to be shocked out of their ruts. Whatever it takes to wake you up, that is the medicine.

The most pure medicine is unity with mind itself. To remove obscurations of the mind's primordial clarity and light we call upon the sacred fire, the sacred energy within the spine.

Ever burning in the spine are the three building fires. There is the blue fire of will, will to be, clear intention to act. In its intention, in its action, there is also reaction, so that one fire becomes two. Then there is the compassion fire, the fire of compassionate wisdom that builds, that understands, that gives sustenance and nurturing to one's purpose, to one's life. And then there is the fire of active intelligence. This is the fire that our time especially calls for humans to shine more finely, to brush from the sacred hearth the ashes that obscure the mind, that clear mind and right action may manifest, action in harmony with yourself, your purpose, and the true purpose of all the people about you, and in harmony with the very land.

When the Elder Fires Above are not carefully tended, obscurations arise. The three fires must break through five gates, five doorways within your body—at solar plexus, heart, throat, medulla, and crown—where energy may become blocked. At the navel you are receiving five subtle airs from Earth herself—five rivers building and sustaining five organ systems in your body. There is the air of the wind that makes your mind and your lungs strong and also has the sound of bells. There is the wood element that feeds your liver, and the fire element of the heart and the small intestines for building. And there is the fire-that-breaks-down, of the stomach and the spleen, and the bones of the Earth, your kidneys and the very bones of your nature. There are also channels of fire that are moving through your spine: in the left side of the spine, moon energy; in the right side, solar energy; in the central column, the central channel. These energies flow up and down, changing direction according to your biorhythm. They never go in the same direction at once unless you are leaving your body for good; when you are ready to go, then they all go in the same direction at the same time.

What is the purpose of the fire? Why does it move up the spine? Its purpose is the animation of a dream. The fire's purpose is your opportunity, your thought, your desire, your feeling to be, to manifest in a certain body. You shape a body that is most appropriate to the thinking you have done, the feeling, the wanting; you get the kind of body that will take you through your feeling and your dream.

The nervous system is the gateway to heaven. The spinal column is the ladder Jacob climbs. The spinal column enables us to be rooted in Earth, alive. By perceiving the breath, which is also mind, we are able to be aware of the sacred pulse of the fire within the body. In Tsalagi tradition you can gain enlightenment in this lifetime, but you must be willing to work very hard. That is the challenge: to put aside your fear and your doubt and truly be mindful all the time, even when you are sleeping: mindful of your breath, mindful of the sacred power within you.

Solar Plexus

The biorhythm in each person's body is related to the spiral of life, related to one's thinking. The obscurations of one's thoughts show in certain places, at those gateways we have mentioned, one of them being the solar plexus. When one is attached to fear, grasping, always angry, feeling envy—"Oh, it's not mine, I want,"—then there is closing in the solar plexus. Bringing the energy of clear mind to this place of obscuration can release the blockage. That gate can be opened by generosity and willingness to give. Then the energy can rise yet higher up the spine.

Many people say, "Oh, in my meditation practice I get distracted, or this or that happens." It is because the channels are unclear; certain gates are holding things that need to be released. The thought that comes to your mind is telling you exactly what it is you need to let go of. And the place where you may feel tenderness or anxiety or pain in your body, it is also saying, "Work to release that pattern of thinking, that pattern of tension." In Native American understanding, everything you think is just as real as the act of spitting water on the floor. Because you thought it, it has already set something into motion. So we are accountable even for our thinking. That is a significant challenge for our time, because the world has begun to think madly, building munitions and things that really have no benefit for the people. We must think of life; we must be willing to live.

Anger is a real energy field present around this planet in this time. For many people energy is blocked in the solar plexus, so there is a dominant thought form on Earth today of grasping, not being able to give, always reacting from a place of anger. Whether you become encapsulated by this energy or understand it as something unfolding, in a process of change, is a matter of choice. A few people activating seed thoughts of complementary resolution and diligently manifesting peace in their own actions will open the gateway for all to know peace of mind.

When I see so many elderly people suffering because of government cutbacks in programs, because of less emphasis on life and more emphasis on war and defense, something rises in my heart that says, "Speak out and call people to attention. Speak out and say, 'This cannot be, that the elderly suffer hunger so that more airplane bombers can be made.'" It is a deep frustration for people in these times to perceive injustice and oppression and suffering and to feel unable to make it right again. Remember that your mind does have an effect upon the outcome of this planet's development; this knowledge can empower you to move from anger and indignation to right action. When you feel powerless to express that which you know, anger becomes accumulated in your body. The anger of a child that has built up over many years may be the words of wisdom that young one sought to express, blocked because appropriate attitudes or structures were not there when needed. Such mistakes of education and acculturation have engendered anger and alienation in many people, educated in a mold that did not acknowledge their inner wisdom.

By abdicating responsibility for our creative voice, our inner knowing, we all have manifested the realities that are so dangerous to the planet today. Accepting the rationale of "them" and "us," we have bought the idea of a "defense" so massive that it threatens all life on Earth. Yet my elders speak as if we can prevent the bombs from going off, that if need be the planes could be pulled from the sky by the hearts of a few good people. In working with people over the years I see that it is so. When seeing discord and illness, the potential for destruction, nuclear overkill, the wise person does not react with fear or anger, feeding the negative attitudes, but consciously responds with the energy of peace.

It is most important that the individual not get caught in the glamour of feeling at fault for the discord and imbalance in the world. That is like the beaten child thinking she or he deserved the beating and then acting out "I'm no good" throughout an entire lifetime—when truly the child's only error is being born in an age of darkness. We have all planted causes to be here in this time; it is wise to learn from the error of these ways and to turn it aside.

It is a subtle use of words and a deeper awareness of one's own power of voice that bring transformation of anger. It is important to recognize the indignation one may have experienced as a child at the hands of adults ignorant of the flower's sensitive nature. It is important to acknowledge, "Yes, this has occurred, and it is now something to pass." There is a way to see anger without being carried away in its wave. It is ignorant to deny your experience, and it is far more ignorant to become lost in it. The discriminating practitioner opens the eye of wisdom to see the anger as a thought form, a form created out of the mind, not the true nature of the person. One can become attached to anger and think, "Oh, this is my definition, this is who I am." One can become polarized in the realm of anger (or even in the mind of the hermit or the caretaker), thinking this is "how it is." To free yourself from the pattern of resonating to anger is to see anger as an energy. Then you can look at the energy, acknowledge it and know it as part of a process, and forgive those who have caused it and forgive yourself for having received it. Anger can be perceived as an energy field in the aura; you can visualize carrying that emotion to the sacred fire within and transmuting it.

When you feel something, acknowledge it as a feeling. Eventually you will come to be empty of that feeling and recognize the unmanifest possibilities, the potential of your nature. Acknowledge that you have a right to perceive reality, that you have a right to feel, and that you do.

Anger can be a place of great entrapment if you do not approach carefully. You can see anger as a wall to surmount, yet it has a place in the universal scheme of things. It is not too far from the "hungry spirit," wanting to express, wanting to understand, wanting to live in the light, yet still wrapped up in the indignation of not expressing right relations.

If you are seeking to be free from attachment to anger, it would be wise to see the pattern of anger in your life. What were the situations that led to your acknowledging anger or accumulating it? What is the means of transformation? Is it to forgive? Is it to write to yourself or others in gentle words, "These things I have wanted to say and have not been able to?" Or can you still the anger simply by visualizing its resolution in your mind? It is a choice. It has much to do with your nature in this lifetime, for each of us comes here with a particular purpose and need for understanding and giving. For someone whose path is the hermit's path, it may be to still the anger, to be empty of it. For another whose way is the warrior's path it may be to see that anger fully and apply it in a way to energetically transform. These are choices one makes depending on one's purpose.

Perhaps you find yourself repeatedly in a pattern of conflict with people, or conflict with authorities. Here is an opportunity to transform this fundamental pattern from conflict to complementary resolution. Look at your pattern and then look to the "keys" in the other people involved; see how your modality may be to their mind an infliction of something upon their rhythm. It is important to respect one another's rhythm and purpose and look for a means of complementary action rather then an antagonistic or adversarial reaction. Instead of "either/or," look for "both/and." Find where the consensual agreements among you are and make a roadway in your own heart for that energy to travel. It can be an opportunity for learning about human relations and about the power of ideation. Will you hold a form of conflict around authority all your life? If there is conflict in your own mind, what *is* the real authority? Empower yourself. Recognize the

209

clear light of reality and your apperception of it. Perhaps the small mind is saying, "This is how it is," and the whole self is saying, "This is how it is," or perhaps it is the two small minds of the individuals; that may be the point of confusion. Yet everything is an aspect of mind, so better to meet with no goal other than communication.

If authority appears to be the issue in your life, then the underlying issue is of surrender to the great heart of compassion, manifesting the many hands of love. The mind is generating confusion and all situations are opportunities to explore it, so better to see situations as experiments and not be attached to the form—because if the opportunity for clarification is not met in the moment, it will come again and again. This is a facet of consciousness that we too often forget. Whatever we set in motion by our thinking, whatever we think about ourselves and the world around us, is going to return to us.

When we feel there is conflict around us, there is; it is part of the planetary mind at the moment. It is also changing. More and more people are speaking out about nonconflicting realities, complementary realities. What is disarmament but the taking down of fortifications that separate us from our beauty and from one another? Thus when we hear the planetary mind speaking of disarmament, it means that individual hearts and minds have been saying, "Let me make peace, let me bring together in my own nature the mother and father." That is the voice that is resonating out on a planetary level, saying, "Disarmament now." It begins with each of us.

Sometimes non-Native people attending Indian ceremonies will see something that confuses them. A medicine man makes a dead eagle's wings flap and heals people of their illusions. How? Because his *mind* is free; knowing this is a dream, acting it out for the benefit of the players and the watchers. When one has become aware of the clear light and has clarified the inner channels, moving beyond the gates of solar plexus, heart, throat, medulla, and crown, then no matter what that person is doing, it is an action that will enlighten, it is an enlightened action. That is why Native people have such respect for their medicine people; they really see and understand what the medicine people are doing. They know that the holy person is a reminder that they, too, can clarify the sacred breath within themselves. Even if the spine is crooked, one can make ways to straighten it so the fire can move correctly. Because spine being crooked is a matter of your thinking, "Oh, well, I don't know, maybe." You can't live in the cold weather with "Oh, well, I don't know, maybe"—you must be awake and certain. If you don't put your gloves on when it's twenty below, you may lose your fingers.

It is just as critical about your thinking. If you don't take responsibility for feeling angry or sad and calling yourself to feeling glad, then you are depleting your life force. When the solar plexus accumulates more of that energy of pain and anger, so much less of the life force moves through your body. Take the time to look deep within.

Let us practice a simple exercise of breathing and movement to free you from these patterns of attachment that block the solar plexus. Nothing to lose, nothing to gain. Only allow the flue to be open so the three fires can rise and move through your spine. It is not a thing you can only think about; thinking sets the vibration but it is not quite enough; you have to *do* it.*

Sit strong upon the floor, right foot over left thigh, hands on knees. Begin to rotate, moving to the left in a gentle circle beginning from the pelvis. Contract and release with the stomach. Breathe deeply. Inhale and exhale through the nostrils. Do not push the energy down; just feel your spine suspended on a string, swinging around as if in a spiral. Feel the stars above your head, yourself suspended by those stars of clear insight. Then reverse direction, rotating in a gentle

*There must be at least four hours between eating and doing this exercise, for it could be very dangerous and injurious to your physical body to do it while the stomach is digesting food.

circle to the right. Then you may rotate at least thirty-six times in each direction. Finally, sit quietly, breathing deeply and restfully.

This exercise is to remove obscurations of the solar plexus, making way for clarification of the heart. Let the thought forms of fear and anger pass. Let the gate of the solar plexus open so that the three sacred fires can rise into your heart.

Heart

The heart is the mind, in Native American thought; it is where the intellect lies. Around the heart are two electrical fields, one going clockwise, the other counterclockwise, ever moving together. These two fields of energy are your purpose, the seed of your life, your dream manifesting in the physical form and held together through the energy of the liver. The heart is the balancing point of heaven and Earth, a retort where the sacred wisdom fire burns. The memory of what you have been and will be resides in the heart as well as being recorded in the medulla. The heart is ever pulsing, ever responding. When the human being feels, "Oh, I don't love, I can't love," the heart becomes occluded on a physical level; there are actual deposits that occur. Reciprocity is balance in the flow of giving and receiving.

To remove obscurations from your heart, call upon the clear light and its insight. Sense the seven stars above your head, their rainbow light cascading down around you. The light fills you and surrounds you, irradiating all your being, all your actions. Feel the light from the stars; breathe it into your heart, through your heart. Send it out as waves of compassion, waves of generous care for all relations. Feel that cycle of energy, giving and receiving.

You must practice very diligently. In the Native teaching tradition the teacher very often gives people assignments to help remove obscurations of thought. Sometimes a person will have to do something over and over again and always be told, "Incomplete. Try again." That is saying, "Commit yourself fully; bring all your energy to it." If only one channel of energy or just a part of your concentration is dedicated to the purpose and the action, it is incomplete. When you attend medicine ceremonies you may hear the medicine people say, "Do this, do it again, do it again, do it again." That is because the person did it the first time without commitment or with resentment, holding back, and must keep doing it until he or she can let go of that resentment, be fully present in the action. So many people give up. But it is your life and you cannot give up. You may think you can, but even if you commit suicide you will have to continue working it all out on the other side of that divide. So better to do it now, better to clarify your channels now, in the physical body. You must be very mindful. The moment you feel some thought of doubt or anger creeping into your mind focus on the opposite energy. You have a choice, you can be certain. If you are uncertain, inhale and exhale and say, "I am breathing." Be aware of that. Acknowledging what you are certain of builds up a store of certainty—then, when the mice of doubt come looking for those grains of wisdom, there will be enough for them to become enlightened, too!

One of the difficulties that obscures the heart is comparison. "This person is doing that. Does it mean I can do that, should do that? Do I have more worth, do I have less worth?" These are questions that make the heart very tired. They actually deplete the lunar energy so that you receive less inspiration, and the solar energy becomes tighter and tighter. Then you wonder why you have no energy. The moment you find your mind making comparisons between yourself and another, stop and evaluate the flow of energy in your body—then you will see, "Oh, this is not good for me."

It is good to recognize how we are in our relationships together, and to do that without falling into comparison mind. Look to see how your thinking establishes certain patterns, how your attitudes or perhaps your connections to the past may be resounding in the moment, and be willing to cut the threads of those attachments. Perhaps the only way you knew love or attention was to annoy other people so they would yell at you. Or perhaps that was a pattern in the past because others did not know how else to relate. It is not necessary now. Now you can show your pure gifts without having to wait for people to correct you. It is your life and it is your choice how you are creating it. The fire burns within you to transform patterns of thinking and relationship. It is just for you to fan the fire.

Grief is another energy that can obscure the heart if not brought to completion. And an excess of grief in the people can sadden the Earth. The Earth depends upon us to return energy, keep things flowing in the cycle. If we hold grief to ourselves we are breaking the flow to the Earth; you feel too full and Earth feels empty. You can return that grief to the Earth. Hug a tree and pour out your sadness. Tell the tree, "These things have happened and I have felt sad. I know life goes on and I cast the sadness aside." It is good to recognize your feelings, to know, "Yes, I am feeling grief." Grief serves a function in our society, a healing function. So that the forgiveness can be made we must acknowledge the hurt—and then let it go into the river of forgiveness. Then we find ourselves replenished with joy and thankfulness for the opportunity of having opened the heart. So grief may be a teacher to you. In having lost something, you will also have something shown to you.

What is happening in one person's heart has significance for the whole world. To hold back the feeling of forgiveness closes meridians in the body, affecting your health and the health of your community and your home, the Earth. So to be able to forgive is very important. It is one of the first gifts we must accept from the spiritual path, the cup with its sweet waters of forgiveness. Making friends again, it is so dear.

Throat

Three fires move through the spine. Heart becomes clear, putting aside all its fear, letting go of others' thoughts. Fires rise to throat center, another gateway. For many people it is something new to acknowledge the power of the voice, to know that one can affirm and say, "It will be so." Thus chanting and singing are very important, and voicing affirmations aloud, because through the throat center what you think is manifested. From the light, the sound, came forth everything we know. The sound of your word, the sound of your thinking, goes out into the world and comes back to you as your reality.

The power of affirmation is a way to clarify the obscurations of the voice, as is the commitment to speak as true as you can; when you say you'll do it, you do it the best you can. Thus you gain more and more voice power and more and more life force. Voice sings out, "I am that I am. I make a dream of beauty, beauty before, beauty behind, beauty all around." That becomes more and more the reality and the doubt that stands in the way of speaking true becomes less and less. The means to say what is, in a way that is beautiful and beneficial, becomes ever greater.

To find your own voice is not to put other voices down. To find your own voice is to acknowledge the beauty and call it forth. Let your voice be clear, that you may germinate a vision of peace and harmony, that the spirit of wisdom may manifest in all your actions, and that it may go around the circle and come again for all your relatives to perceive enlightened mind, the clarity of the great light in its vastness. Even a glimpse of it is enough to send people on the right course.

Medulla

Fires in the spine now rise up through the medulla, at base of skull, where the obscurations of the past, the early part of this lifetime and other lifetimes, may hold you back. Many people do not make it past the heart; in this time if the mind can come to the throat, that is wonderful for the people— with a few seeds of enlightened people it will go all through the Earth. So whatever you can do, do it now. And to clarify medulla is a powerful step on the Beauty Path.

Many people are responding from other lifetimes in relationships in the present, still stuck in the anger or fear of another life experience. How to clarify those old patterns? Focus on the violet infinity symbol in the medulla center. See the light, know that whatever has occurred has occurred, and so it is. What is in the now is clear light; no need to feed those thoughts of doubt or retribution. See everything in the moment. In the process of clarifying the medulla many things will come to your mind, and that is good. Simply notice them without attachment; no need to get excited about them. Just be certain that you are not repeating those patterns in this time.

Crown

Something most wondrous happens in that clarity of non-attachment to the pain of the past. There is a great buzzing and all kinds of energy felt at the top of the head, the crown. In the Tsalagi practice a depression actually occurs at the crown, emitting fluid; there are also other places where fluid comes out of your head. That is how the teacher knows you have accomplished a certain level of insight or realization. Someone can tell the teacher, "Oh yes, I understand, I got it." The teacher will say, "Come here, let me feel your head. Still hard. Soften it. Let the light come in."

So in conclusion I say to you, be mindful of your breath. Know that it is stirring those three sacred fires ever burning in your spine. Know that you can attain enlightenment in this body in this lifetime, by clarifying those channels through your body, by being attentive to your thought, word, and deed, by acting with generosity and compassion and patience—and by working very hard.

There are many glamours in this form-filled world. There is the glamour of position, status; the glamour of abundance or not-abundance, the glamour of health or not-health—many ways in which one can become caught at a critical point in the spiral. Everything is a field of consciousness in motion. How we relate to this field of consciousness, of mind, is a matter of discipline. The development of discriminating wisdom is a process that can only occur within the individual. We can share techniques and practice, but the process is your own will and your own diligence.

What cause shall you create? Shall you see the world in terms of complementary forces, balancing? Mother-father, yin-yang, sun-moon, these are elements of creation, and from these elements forms manifest. The three sacred fires—will, love (which is wisdom), and active intelligence—are the form-builders through which the Beauty Path unfolds within us.

The power of the voice, that is the power of the will. It is the power of mind attuned to sacred harmony, sacred law. Everything resonates to the sacred law. The quartz crystal is hexagonal, occasionally with an extra facet; that is the law of the crystal. A human being has two arms, two legs, a head, six senses; that is a law, also. And it is inherent in the law that unmanifest potential shall come into form in alignment with the sacred principles of will, love, active intelligence.

Form-building, seeking order through harmony, through harmonic interaction, is a relationship. Our thought creates our environment and our relationship with that which we have brought to form. Knowing comes through repeated ex-

217

perience of what is happening, what is correct. We inhale, we exhale. We know that. Eyes perceive light, ears perceive sound. Through the experience we can say we know. The feeling of the heart, to know through devotion, to be touched by the intuitive reflection of ideal form, that is a way of knowing. To realize through continued practice, through regular chanting and prayer, that is another way of knowing. Through chanting alone we can renew the wave of harmony because the sound carries energy of transformation.

TRANSFORMING ANGER

I would like to share with you a simple exercise for looking into the mind, seeing where there may be seeds of anger and transmuting those seeds, offering them to the fire. It is a wise person who is attuned to the fullness of life, realizing that anger is but an aspect of life. No blame, no shame; simply an emotion. Not one's true nature.

Feel the light spiraling through you. Be aware of the third eye in the center of your forehead, the heart, the crown center, the light. Sense yourself as light. As you contemplate the light you move into yourself, and in that movement you may meet one of those basic energies that can hold a person from full enlightenment. Let us meet those limiting thoughts and transmute them to forgiveness with the clear insight of reality, with the eye of discrimination. See the limiting thoughts of mind, see the thought forms of anger in your life. Shine your wisdom light through them, tracing the stream of your experience until you see the pure seed of your creative potential that may be hidden in the confusion. In your mind's eye, recall the moment when that creative energy may have become blocked or obscured. Go back there and remove the blocks, let the wisdom stream flow, freeing your creative potential from the world of anger. Affirm, "I am that I am. I speak the

218

truth of my experience. I realize my vision of beauty." Bring upon the light of clear consciousness the energy to transform what may have been a cause for indignation in the past, of trepidation in the present, of fear of stepping into the future. Let us clear from our light bodies the thought, the need, that creates anger and cries for forgiveness. Chant the Heart Chant [see page 197], sending the thought of forgiveness circling forth from your heart, from your whole being. See all your relatives and friends surrounded in that light.

Many Native prayers end with "All My Relations," that is to say, "May the good, the beauty, be realized by all my relatives, by everything that lives, walks, flies, swims, or creeps." Ah-ho, it is so.

May you continue to seek and cultivate within yourself the wisdom of equanimity. Recognize that from emptiness comes form, and let yourself be attuned to the clear light of its unfolding. The opportunity of human life leads to the fullness of enlightenment. Let us recognize ourselves, recognize our own energy, how we think and how we feel, and cultivate within ourselves those thoughts that are most productive to our continued evolution. Let us acknowledge our gifts of love. Let us ever cultivate the light of clear mind.

HE! HAYUYÁ HANIWÁ. IN TRUTH YOU WERE CONCEIVED.

Earth Mandala: The Teaching of the Crescent Moon

Upon the altar of the heart is a crescent moon, symbol of the life path that all beings walk. It is part of the circle. The crescent with its path drawn atop represents our sojourn in the form realms, and the other half of the circle represents the formless realm.

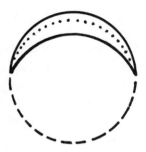

When I was young my father made this form out of earth and talked to me about the gift of life. This is the teaching of the Earth Mandala, of the crescent moon.

Showing me the simple earthen form, my father said, "This is the path that all beings walk. Whatever our nationality, wherever we have come from, we all are born of a woman, we all walk along the road of life, and we all exit through the gateway."

The gateway takes us again into the emptiness, into the Mystery whence we have come. Each being enters the realm of form from the emptiness, through the gateway of birth, to which one is drawn by desire, intention to be. Birth is the tip of the crescent, placing one upon the path of life, and the path travels around the crescent, completing the circle.

We choose a family wherein our gifts may flourish, through which we can complete a cycle of learning. Even when we are within our mothers we begin to hear and feel our family around us. In the time within the womb the young person is sensing the qualities of its parents' minds and comes to love one parent greatly and the other less so. Boys love their mothers very, very much, and daughters' cohesiveness is in mental relationship to the father. So there begins the dance of the sun and the moon. As the child moves within the mother's body it is experiencing her thoughts and responding to the thoughts directed by other people toward the mother. For this reason it is very important that mothers-to-be have a loving support system and an environment as free from anger as possible.

The time of the woman's carrying a child is a most precious time. To be a parent is a precious gift. Always we can hear the sound of the children in the community. The babies, they keep us going, and each of us has begun in that same way. We come here wearing nothing, possessing nothing. We only have within our hearts the secrets of creation and a gift to offer our family, our friends, our nation, and the planet.

The child's first smile is a most wondrous moment, for the child is reaching out and recognizing relatives. This is a time of celebration and gift-giving by the family. Gifts are given to those elders and wise people with whom one hopes one's child can council. Three years of age is another time of celebration, and after that the cycle is from seventh year to age fourteen, twenty-one, twenty-eight, and a special celebration when one becomes a grandparent and reaches age fifty-one.

In the first three years of life we learn to understand communication and the power of a true voice. We also learn how to live in harmony with our relations. In the early years of a child's life certain characteristics begin to become recognizable. Those characteristics are signs of that child's special gift, and they will grow and flourish into adulthood.

The child is a precious gift and a precious moment; most learn to crawl before we learn to walk.

In these early years we make good our relationship with our parents, our family, and it is the fortunate child who has an extended family with which to relate.

Then we come a little further, and by age six we are very clear in our language and our ability to speak the truth and to understand what is good, and we have an idea of what some of the gifts are that we may offer to our circle of friends.

At the age of seven we come to be fully present in the body; our potential to be is now grounded through the roots of the Earth. It takes seven years for the person to move fully into his or her body.

We walk along the road, and in the time from age seven to twelve we are learning how to relate to an extended group of people. We also have learned some particulars about maintaining a healthy life. We learn that what we do returns to us.

221

We also learn to play with one another, to work together, and this is setting the foundation for the rest of our lives.

At twelve to fourteen we begin to feel the stirring within us of the energy of the South, the gift of generation. The grand-mothers of the South carry the seeds of procreation, just as each one of us does. Those seeds of life begin to blossom that we, too, may become parents of our own reality. This is a most precious time. When the young girl comes of age, that is a time of honoring; when the young man has seen clearly his purpose, that is a time of honoring.

Now we walk a little further, making our bodies and our minds stronger that we may benefit the people and the land. And we come to the age of twenty-one, where we have an understanding of our gifts and a desire to share. At twenty-one there arises from the East the wind of inspiration, that we may be inspired to bring forth our gifts. Also at twenty-one we are certain: "This I know, this I have to offer, and this I need to do, that I may make that gift more real."

We keep walking along this sacred wheel of life, and we reach the place where we see our other half, "the one who sits beside." That is the name for the husband or the wife. We begin to find our friend and our mate. Each of us has within us both mother and father energy, and also we seek to hold hands again with that starmate, that person who began the dream with us.

We procreate and bring forth children, and we seek to create an environment of beauty and peace. Every family wants to have a home; everyone wants to live in good rela-tionship. The early years of the family's growth are to make the family strong, and it is a most sacred time. In this time the parents have a responsibility to speak to one another with love and never to go to sleep with anger in their hearts, lest the preciousness of their children's lives be tainted with anger. So being a parent is an opportunity to serve. It is also a re-sponsibility and a duty to bring forth beauteous beings for the benefit of the land and the nation.

At fifty-one we become an adult. It takes that much time to begin to understand the mysteries within us. At fifty-one, understanding cause and effect, our voice arises clearly. At fifty-one we may look to the Western gate and decide what negative thoughts and attitudes can be cast out so that we may resonate a song of peace and harmony for all people, so that they live without fear. At fifty-one we decide, "Shall I continue for the benefit of the family, the clan, the nation, and the planet?" At fifty-one we commit ourselves to bringing forth beauty for all people, and one may begin to become a grandparent at that time. At fifty-one, in the Tsalagi tradition, we become an adult.

The potential for human life is a total of 127 years. That is the gift that is within our genes. When we walk in harmony upon this Beauty Path, when we keep clear our relationships with one another, the life force is not dissipated and one may walk along to 127 years.

This medicine path all people walk. Even the creatures that fly, crawl, and swim have a medicine path that they walk upon the sacred Earth. The Earth is our home, our foundation.

As we walk along the path of life we begin to recognize certain qualities from the directions that help us refine and clarify our consciousness. From the North we begin to see the cause and effect of our action. In the North we see the purity of clear mind; the Buffalo Maiden and her wisdom, her offering of good relations, comes to all of us. The North clearly mirrors the wisdom of things as they are. As we move around the Medicine Wheel, in the East the sun arises, even from the empty space of dark night the sun arises, illumining the beauty and the opportunity of life. In the South sprout the seeds of regeneration. In the South we understand what it is to plant seeds of good cause, to make clear and powerful relationships. And in the West we learn from the Dancing Bear how we may cast our doubt and fear, that we may truly be a friend for all our relatives.

So this is a simple teaching. And this was the way that my

father showed me about the gift of life; this was the way that his father and mother showed him about the gift of life.

When we were young and asked, "Why can so-and-so do this and I can't?" or "Why is it this way?," the teaching of the crescent moon would be referred to, and occasionally the crescent would be drawn on the cabin floor or outside for us to contemplate, to truly understand the beauty of the different stages of life. The most beautiful lesson that our elders taught us was not to rush, to know that everything flowers in its own time, and that each of us is a unique flower and cannot expect our blossom to come at the same time as another's. There were certain common factors, such as the seven-year-old having muscular strength that was not available at age three, yet one seven-year-old might prove to be very agile and another one cautious. We were taught to respect these variations. Through our extended family flowed the blood of many races and peoples; the children were truly a flower garden of unique and precious blossoms.

Every nation has a different way of describing the walk we take through life. Nevertheless, we all know that we came here naked and without possessions and that we will leave without anything. The greatest wealth that we may experience is to have good fellowship, good friendship. That you can take with you into the afterworld, into the invisible realms. And the greater the joy and the good relationship generated in our lives, the longer we may stay in those empty, quiet spaces. Or perhaps one chooses to come very quickly again and again around the sacred hoop until all families and friends realize themselves in good relationship.

So this teaching of the crescent moon is something very simple, and I pray that it is of benefit to you. The Medicine Wheel's message to each of us is that we all walk around the circle of life. Its application is a reminder of the sacredness of the steps along the way, and what we may hope to understand and gather in the certain stages of our lives. In the Medicine Wheel we see revealed in every action in every stage of our life that we have a relationship with the Earth, that we are walking a path with others. Each human is born and each one dies. This unites us as human beings. So the Medicine Mandala is like a road map; it makes the way a little clearer when we see the certain signposts of life.

May you apply these teachings in your life for the benefit of all people.

My grandparents and great aunts had powerful means of expressing the relationships of mind, spirit and body. The three most common analogies were:

1. *The body is a robe stitched together by desire, thought, and action,* the cloth a gift of the three Elder Fires Above, the triune nature of deity, which creates all form.

2. *The body is a temple wherein the sacred fire of wisdom burns.* The altar is composed of compassionate and generous deeds; the stairs to the temple, stages of learning at various ages of one's development, are sometimes described as follows:

   a. Desire for birth, or intention
   b. Quickening—first movement within mother's womb
   c. Dreaming relationship with family
   d. Birth
   e. First smile
   f. First words and laughter
   g. Crawling
   h. Walking
   i. Sense of being in a circle; basic tendencies shaped (age three)
   j. Friendship (age seven)
   k. Generosity
   l. Skills developing; learning, gathering (age fourteen)
   m. Cultivating; planting seeds, developing family (age twenty-one)
   n. Harvest with others; sharing community gardens (age twenty-eight)

o. Family and community building

p. Sharing life's experiences as elder in council and teacher to the young (age fifty-one and beyond)

The bricks of the temple are composed of elements shaped and formed by the three Elder Fires Above, held steady by the mortar of four cords connecting all realms. The altar was described as two triangles, apex to apex, which represented wisdom, and upon which was superimposed the crescent moon symbolizing the life path that all beings walk.

3. *The body is clay shaped by Creator, infused with breath, the wave carrying mind.*

The weaving of a sash or rug was an opportunity to teach us children about the fibers of thought interweaving and creating something of beauty or something flawed through lack of skill or clear intention. That which was produced by one's hands was considered a mirror of the beauty or confusion of its maker. It was said that "cords" composed of seven threads each held our bodies together, woven upon the tapestry of life, which included the whole universe. Three major cords within the spine connect one with heaven and Earth. From these cords, twenty-one threads radiate through the body as conduits for lymph and blood. Through the navel five cords enter from the Earth, containing thirty-five threads, which sustain five organ systems (liver, heart and small intestines, lungs, stomach and spleen, kidney and bones). Each of these threads is also composed of three-plus-four threads corded around each other. All these threads are in constant rearrangement according to our thoughts and deeds. In Tsalagi worldview life begins in beauty. One's thoughts and deeds may be discordant, thereby putting beauty into disharmony. The tapestry of beauty can be rewoven with remorse and purification and then development of clear mind and clear action.

226

When the analogy of body as temple was being expressed the emphasis was on maintaining clear burning of the Wisdom Fire upon the altar. Discordant thoughts and deeds hinder the Wisdom Fire's burning by constricting the wind pathway or heaping ashes of impure deeds upon the fireplace.

Each brick of the body's temple represents constitutive thought and action. With inappropriate action the mortar of relationships weakens and bricks fall away. So the temple's stability—physical body's stability—is the result of harmonious thought and deeds. It was said that 127 years was the lifespan of one who walked in beauty.

The story of the red clay people was often related to children as an explanation for birth. "The One Who Makes the Breath" blew into the clay figures, infusing them with life and mind. Through this breath all beings are connected; the breath carrying the sacred mind permeates all. This was a reminder to us children to treat the small creatures kindly, as our lives were tenuously linked to our bodies through the One Breath.

To caretake the gift of the human body properly, massage, exercise, dance, and herbal preparations were a daily part of our lives.

The first lesson was to breathe through the body as the leaves move through the trees, filling the belly with breath so that the essence of Mother Earth food entering our navels could be properly "cooked," releasing strong energy for the body and mind. The belly was conceived as a cooking pot, heated by the Earth energy, cooking and releasing energy for life action. Chanting and dance were means of instruction in full breathing.

Just as smoke rises in a spiral and leaves dance in a spiral, spiral motion of the joints (shoulders, fingers, waist, hips, knees, ankles) opens the flue in the spine so the three fires may burn brightly. Breath, water, food, and inner and outer motion maintain the body in harmony.

When the child is born, the grandparents massage the little

one, gently rotating the fingers, the outermost joints; then rotating each large joint of arms, shoulders, toes, ankles, knees, hips; then gentle stroking the spine, legs, chest, stroking toward the heart, so the child's potential may manifest and baby's spirit be fully incarnate.

As the child grows, he or she is carried around with mother or older siblings, always part of the family doings. Children are encouraged to join in, yet crying is discouraged, by holding the mouth and stroking; eventually the child calls for attention by means such as laughter or shaking a plaything. To the Tsalagi and some other Native peoples, noisy or boisterous behavior predisposes one to self-centered actions. Thus children are encouraged to develop subtle means of communication and self-sufficiency. Tsalagi children often speak at an early age through participation in whatever is happening.

Objects are hung from the rafters for the very young (up to two years old) to play with. Bells, bones, and mirrors hung from strings develop eye-to-hand coordination and muscular development. Young ones learn to create dolls and toys from foods in the garden—gourds become rattles, corn husks become dolls, dried apples become the faces of old people. Thus nature and everyday activity are seen as sources of joy.

As the children learn to walk they are invited to dance and play drums and rattles. At this time our grandparents began teaching various exercises for mental, physical, and spiritual development. We were invited to imitate the wind moving through sky, tree, and water. There arose common motions of spiral rotation; our attempt to imitate the wind engendered great flexibility. Imitating the birds, deer, fish, whatever we saw, became a way of learning about our own capacities. As we would tire of this game our elders would come forth and demonstrate a song to match a set of movements. They would sometimes invite us to hold a broomstick and leap through. To do so required steadfastness of mind, fleetness of foot, and the balance of a bird.

Our games became offerings to the Adawees of the directions. We ourselves became the winds and rains sustaining the Earth. We soared on the wings of imagination as clouds bringing sweet waters to Earth. This movement transformed the child's vision to the vision of open sky.

Movement itself is transformative. The body's wisdom is made manifest through action. In Tsalagi practice, each movement begins with breath, in the spine, and spirals from inner to outer motion.

Everything is well, everything is whole, according to the Tsalagi worldview. Healing is a matter of recalling the wholeness and purifying the body so that spirit may fully manifest in this temple. The cornerstone, bottom of the foot, ball of the foot, is very important. Most Americans have been trained to walk on the heels, but then one is really not being fed by Mother Earth. When stepping first on the balls of the foot, the body is supported and there is a lifting from the hips. Many of our playful dances, such as grass dances, as well as our more sacred dances begin on the ball of the foot, moving gracefully with the drums and shakers, toe, heel, toe, heel. The step seems to give one a sense of ease with "hill and valley." One feels swift and quiet dancing toe-heel, toe-heel. Occasionally my aunt Hattie would comment on "So-and-so walking on his heels like he wants to rule the Earth." She thought those who walked hard on their heels were dangerous, angry people. She said the noisier the step, the greater the imbalance; the louder the voice, the weaker the person. So in our dancing and singing we sought to maintain harmony with one another and the Earth, gently placing our feet upon the Earth so that we left no scars on her bosom.

Harmonious flow fed by breath ensures the continued flow of Orineida, sometimes described as Nuwati. Orineida is "subtle mind uniting all things"; Nuwati is the "sacred medicine that permeates all things." Breath is the wind fanning the fires within our bodies so that healthy activities may come forth.

We were taught to give particular attention to accumulating energy through the right nostril and breath through the top of the head. As we danced we were encouraged to note the energy descending through fontanelle and ascending through ball of foot. First releasing through left nostril any accumulated confusion or mucus as compost, then giving thanks to Earth and heaven with each exhalation. Right hand and foot giving, left hand and foot receiving, breathing in, breathing out, breath warming the "good heart," that our deeds may be beneficial for family, clan, nation, and land.

The navel is the base of our operation, because from here we were fed in utero by our mother, and through the navel we are still sustained by the Earth. As we receive the energy of the planet, we are also giving something in return. Five qualities, five airs come in through the navel area. In Native American teaching wood is the foundation. Like the tree firmly rooted in the Earth with its branches flying freely is a well-integrated human being.

It is said in Tsalagi tradition that "all is well." Within the idea of illness is the cure. Each organ system maintains balance by moving in harmony with a fixed tone, a tone of optimal health. This tone may become distorted by impure thought, speech, or action and may be restored with the proper sound formulas and herbs. Many illnesses result from discordant emotions, which may be brought to resolution through chanting, prayer, and certain exercises to restore patterns of thinking and action to harmony.

Illness manifests when people have forgotten their wholeness, when particular patterns of relationship or action have obscured the flow of love in their hearts. The challenge of releasing energy from a state of disease into balance has been approached in many ways. It is better to think of "healing" than "release." Healing calls discord into harmony through transforming the seeds of disharmony, the source. There are many modalities for release of energy, yet the discordant seed-thought may still be left intact. One may go through years of therapy, for example, screaming, crying, going deeper and deeper into one's "story," and still not free oneself of the pattern of incorrect thought. Discordant thought is always seeking resolution. When one focuses on the pain without calling on the quality of will to transmute a painful situation into constructive pattern, then the pattern that brings pain will repeat itself continuously.

Thought is carried upon the breath. There is an immediate change in the breathing pattern when someone experiences some kind of shock or conflict. Attuning to the flow of breath, we are able to remove any obscurations and to transform patterns of confusion. Visualize the breath moving through the body, washing away inner hurts, bringing the energy of light to replace destructive thoughts with constructive affirmations.

The breath feeds flesh and bones so that one may actualize one's potential. Movement is initiated by the breath. Just in the way you start your day you can experience the power of breath and movement to bring harmony and to clarify mind.

On first awakening, still lying in bed, begin to stretch, gently rotating wrists, ankles, then stretching the spine, enabling you to be more present in flesh. Stepping out of bed, continue to stretch. The breath, guided by mind, spirals outward from the spine and the movement becomes large, rotating the neck gently, then shifting weight from one foot to the other, rotating the hips, aware of the small of the back. You are supported by the light, by the breath.

Each morning my grandfather and great-grandfather, and occasionally my grandmother and great-aunts, would begin the day by doing a dance. The dance, they said, kept them young and showed their appreciation for life, in that it was also an offering. They called it the Dance of the Directions.

Before speaking to anyone or taking a meal, these older people would dance. Sometimes they appeared like fluttering clothing moving in the breeze. We were told that they swam in the brook before we children awoke and that even in the winter they would swim in the cold water. As we watched them dance we saw the elements of the exercises and games they had taught us.

One first greets the rising sun with a prayer or song of appreciation that a new day has arisen, and one is thankful for the glistening dew on the grass.

One begins the dance facing the east, hands upraised, greeting the sun coming over the horizon, receiving the rays of the sun, then bringing hands down to body, caressing heart and area between solar plexus and navel. Then the hands are brought together as in prayer; the more supple ones of the elders would bow so low that their heads would touch their knees. Rising, their arms would reach out as if carried on the air itself. One would see right hand giving, left hand receiving, a human being in good relationship with heaven and Earth.

Although the old people were not looking at each other, their movements were in unison, and sometimes so slow or so fast that one was not quite sure how they arrived in position. Even the oldest person would lift his or her feet high and step through space with the grace of a sapling dancing with the wind. They would make the same pattern of steps to each of the four cardinal directions, repeating this pattern four times to each direciton. During special days the dance would continue all day, on a platform.

We children often wondered how these old people sustained themselves. They did not appear to tire, they seemed invigorated by the dance, and they all said the dance kept them young. Even at ages eighty-six and ninety Aunt Hattie and Aunt Leila move with great suppleness and grace. They said that by having the gift of a body we had certain responsibilities to maintain that body so that the spirit of clarity could move through it easily, and this offering of dance in the morning was a means of maintaining the body's health and integrity.

Each of us in our busy days can take a bit of advice from these ancient people. Treat the body kindly. Allow the joints to be supple, rotating shoulders, head, knees, ankles, even wrists and fingers. Imitate the movement of animals. This is the simple medicine of the Tsalagi.

The movement as an offering enables the pathways of life force to remain supple so that one's intention may manifest in a way that is beneficial to oneself and all one's relations. By allowing joints to move in the sacred spiral, one allows right and left hemispheres of the brain to communicate, to exchange information more clearly. As my relatives would say, "The spiral is the angle of life—and if you don't dance and sing, your brain will be only partly awake." So the flexibility of the spine and the large joints of the body also expresses a flexibility of mind.

The movement is exploration, that one may understand the life force moving through oneself and be aware of the ascending and descending currents of energy in the spine, and through the spinning outward of the hands one perceives the sanctity of giving and receiving. As my grandfather said, "I dance to live."

ᏣᎩ ᏣᎩ ᎮᏭᎳᎮ

Tsá gi   Tsá gi   hi   wí   la   hí

Upstream, upstream, you (must) go

ᏣᎩ ᏣᎩ ᎮᏭᎳᎮ

Tsá gi   Tsá gi   hi   wí   la   hí

Upstream, upstream, you (must) go

ᎦᎢ ᎦᎢ ᎮᏭᎳᎮ

Gé i   gé i   hi   wí   la   hí

Downstream, downstream, you (must) go

ᎦᎢ ᎦᎢ ᎮᏭᎳᎮ

Gé i   gé i   hi   wí   la   hí

Downstream, downstream, you (must) go

Há- ma má   há- ma má   há- ma má   há- ma má

Let me carry you on my back

ᎤᏓᎭᎴᏱ ᎮᎷᏄ ᎮᎷᏄ

U dá ha lé yi   hí   lu(n)   nu   hí   lu(n)   nu

On the sunny side, go to sleep, go to sleep

ᎤᏓᎭᎴᏱ ᎮᎷᏄ ᎮᎷᏄ

U dá ha lé yi   hí   lu(n)   nu   hí   lu(n)   nu

On the sunny side, go to sleep, go to sleep

7

DIAMOND LIGHT

IN our hearts we look to see divine presence. The crystal is the symbol of that perfection, which is within us. These teachings on the crystal come through the Pleiades, the Seven Dancers constellation, through the ray of the Tsalagi medicine to the priestesses and priests who maintain this sacred tradition, and from the constellation of the Bear. We Ywahoos are crystal keepers, and the crystal teachings were passed to me by my grandfather and great-grandfather.

These foundation teachings are now being made available that people may understand the power and sacredness of the crystal energy. They are from the general teachings, which are appropriate to all people, and it is hoped that through them the reader will gain a clear perspective of the crystal mind within and a willingness to bring forth that wisdom for all beings. May these teachings help to balance the incorrect use of crystal energy that has become a glamour in this time.

In the traditional system of the Tsalagi only certain people directly handled the crystal, those who had realized stability of mind and demonstrated purity of action. The caretakers of crystals have the responsibility to maintain equanimity because the crystal will amplify whatever thoughts or emotions are in the continuum of the people interacting with them.

In these times much false, confusing, and dangerous information is being disseminated about crystals, and these sacred stones are being misused by persons who have not transformed ignorance and greed to right and generous action. In our tradition students prepare very diligently and over a long period of study, practice, training of mind, and purification of action before working with crystals. It sometimes takes twenty-one years to refine and strengthen the nervous system to optimal balance so that one may handle the potential of quartz crystals. Many people are now teaching crystal workshops and practices whose subtleties they really do not understand. This is dangerous, for crystal energy is as volatile as the atom bomb, and when you work with the crystal whatever is going on in your mind is going to be amplified.

Misuse of crystal energy can be as destructive to the physical and light bodies as the use of drugs. Many of the so-called "enlightened crystal teachings" can potentially kill a person. It is especially dangerous to place crystals upon one's energy centers or to sit within certain configurations of crystals without having established stability of mind and purity of action. Such "crystal games" weaken the etheric web of the body and enliven negative thought forces that may seek to live and act through the body. Crystal energy has the potential to disturb the electron spin and the molecular cohesion in any form. This potential of the crystal is greater than that of the largest nuclear weapons currently in use. Damage that can be wrought to one's body in the present also affects future lives.

Each crystal taken from the Earth maintains contact with the heart of the Earth. In many ways the crystal is like the "Eye of God," reporting to heaven and Earth the thoughts and actions of humanity.

For all these reasons the Ywahoo lineage of the Tsalagi Nation emphasizes the development of mental stability, mind of altruism, and strong community relationships, so that one does not get a large head, thinking he or she has dominion over anything. Rather, one cultivates a mind of good relationship and responsible action.

Many people today read about and have the good fortune to participate in Native American spiritual practices. Unfortunately, people often misconstrue the directness and apparent simplicity of Native practice and ceremony, believing that they themselves can perform such ceremonies or practices. The Native rituals of the pipe and the purification lodge and work with the sacred crystal, many of these deeper ceremonies and practices are meant for Native people who practice them in relationship with the sacred cycles of Earth and heavens that were given them to maintain. In these times the external trappings of these mysteries have become extrapolated into "New Age" practices for religious or social gatherings. Such activities have harmful effects upon those who participate and also further denigrate and rape the wisdom of the Native people. The teachings presented in this book are conveyed to clarify whatever misconceptions there may be about Native American wisdom and, most significantly, to rekindle the fire of wisdom in the hearts of all the people, that we may plant seeds of good unto seven generations. These crystal teachings are intended particularly to release some of the suffering caused by crystal misuse. In that each crystal is of the Earth, the energies amplified by the crystal also affect the heart of the Earth. May all those attracted to the "glamour" of the crystal cultivate the crystal-clear mind in thought, word, and deed.

First understand the nature of your own mind. If you follow a regular meditation practice, you may place a crystal on your shrine and in time you will become more clear; as the channels are clarified, especially the three main channels, then one is able to work with the crystals. They are wondrous gifts from Mother Earth. Remember that the crystal is a living being, a conscious being. It is mind made concrete. A crystal is not an object or a thing; it has an effect upon you and you upon it. It is more like a friend than an object. With this attitude you will have a good friendship.

Realize that the crystal is a mirror of your mind. First bring mind to stability and purify mental and physical continuum—then converse with crystal friend.

What follows is an outline for developing good crystal relations.

The rock crystal or quartz is basically silica dioxide. Its medical properties are astringency and toning of the body. Crystals work within the body through resonance coupling, in a process similar to what happens when sunlight touches the skin, forming vitamin D_3; there is the direct action of the light and its response within the body. The etheric web of the human body is very much like that of quartz in that it is hexagonal, and one photon, one beam of light, coming through a space in this hexagon becomes two; each time the light hits one of these spaces it doubles. This suggests the great potential human beings have to generate energy. Human beings have the capacity to turn and transmute the elements of this planet. The rivers can be made pure again. At this time the Earth is waiting for us to remember, to call the elements again to peace and balance. That understanding comes first in our own hearts and minds.

Quartz crystals are activated by sound, by heat, and by pressure along the axis. Activated crystals send out a field of energy approximating five cubic feet per pound of crystal mass. A crystal that has been activated will pulse energy along its axis, amplifying whatever thought energy is carried on that pulse. While holding a crystal you may have sensed a pulsing and an expansion of energy. That very energy pulsing is how the quartz crystal has become the basis of technological society, from the simple wireless radio to the complex computer, and how it resonates the light of clear mind.

How to communicate with the crystal? Heart to heart and mind to mind. You become one with the crystal. The crystal is alive, just as you are, and we can never think of abusing its energy because we ourselves do not want to abuse or be abused. This beautiful living being shares with us according to our respect and willingness to accept the beauty of ourselves. It reflects the beauty to us; it shares its wisdom; it shows us that the wisdom is ourselves and the basic pulse of life.

From the sea of nothingness arises a sound—*A-E-I-O-U* —five tones, five winds, five breaths coming forth from the emptiness. Those simple sounds have a great significance for people from many traditions; they are related to sacred sounds practiced in the Kabbalah, the African religions, the old Christian chants, the Buddhist chants. That primordial sound means, "From the circle of light-sound came five points, five rays of energy, much like the crow's foot." In certain crystals (fluorite, for example) the crow's foot is very apparent as the light moves through. Just as everything in the universe reflects that one sound, that one light refracted into many forms, so in sitting with the crystal we again recognize the One, the essential unity, within ourselves.

It is good to sing your spirit song or prayer while communicating with the crystal. The crystal's musical resonance is very significant. Music, mathematics—whatever system you are studying, it is all basically built on one truth. The energy vibration of that One Truth moves in thirds and fifths and octaves, and so it is with the crystal.

The discipline of meditation is important for all, and especially for those who are called to be healers and to work with the crystal. To discipline our own energies, to understand our own process without judgment is very important, because any thought of self-dislike, separation, fear, or anger that is held in your mind is amplified by the crystal. So the first step is to clarify your own consciousness. The means of clarification is contemplation of the light. Recognize that all forms are vibrating atoms. Through resonance, conscious interaction with your environment, you perceive no separation of inner and outer expression.

In attuning with the crystal you may sense continuity and expansion of vision, seeing the threads by which the inner vision manifests through your interactions. Sometimes when you tune in to the spiral motion with the crystal there is the tendency to become drowsy. When the mind is focused beyond the drowsiness there is a sense of great light and great energy. The more you practice, the stronger the sense of the light.

Spiritual practice builds the foundation of stable mind. The crystal is a symbol of steadfast clear wisdom. In that the crystal responds to thought energy and amplifies such energies, the wise person cultivates ethical thought, word, and deed. One who meditates while maintaining thoughts of an angry nature toward another person is planting seeds of discord in his or her own continuum. Therefore it is wise to cultivate the mind of compassion and altruism so that the finer qualities of the human condition may be amplified and brought to fruition. It is within ourselves that we seek perfection, and it is our friends, the crystals, that enable us to see it. The crystal amplifies the Creator's eye within you that you may see the true light and feel the true vibration within.

The quartz crystal is the crystal of will, the desire to be. It calls forth your will to be whole simply by its presence in your environment, stimulating a process of transformation at many levels within you.

Rock crystal may release toxins from within your body, helping your body to let go of certain accumulated products of metabolism. Tasting an acid tone may indicate an imbalance of amino acids; if there is a bitter taste or a taste almost like fecal matter, then the body needs better elimination.

The crystal also works on the parasympathetic nervous system through the optic nerve. The eyes absorb light energy beyond the visible light spectrum. The peripheral vision is more sensitive to the subtle energy of life, such as auras; energy is absorbed through the peripheral vision, and even if the person is born blind or the body has been traumatized, the subtle body still has those functions. The peripheral vision's reception of light directly affects the pineal and pituitary glands. We can visualize a little cup within the mind which is receiving the subtle energy and distributing it throughout the entire endocrine system. Some people say the pineal gland receives the violet light, and others say it is received through the pituitary; one or both glands may receive the violet light depending on the individual's purpose and stage of development. Those who have a strong meditation or music practice can receive violet light through both glands, as can chemists, whose minds are disciplined through study of the law of octaves. So through resonance coupling, the power of the crystal resonates within us and the energy of the crystal is directly perceived through the skin.

Many people can receive this light energy from the crystal through the cheekbones, the sinus cavities, and the sternum. Blind people can perceive depth and distance through the facial bones; it is the same with this subtle energy amplified by the crystal. In the practice of meditation one may notice a tingle of energy moving up the nostrils through the sinus cavities. A connection is made and the energy is balanced in a particular triangle: the energy centers of the head, crown, pineal, and medulla operating in harmony. Another triangle that will become balanced with disciplined practice is composed of throat, heart, and a subtle center above the heart (some say it is the thymus gland), which comes into balance when the crown center is activated. Through the balance of the thymus energy, it is said, one may transmute not only ill thoughts but the very base metals themselves into gold, and import into this moment anything that may be required by the people. The universal abundance manifests through united heart and mind. When heaven and Earth unite in the heart, then we call to ourselves what is necessary. When berating what is present, one calls forth hard times. So one need never be hungry in the bosom of Mother Earth. It is a matter of recognizing the abundance there.

Crystals make very clear what one's consciousness is. For some, when they begin to work in the light what is drawn up is the doubt and fear, that which needs to be transformed. And here we must be vigilant and sturdy, and maintain cer-

241

tainty of purpose and balance so that what needs to be transformed can return to its natural source. Every anger or pain need not be articulated. To see it without judgment and let that energy return to the stream is cleansing in this time. Here is where the gift of the crystal is very important. Crystals bring to the forefront of consciousness actual moments when the flow of life's energy has been impeded, as if on a screen. Crystal gazing makes apparent the stream of one's mind. Memories once encapsulated in confusion become transparent, freeing energy for constructive action. As transparency develops, energy that sustained a wall between idea and action is released. Many feel energized after crystal meditations.

Illness develops when life energy is impeded in its flow. Illness manifests as elements of society fighting among themselves, people destroying the Earth. These are qualities of illness and imbalance. As individuals find the balance in themselves, maintain and act in harmony, the crystals resonate that song and help in the healing of the planet.

The crystal is vibrating faster than the speed of light, neither solid nor liquid. You can hold it in your hand and look at it, but its definition defies the language that exists in this time. We speak of the crystal as maintaining the sacred sounds of Galunlati, the realm of ideal form. Through the seed song, through the vibration of thought, we have precipitated the world as we know it today. Each of us is attuned to that sacred crystal in the heart of time, in the heart of now.

The relationship of the individual to the crystal is the relationship of the individual to the stream of clear mind. Quartz crystal has six sides, as does the etheric web of the human body. Through both forms mind energy moves, doubling each time it hits a corner of the hexagon. Human beings, like crystals, are energy generators. Just as the crystal emits negative ions that carry away the unhealthy charge around the environment, so can we, through clarifying our own thought and our own nature. It begins very simply, by acknowledging the up and down motion, the vortex of sun and moon within our own bodies, and recognizing the cross-current of East and West through which the world is made manifest.

Crystal is stimulated by sound; voice, thought waves stir the crystal to generate a field of energy around itself. Human person, your thoughts, your desires are creating a field of energy around you, determining the reality that you live in this moment. So we are no better than the rocks; we are like the crystal.

In this time within the heart of the Earth there are many crystal fields that are being stimulated by energy from the planets around Sirius, by energy from the Pleiades. This is happening so that we may all recall our home in the stars and may each trace our roots again to the Great Tree of Peace, the Tree of Life. The only way we can trace our roots and recognize the seed of star mind within ourselves is to look within and acknowledge that what we see around us is a reflection of our thinking, that what we are experiencing is a result of causes we ourselves have set.

To recognize our home in the stars is to prepare all nations upon this planet for a leap into the realization of our universal relationship. For this to manifest we have certain duties as individuals. First we must be a strong vessel, a whole vessel, a worthy cup. We are to clarify any breaks in our auras, any disturbances of mind, that we may hold the light aloft for all of our relatives to see and recall that we are dream weavers together.

How do we clarify our own aura? First we recognize that we are moving with the tides, that we have cycles of energy rising up and cycles of quiet; people call these biorhythms. Lunar energy, solar energy, Earth energy, and the energy that unites this entire quadrant of the Milky Way, these are four factors that are also the Adawees, the energy of the directions, and the constituents of consciousness that they express are what enable us to be here as we are now. The wise person recognizes that from the North we see the seeds of our ac-

243

tions. We recognize the causes that were established in the past without blame or shame; we simply see that these causes bring forth these actions. And we learn in the quietness of the North to look upon the lake with its frozen waters of mirror wisdom, that we may see things as they are without distinction or separation. Then the mind becomes less and less reactive; one understands that these feelings that arise and fall are just feelings. There is an essential nature, there is a stillness.

To understand the nature of one's mind, that is the greatest gift of this time. In understanding our own nature we begin to see that we create fields of energy around ourselves. It is the potential of the frozen water to become a stream and run to the ocean. Like the salmon, we came from the emptiness, we were spawned in that great lake. The waters thawed, the seeds became ripe, and the salmon made their way out to the ocean of experience, where we all bump against one another. There are many illusions in that ocean, and like the salmon we also look to find our way home again. We may encounter many obstacles along the way—but the salmon have returned to the east coast, and that is a sign that we as human beings are returning to clarity of mind and right relationship. We are making ourselves more clear. We are acknowledging the power of thought and prayer, and we are making strong our auras.

As human beings we are fed by Mother Earth, receiving through the umbilicus the elements of life, sound, air, fire, earth, water, the wood of the trees enabling us to be rooted in the now. Many humans feel suffering because they have a hole somewhere close to the navel center and are not able to keep all the blessings that Earth is giving. Sometimes one even picks up through the navel that which has been thrown away by others, causing confusion in one's mind. For this reason we have a practice that helps to keep the navel center strong and intact. It is a simple practice that stimulates the lymphatic and endocrine systems to put forth elements that are beneficial to you. When you are feeling constricted your body will release elements that are harmful to you. So it is wise to give the body gentle thoughts and gentle movements, it is wise to trust yourself in the moment.

Begin by kneeling, spine straight, hands on knees, right foot over left. Sense spirals of light moving up and down the spine. Now bring your hands together before you as if in prayer. Inhale and rise up on your knees, exhale and sink down. Inhale up, exhale down. Gentle movement, like the breath, with the breath. Sense yourself suspended by the breath, carried by the stars.

This simple exercise clarifies the energy of your emotional body, mental body, etheric web, and physical body. In the physical body, the spine is aligning through the breath and the lifting motion. The etheric body communicates more clearly through the spine with the emotional and mental bodies, in that the etheric body is a web, a conveyor of all your relationships of this world. On a more subtle level changes occur within the spine, within the head centers, and eventually, as one continues this exercise and the Sunray Basic Meditation and Diamond Body practices, changes are felt in the skull and sacrum; the plates of the skull move and become flexible again like a baby's, and the sacrum elongates and flattens out. The spine seems to have more air after this exercise, because one senses oneself supported not only by the muscles of the body but by the breath as well. This is a good practice to do regularly—if possible, three times a day for fifteen minutes would be very beneficial.

The position taken in this exercise is like a prayer position used in many spiritual practices. There is a reason for the poses people have always taken in praying, sitting on the knees or in the tailor's position, or in half or full lotus. All around the world these positions have shown themselves to be good tools for stabilizing the mind. Subtle differences in position in different cultures point out the effects of bioresonance, how a certain environment affects our thought and even our physical development.

To the Tsalagi, bioresonance is a very important concept in the *Elo*, the philosophy and tradition of the People. Bioresonance acknowledges the mutual responsivity and responsibility of individual and environment. Every individual has a gift, and it is in relationship to the environment. You may not see your environmental relationship as hills or water systems, but you can certainly see it as a neighborhood. As individuals, family, and group relate, how you maintain your practice has an effect upon your neighborhood and your environment. One person, a few people make a difference. Just by making our own natures clear, by keeping our own auras in good repair, through the resonance of our stability the neighborhood, the environment will reflect that stability of mind. So in the Tsalagi tradition we see ourselves as having a spiritual duty to keep our hearts and minds clear, to benefit all beings by our clarity.

When we were children, if we thought something that wasn't nice our elders would pick up on it and correct us. They said that to think something was just the same as doing it and that we needed to take care of our thinking. They taught us to understand the source of our actions and to know that whatever we thought about another was going to return to us. So it is wise to look for the best and when errors are made to remember that we are all in the process of changing. By acknowledging beauty, by seeing beauty, we create the vortex for it to actualize through every aspect of our existence.

Mother Earth will nourish us as we nourish her. Reciprocity: whatever is set into motion by our giving nature is returned to us. If we withhold anything from this being, the Earth—our heart, our right action, our care and respect for other living beings—then she, too, will feel dry and be unable to give.

Ease or dis-ease manifests in us in relation to the clarity or obstruction of our energy meridians, and the same principles hold true for the Earth and the social fabric of our lives. In groups of people with occluded heart center, for example, the flow of life force within the people and Earth will be affected.

246

If there is an occlusion in the heart, the individual has a heart attack or stroke; Earth has an earthquake. When humans keep the heart open, the vortex of light moving freely, then the ley lines of the Earth move freely.

There was a time in the early 1980s when many of the Earth's ley lines were very blocked. Certain people prayed and did ceremonies in these places to restimulate and balance these meridians, as if we were placing acupuncture needles in her back; through this she has reached a level of greater health.

Reciprocity is a most important principle to understand. When we give, we receive. As we recognize the cycle of reciprocity we are able to free ourselves from attachment to blame or guilt. We can just acknowledge, "Oh, I will plant these seeds of good relationship in this moment, and the results will be good for all my relations."

The crystal brings the gift of vision. The ideal of the medicine person is to be so that one with all of Creation that her or his prayers resonating with the crystal further amplify and resonate this peace and harmony through the human family and the body of the Earth. Crystal understanding is within each of us. As we first touch the cyrstal and meet it as a friend, we realize how much of our own thinking is calling to be transmuted. In this time the crystals stand by to help each one in that process of transmutation. Life is a continuous process. At some point every clear crystal was opaque and through transformation became clear. So it is with the consciousness of the human being. From the carbon of experience comes the diamond of complete assimilation and understanding.

MEETING THE CRYSTAL FRIEND

The relationship with the crystal is one of friendship. In meeting the new crystal friend it is important to give thanks to the crystal by placing an offering of a few grains of tobacco or corn directly on the stone, after having run it under fresh spring or brook water for about twenty minutes. Then burn some cedar and pass the crystal through the smoke; let the incense go around and through every part of the stone. Then wrap the crystal in a soft, dark cloth and keep it covered for two weeks, from the new moon to the full moon. Place it on your shrine, your mandala of clear mind. Every night, with the crystal still wrapped, take it to your heart and make communication with it. Sense the spirals of light, ascending and descending, heaven and Earth meeting in your heart. Visualize the stars above your head filling you with light. As you visualize the light, communicate with the crystal; sing the Heart Chant (page 197) or some hymn or chant with which you feel resonance. Soon there will be some connection with the crystal. When it is infused with this energy of your prayer, it will hold this energy and play it back for you if you forget. After the two weeks have passed you may uncover the crystal during prayer and meditation.

In attuning with the crystal, hold it in the palms of your hands, sensing the continuity of life, of light, moving within and through the stone and you and all beings. The crystal mirrors what is. Subtle things happen in the body when one is holding the crystal and calling upon the vibrancy of the spiral, ascending energy of Earth, descending energy of the heavens, yin and yang, mother and father meeting in the heart, energy flowing down in great cascades of light from the stars above the head.

Trust your own perception. It is very important to trust the vibration, whatever you sense; that is the only means of understanding what the crystal has to say. The energy you feel is the crystal's message to you, and as you practice and understand more in yourself, the clearer its message will be.

When first meeting with the quartz crystal align it toward magnetic north, holding it with its largest face looking north. Attune to the energy of the north and sense it flowing through the crystal to you, through you, and back again to the crystal. Sense the cycle, sense the flow.

In communicating with the crystal we see it becoming brighter and clearer. The crystal is singing, and one can sense

248

a stillness, a subtlety in its energy, its song. It is as though thoughts and their overtones become more clear, as though meaning becomes clear in many realities. It is through the six sides, the mirrors of ourselves, that this fullness is amplified and resonated.

What we experience in crystal communication is thought of as a right-brain activity. At this time humanity in the western world is calling out for a rebuilding of the bridge between the right and left hemispheres of the brain, a rebuilding of the Rainbow Bridge. The crystal is a friend to assist human beings in that process.

CRYSTAL MANDALA

In the teaching that was passed to me I was shown drawings of triangles with ten points in them. What do those ten points represent? Circle, completion, wholeness. Those are the qualities of the number ten. Within the circle is the inherent energy, the potential; and the manifest energy, that which takes form.

The quartz is basic. It is the seed of life, reminding us of the will. In the circle of life, the quartz relates to the North. From the North comes intention, the very essence, the pulse of life; will to be, action, the understanding that comes from having lived through trying times. From the white light, from the quartz crystal and the diamond (which also symbolizes the will energy) comes the realization, "Ah, so I am."

As we move around the circle we come to the second tone, from the Northeast, the wisdom and love that grow as two flames of one bough, symbolized by rose quartz and carnelian. Red coral also carries this tone. One would call upon the energy of rose quartz and red coral to reawaken a heart stilled by grief, and we call upon red coral when the body is in great trauma, such as through great loss of blood. It has the quality of drawing out excess heat and is useful when there is an infection in the lymphatic system. Rose quartz is refreshing and renewing to the cells of the body.

While holding the rose quartz, sense the movement of light within yourself. Sense the cycle of energy from Earth and heavens, meeting in your heart, and sense the stars above your head, those subtle energy centers and the ones within your body. Commune with the gracious resonance of love-wisdom as it stirs your heart to compassion for self and all relations.

Rose quartz has a different energy than clear quartz. It is more subtle, resonating a sense of spiritual devotion, caring for many. The energy of the Northeast, like the energy of the South, inspires and prepares the way for something else to come. The wisdom of the Northeast opens the door for the way of active intelligence, for the rising of the sun, for the voice of the wind to stir the mind to know that it is.

The crystal's polarization, the way it receives the light, determines how the spirals of energy meet around particular planes and call from within the wholeness of white light the colors needed by the individual. The pink coloring gives rose quartz a different polarization, a different vibration from that of clear quartz. The healing energy of rose quartz is in the flow of the gentle fire, the building fire. It is recognizable in relation to the reflexes of small intestine and circulatory system.

As we continue moving around the Medicine Wheel we come to the East, the place of active intelligence, the birthing of "I am that I am." It is the yellow of the topaz, the gold of building in transformation. The true topaz aids in the process of remembering.

From the Southeast comes the song of harmony and family building, the vibration of orange. Orange jasper relates to the form building of the solar plexus and will infuse the body with solar energy when it has become depleted.

From the South sounds the fifth note of green, the color of vital energy. Within the green is the red, so it is the seed of new beginnings and also concrete understanding, knowledge gained through experience. The watermelon tourmaline is a crystal of change in this time. It holds a negative and a positive charge, good for balancing the yin and yang in the body, the solar and lunar forces. Even more important, it enables the physical body to adjust to radiation bombardment, because its magnetic energy shifts the electron spin in the body to a cycle appropriate for transmuting energy, so the wastes of radioactivity are carried out of the body.

The emerald has a very different energy from that of the tourmaline, yet it is also the fifth note. Green is the center of the rainbow, the place of perfect balance, so the emerald is adaptable and has its place in many parts of the circle. Emerald and tourmaline are the most resonant of crystal beings. They have cycles of initiation just as human beings do. They are very receptive; their magnetic energy has the ability to draw forth at this time the energy needed to transmute consciousness and enable humanity to move to the next ray, the next sound.

Another member of the quartz family which is related to the tourmaline in its power of physical healing is the heliotrope (bloodstone). It is basically quartz (silica dioxide) with some iron and aluminum in it. Its crystalline structure is amorphous, like the opal; it has many lines of light. The green heliotrope is helpful in drawing swelling and poisons from the body. It will staunch the flow of blood very readily. It is also valuable in the treatment of liver ailments, as is the emerald.

Around the circle we come to the sixth note, the place of devotion. Christ energy is symbolized by the ruby, deep belief and understanding through direct experience. Ruby and garnet are stones for understanding the solar energy of ourselves. In the Southwest we meet the heart irradiated by devotion and set ablaze by the knowledge of our transition and transitoriness. As we approach the West, the gate through which we leave to enter the light, the knowledge of life's continuousness is represented by the ruby and the garnet. This devotion can be the key for the heavy learning that comes through the swinging hand of Saturn. If a person is overwhelmed by emotions, carried away by moon tides, then one may call upon the garnet and the ruby to balance the solar energy within the consciousness and the physical body.

We come around the circle to the West, to the place of transmutation and transformation. The animal of the West is the bear.* The black bear has taken the experiences of life and freed itself from wanting. It continues around the circle or leaves at that time through the Western gate, through the sacred ritual and the astringent, synthesizing, transforming energy. This energy is carried in the amethyst. The purple amethyst has the blue of passive, receptive understanding and the red of activity to move into another dimension. Its healing action is astringent, pulling from the body that which occludes its wholeness. It is basically a quartz with a bit of chromium and magnesium, which give it the purple hue.

In the West one makes a choice: is life for oneself alone, or does one continue into the older hills and become an elder to carry the people forth? In that process of choice one comes to the Northwest, where the experience of life is transmuted to metal, transmuted to gold, involving the basic sky stone, the lapis or turquoise. Both of these stones represent the day and night of our consciousness; through the experience of mind, the threads of gold and the threads of transmuted feeling move through other dimensions.

The magnetic flow of energy, the song of the universe, has many dimensions. Thus it is that some stones are not to be worn or worked with all the time. Perhaps a stone that you have worn for years will call to be put away; when that particular chemical substance is balanced in the body, one no longer has to call upon it to resonate from a stone. And often a stone will die when it has done its service to you. The color may become totally lifeless, or it may crack and burst. Opal and turquoise will do that.

The quartz is composed of tetrahedrons, three major and three minor. Think about the song of life, the tetrachords and

---

*East is the new sun of Nutawa, inspiration; South, the Grandmothers; North is the buffalo and the frozen mirror lake.

the tones and how they build: first interval, third interval, fifth interval. A song may be played in many keys, and crystals possess different properties. Crystals may be attuned to particular frequencies to benefit one's development. The land from which a particular stone is mined and the method of mining affect the crystal's stability in resonating an idea.

The shape of the quartz crystal, its hexagonal structure, is the double triangle or the Star of David: "As it is above, so it is below." Some crystals have a seventh face, usually appearing as a triangle. This indicates a mother crystal if the vortex of the energy is spiraling to the left or a father crystal if spiraling to the right. The left-turning crystal is able to draw pain from the body and the right-turning crystal is energizing. The mother and father crystals are very significant in terms of healing duality in consciousness. There comes a certain stage in one's understanding when one calls to transform the limitations. In the period when one is conscious of duality and seeking to find balance, the right and left crystals are very helpful.

Principles of crystal healing and attunement are relevent to all aspects of our life and our consciousness. It is not just crystals that we are talking about. It is a whole process of evaluating and moving through life. It is recognizing the principles of triangles and understanding the significance of the triangle, in that this is the way in which we build.

On different days there are different alignments of energy, and in this way certain crystals and gemstones have come to be associated with particular days of the week:

Monday: Pearl

Tuesday: Amethyst, tourmaline
           The energy of magnetized steel, a day of charging, a day of action. For healing practitioners, having these stones in the room when massaging or treating enables a greater flow of energy. They also make a natural egress for the unhealthy energy of doubt and limitation.

Wednesday:	Agate
Thursday:	Amber

Amber is petrified resin from coniferous trees growing by water; that which has been collected from China is very dark and red and strong. Amber is the accumulated solar essence of a living plant. You may place it in water in a glass or enamel cup (never aluminum or steel) and set it in the sun for two weeks; to drink that water is very efficient for correcting body illnesses.

Friday:	Turquoise, lapis lazuli, beryl (aquamarine or emerald)
Saturday:	Obsidian and leaded crystal; the energy of Saturn
Sunday:	Ruby and chrysolite

The yellow stones relate to the stomach, the spleen, and those fires that break down to build. The green stones balance and tone the liver, the wood element within your body. The liver is the door to your spirit's entry into the flesh. This is also the key to assimilation. The red stones are strengthening and toning to the blood and circulatory system.

These words will mean more to you as you meditate and become familiar with the energy of each stone. The crystals don't do anything for you; they only amplify what you are. Cyrstals try to help human beings in healing because the true destiny of human beings has been forgotten.

In this abundant world, in this home that has been given to us, it was said that we would always have enough of everything, that the elements themselves would respond to us and grow corn out of a rock, if need be, and that there would be enough corn to feed everyone, no matter how small the garden was. Some people are recalling this promise now and finding the means to realize it; this is the success of Findhorn. Through affirmation and communication with the devas, the beings who oversee the flows of energy in the plant kingdom, the people of Findhorn Community in Scotland have been able to grow magnificent gardens on what was once a sandy beach.

Everything has its place and time. Everything here is a gift and is sacred. It is our meeting of it that makes it holy or unholy. Within itself, everything is truth.

Every crystal belongs to a crystal family. Meeting one quartz crystal is the same as talking to one dolphin; all the other dolphins know about it. It is the same with crystals. So in first moving around the wheel we sense the crystal in ourselves individually, and then we see more and more, the immensity of our own consciousness. The crystal is a silent witness to the ever-present gem of wisdom in yourself. In many other ways the crystal is a door, but first the mind must be free of anger, of pain, of doubt. Then the crystal door is opened to you.

How is it that evil comes into the world? Evil comes, as my grandparents told me, from people having pride and thinking they have dominion over creation and others. In the Tsalagi creation story about Star Maiden, it is told that when she came to Earth she inhaled a wind and became pregnant and bore two sons. One of them wanted to do things in the right way, and the other one was cloudy and stormy, wanting to argue and do things in another way. And these twins fought within their mother, and she died giving birth to the storm-making one because he came out from underneath her arm rather than in the natural way. And from her body came all the good things that we know. This is one explanation that was given to us as children as to how evil originated. The real lesson in this story is that when we want to argue with the natural plan, when we become so arrogant that we seek to go against the order of things, we bring forth a negative energy. When we act without considering how our actions will affect others, when we act in a way that may cause harm to others, in this moment or three generations from now, then we are planting the seeds of evil.

Thus evil is a misuse of the sacred power of life, relationship, knowledge. In the Native tradition there is no power over, no dominion over creatures, over Earth, or over others. We are caretakers of one another. That is another way of looking. In the past one may have thought power was somethng to be used for or against. In reality power is to be fully present in the moment. It is a sacred energy, and its manifestation is the result of our clear relationship with our own thought and our clear relationship with one another. The power of right relationship is the power to call forth peace.

When we make peace in ourselves we open the door to the Most Great Peace. When we can cast aside doubt and fear and recognize what is within, the gateway of peace will open. When the gate is open and throughout the Earth all creatures honor life, then beauty will manifest in the hearts of each of us, and our society and our planet will know a new day, a new age. To live ethically is the opportunity. Ethics is the science of right relationship, and in right relationship the inherent patterns of peace and harmony are revealed. To see the whole pattern, that is a glorious step for human beings. In committing yourself to be the light that you are, to resonate as a whole form, you begin to see the cycles and patterns more and more clearly.

Let us watch the developments that will be occurring in the coming years. Let us be observant and yet very firmly seated in the light of our knowing. For we shall see many things. We shall see many coming just to the point of realizing their wholeness but somehow unwilling to surrender the ignorance, so leaving a space, an opening. We can only know about the light by the energy. Look at the plants in a room: if they are drooping, energy is draining somewhere. We can mend those energy leaks. It is a matter of choice.

And in the dynamic of the light we shall see thought forms in the heavens, be they angels or demons; we shall see them in the sky. The point is ever to recognize the stillness, the balance, and the beauty. These are great times of change. My uncles told me that during the Second World War many soldiers in Normandy saw Christ in the sky, and at various times soldiers would see armies fighting in the sky, because 1935 was the opening of the ninth and final stage of purification. Now we see that cycle completing. And one of the promises made by the ancient Native calendar of this continent is that we shall see, that everyone will sense the right and the wrong, the yes and the no. Each one will sense clearly the choice.

The first step is to find peace and balance within ourselves, to put aside those energies of doubt, of anger, of separation and fear that keep us from manifesting our whole potential. It is a process that each one of us goes through; no one can do it for you. Someone can reflect your beauty, someone can inspire you, perhaps someone can set the shape of a possible future and you resonate to it. Yet it is for each of us to sing out the light. It cannot be done for you. You cannot abdicate the responsibility of your holiness.

Long ago there were people walking in the sky. In this time of illusion many have forgotten how to walk in the sky. As I visited the Sun Dance some years ago the old people were saying, "Dhyani, it is time that people walk again in the sky." I said, "Oh, that is so. How shall it be?" "Remind them of the spirals of light." Remind the human being that there is neither up nor down, that this is the dream we share. And as we recognize the gateways of North, East, South, and West, we give ourselves a place in space, an opportunity to decide where we go, how we go, and a reminder that we are shaping tomorrow with this moment. I ask you to be a skywalker. Let us call forth our unmanifest potential of right action, that it may happen now.

Native people are very pragmatic people. Meditation is done to benefit everyone. And the mysterious things, the "powers" that arise, they are secondary. What is most important is to understand the nature of your own mind and to realize that what you are thinking is going out and touching others and will return to you. We have a spiritual duty to ourselves and others to clarify our mind and to put aside attitudes of discord so that all beings may be happy. Sometimes we suffer with thoughts of anger and pain. Sometimes we feel we are not good enough. The very fact that we have been given a human body and the gift of breath means that we have gathered enough merit for that and therefore we are good enough. So let us put aside the sense of doubt and the feeling of not-good-enough. Be thankful for the gift of mind, the gift of life, and appreciate the merit of others' lives.

Often as people come closer and closer to understanding their true nature, they find themselves distracted and annoyed by things, or deep fears come up that they had not known were there. When these fears and other uncertainties of the mind arise, it s a great opportunity to see them as they are, just thought patterns, and have no attachment to them. Fear is an energy that can only be fed by itself. If the ignorant and hungry spirits have been feeding on you and they see that you are no longer going to generate that energy of confusion, they may make a lot of noise in your mind. Eventually your mind realizes, "Yes, I have created this noise, I have created these hungry spirits, and I can sweep them out."

It is all a process of change, of transformation, of refining transparency. There is no light without darkness. Many feel that darkness denotes something negative, but in the nighttime the stars twinkle and in the nighttime the dreams grow, and those dreams determine our tomorrow. So nighttime, daytime, they are parts of the dream. One is neither bad nor good. It is how we approach those times that determines their value in our own life. So let us not fear the dark.

In my training as a young girl there were certain times when I was left alone in the woods without anything except flint, not even a blanket, so that I would understand the nature of my own mind. There is a shadow side. It is the fears you have not looked at in the day and have not clarified at night. They accumulate and become a shadow. That is why our elders taught us the means of clarifying the day before going to sleep, making peace with oneself and others each night.[1] If we don't make that peace the shadow gets larger and larger, and before we can break through the confines of the illusion of "I," we must grapple with that shadow on the threshold of realization.

Very often the shadow is your creative potential that has been set aside, so as you are falling asleep, make a great effort to open clear communication with divine mind. In some of our ceremonies we are engulfed by the shadow and thus understand the emptiness, seeing that night and day, in and out, are but constructions of our thinking. Better to give thought orderly channels to flow in, a structure of harmony and beauty built with pillars of faith, compassion, diligence, and generosity.

In contemplating the crystal you can sense the shape of it, the movement of the atomic structure. That, too, is consciousness, and the atoms of consciousness are ever moving within us. We are in relationship to all that goes on in this universe. In this and all dimensions there is a practice of seeing the attachment and stilling the various responses that are formed. One can commit oneself to singing the song that stirs the current of enlightenment in all beings. It is a process in which choice is very significant.

There are certain rare crystals that have a ninety-degree angle; usually they are twin crystals.[2] In New York State one can find such crystals growing around Watkins Glen. They come out looking like crosses, quite beautiful and very powerful. Seeing them, you realize that they are living beings who have made decisions about the form they carry. In the form expressed are also revealed dimensions: above, below, within, without. And those dimensions are cycles within cycles, as in our Native sacred calendar where the wheels are interlocked: the wheel of Mars, the wheel of Venus, and one wheel for which there is no planet apparent, a planet behind the sun.

As we look at form and energy in the crystal, we can look at form and the radionic activity of a thought form or a feeling within ourselves. We amplify what is happening. It is there. In the perception of it we begin the transformation. So the form of the crystal is a guide, a road, a sacred mandala of mind. Quartz crystal has six sides, yet those six sides can be fused and shaped in many directions and actually create many turning faces, or facets, simply according to the energy that is available to the growing crystal. This says something about human development, for there are subtle energies necessary to our full growth and development also, and they may or may not be available in the early environment. In these times there are many people who have forgotten their sensing along the clear and resonant lines of orderly, coherent, harmonious development. Just as those lines are the basis of crystal structure, they are also individual structure, family structure, social structure.

We can learn to apperceive directly the energy of ourselves and to recognize it as crystalline structure. Thus we become able to remove the stress that distorts the crystal overtone, enabling the molecules to perceive other relationships, create different combinations and forms. What is stress? Is it one's creation, or is it a process? Does one continue to suffer, or does one recognize and bring forth the jewels and the joy of clear consciousness? The line from one to three, from here to there, is infinite throughout the universe. One can decide, "Yes, in this way it will harmonize," always recognizing what is the greater good. In terms of the crystal, a generator, the greatest good means the greatest refraction of light. We, too, are generators. We, too, are responsible for choosing to create forms that will refract that greatest light for all beings. Let us remind ourselves and the Earth of that sacred choice, of that sacred signature. There is a pattern unfolding. Let it be one of beauty.

So a new age is beginning, a change in cycle, a change in rhythm. The rhythm determines the day. Is it short? Is it long? That is the pattern. It is important to know the rhythm of the seeds within ourselves, for there lies the basic pulse. In our body there is a fire that turns things from yellow to white, that breaks down and brings forth new constituents of building. The crystal, too, has a process of extraction and refinement; it has an abundant consciousness. Energy is never lost, it is transformed. And so it is with us. It is not just the crystal that seeks to be polished and refined; we also are seeking to manifest our full potential. And just as the crystal has its ideal form, so, too, does enlightenment require the proper latticework of our consciousness.

The same awareness of form that a child has, knowing the form from within, is what we are reaching for. Learning to speak true, to affirm our vision, is just a recognition of certain patterns, certain sounds, certain realities, and learning that we can choose to be in a certain part of the wave or even attuned to a particular frequency and maintain an area of illuminated consciousness within that space. This means understanding vibration and realizing that there is in every aspect of life a cycle, a process. It is by being attuned to the larger cycle in the sacred wheel that we draw ourselves and our environment more and more into harmony.

CRYSTAL MEDITATION

Place before you a clear quartz crystal that you have cleansed and fed. As you are looking at the crystal look also into your heart, and let your voice rise in the Heart Chant. It is a simple chant that unites the heart, wisdom of love; the throat, indigo of creation where thought becomes action; and the inner eye, that gold of discriminating wisdom. The melody and the rhythm are resonating the form through which the crystal may send its energy. Even the tones are weaving. And the crystal itself weaves a superstructure of molecules in motion, stirred by the sound of your voice and the energy of thought.

Sensing the stars above you, within you, feel yourself irradiated by their rainbow light cascading down. With the starlight weave awareness of interlacing dimensions, weave a world of beautiful form.

261

Now take the crystal in your hand. View its form as a process in creation. How many sides does the crystal contain, how many faces? Feel the dimensions with your hands, through subtle communication. Let the sense be full, let the fingers become eyes in the air. Sense the subtle current passing within yourself, through yourself, in interaction with the crystal.

Now, just as if it were a radio receiver, let the crystal amplify the wisdom within your body. Sense, visualize the flow of the five sacred energies: the green of the liver, of the wood; the red of the heart; the orange of stomach and spleen; the white of the lungs; the dark blue-black of kidneys and bones. Let these riverways guide you to the wisdom of the crystalline structure within yourself. There is a perfect pattern encoded within every aspect of your being. To recognize it, to resonate to it more and more, this is transformation.

And now be aware of your body's response, of vibration, taste, movement of light, energy. Simply by having crystals around, especially when the room has been charged with a sense of meditation or prayer, there is a chemical reaction in the body. Prayer is an energy that the crystal very easily attunes to. With prayer, especially chanting, there is a certain pattern of memory that the molecules will assume, just as the body's muscles, through a set of exercises repeated regularly, assume certain patterns. Through a repeated frequency or a certain type of energy the crystal becomes even more sensitive to that energy and its reponse, attuned to the regular pathway being created for that kind of communion, be it through clapping, dancing, singing or spoken intervals of sound. The more the crystal hears it, the more its memory of understanding is attuned to it, building a memory structure. Then the energy around the crystal extends yet further. And in yourself there is a nectar produced during meditation, hormones dripping down from two little ducts at the base of the skull to the back of your throat. When this is happening sound becomes light and you sense through all your perceptions, realizing the many doors of consciousness within yourself.

Our sacred power is our prayer power and the clarity of our thinking. Thus chanting, calling upon the right sounds, is the basic means to clarify the channels of life force within one's own body. Through the clarification of our own channels, through the bioresonance of the Earth, the atmosphere, we are able to make even the environment more clear, more pure. It is said that even the polluted waters can be made clear again as we clarify our hearts and minds. It is through the energy of sound and the energy of the crystal that this happens.

Crystal is a mirror of the inherent clear mind. By its very presence it is clarifying. To the Tsalagi it is the sacred sound that is the greatest healer. The sound structure of the crystal resonates, recalling to its optimum resonance and pitch the sound within yourself, the note of your perfection. The crystal is a tuning fork, ever resonating the sound of Creation within each being.

Indian mind always looks to the whole. So crystal is not "applied" to the body or placed on particular energy centers. Treatment of disease is never to a particular energy center but for the whole being, sensing that person as a continuum. If we are thinking "part" then we are giving energy to the problem. It is better to know the wholeness. In working with others, always remember that you are a whole being in relation to all beings. Your energy centers are in relationship with everything in the universe. So to sense the balance, sense the light moving through yourself and your consciousness in tune with all that is. You are light.

The eye of God looks through the eyes of the children. Consider how your thought and action affect those yet to be born. Let each one choose, like the crystal, the structures of thought, word, and deed that will reflect the greatest light.

263

EPILOGUE

Here are some tools for emptying out your fireplace. Test these words and meditations as you would test the food you buy for your family. It is fresh, is it suitable, is it beneficial? Is it good medicine for you and your relatives? If the medicine is good, then take it.

To understand Mystery,
Observe mind.
Stilling fear, mind moves clear.
Sing a song of equanimity,
Awake within serenity.
Affirm your voice
and choice.
Magnetize a potent dream—
World alight,
Illumined peace.

NOTES

Preface

1. As examples of this pattern of cyclical reincarnation of specific wisdom energies, consider the birth of the Pale One in 873 B.C.; of Wotan 700 years later (see Introduction, n.3); of the Peacemaker in 1573; and of a possible contemporary incarnation of the same wisdom in 1983. Shearer discusses the "echo system" in detail in *Beneath the Moon and Under the Sun.*

Introduction

1. The reference is to the fifth generation following the Forced Removal in the mid-1800s, when the Tsalagi people were forced to leave their homelands in the southeast of what is now the United States. Estimates vary as to the numbers of lives lost during the Trail of Tears of 1838–1839. Woodward, citing Foreman, notes that "out of the total of 18,000 Cherokees who went west after the Treaty of 1835, about 4,000 perished, either in stockades prior to removal or on the journey west" (*The Cherokees*, p. 218 and n. 39). For further information, see later in this Introduction; Grant Foreman, *Indian Removal;* and Thetford Denton, *Tsali.*

2. Inspired by leaders such as Mad Bear, "Firebrand of the Fifth Generation," for example, whose Unity Conferences (1956–1968) and brave example reawakened many to their sacred duty as members of Red Nations. See also Rex Weyler, *Blood of the Land.*

3. Some 700 years after the Pale One, another teacher came among the Tsalagi, again reminding the people of their sacred instructions and how to fulfill them. He was

called Wotan. His glyph is variously given as ⊥ or T. He was miraculously conceived and then born in the normal way; due to his great promise he was raised from a young age within the temple, realizing the high priestly attainment of Wind Master. For a long time he meditated inside the cave of an inactive volcano. At some point he was burned; he lost his skin pigmentation and thereafter wore a mask. Wotan was of a highly realized consciousness, with a mind both vast and quick. As soon as he saw the Pale One's teachings demonstrated, he was able to realize them. He was a wise teacher, adjusting confusions in understanding of the calendar and the mathematical system. Because of Wotan's great attainment and his lack of skin color, it has sometimes been thought that Wotan and the Pale One were the same person. For this reason one may find different dates ascribed to the Pale One's visit, 2,000 or 2,700 years ago; he was actually born 2,860 years ago, in 873 B.C. See also Shearer (*Beneath the Moon and Under the Sun*, chap. 11), who speaks of Wotan's incarnations among the Mayans.

4. "Medicine," in the Native way, means one's holy power to do good for the benefit of all.

5. According to the sacred calendar, time flows through different "worlds," each lasting 1,144 years. Each world consists of thirteen heavens, periods of harmony and order, and nine hells, times of disharmony and darkness. Each heaven and hell is fifty-two years long, and together they constitute the twenty-two equal time periods that make up every world. The Fifth World, the last of nine hells, came to an end on August 16, 1987. With the opening of the Sixth World on August 30, 1987, a new cycle of thirteen heavens has begun. (See Shearer, *Beneath the Moon and Under the Sun*, p. 99).

6. According to Tsalagi prophecy, after the Great Flood the four clans in the center of the Earth parted and traveled

to the four directions. The fair-skinned ones went to the east to find means of easing the lives of the people; they became parents of invention. Those who went to the north sought clear ideas to further the Creator's instructions. The clan that went west learned of death and mind transmission to heavenly realms to preserve the wisdom learned in each life. In the south the lessons of growth were sought that the people might manifest abundance. Three of the clans returned to the center of the world at the appointed time and shared their insights. One has not yet returned; the people still await the return of the pale brother from the east, bearing the wisdom of inventions that will benefit all beings. When Córtes arrived, he was thought by many to be the fair-skinned brother arriving from the east; hence the welcome he received among those he subsequently destroyed.

1. The People of the Fire

1. The Four Corners area comprises the Colorado Plateau, Utah, New Mexico, Arizona. The Hopi communities there are the oldest continually populated communities in the world.

2. Mooney gives a brief account of language relationships in *Myths of the Cherokee* (p. 15ff). See also Woodward, *The Cherokees*, p. 19, and Lewis and Kneberg, *Tribes That Slumber*, p. 156.

3. See Woodward, *The Cherokees*, pp. 23–24. Woodward recounts the capture and escape of the "Lady of Cofitachequi" but mistakenly refers to her as the "niece of the chieftainess of Cofitachequi." She was herself in fact the Principal Chief.

4. See Introduction, page 4.

5. The Tsalagi have been creative and resilient in adapting to the encroachment of European colonial law and cus-

tom upon the traditional culture. On the surface it appeared that they were agreeing to the changes being imposed upon them. However, there developed an outer system of tribal law and government, which dealt with the colonial society, and an inner system, which dealt with the people themselves. Thus both harmony and integrity prevailed. See also Strickland, *Fire and the Spirits*, p. 183.

6. See, for example, the works of Vine DeLoria, N. Scott Momaday, Tony Shearer, and Rex Weyler cited in "Readings."

7. See Paul A. W. Wallace, *The White Roots of Peace.*

8. See Preface, n. 1 and Shearer, *Beneath the Moon and Under the Sun*, p. 99.

9. See also Strickland, *Fire and the Spirits*, chap. 11.

10. Ley lines are the channels or meridians within Earth through which energy flows, similar in function to the acupuncture meridians of the human body. Places where major ley lines converge are places of heightened energy receptivity where much benefit can be given to Earth by right prayer and right action.

11. Shearer, *Beneath the Moon and Under the Sun*, passim.

2. Voices of Our Ancestors

1. Some say he also carried her head, which became the sun. The Tsalagi view the sun as female. In oral histories (and even in the *Popol Vuh*) there is reference to one of the sons carrying his mother's head into the sky. See Girard, *Esotericism of the Popol Vuh.*

2. Communication from Joe Washington, spiritual leader of the Lummi Nation.

3. Adapted with permission from Shearer, *Beneath the Moon and Under the Sun*, Plate 91, p. 99.

3. Renewing the Sacred Hoop

1. This meditation derives from the meditation practice of the Ywahoo lineage as taught by Eli Ywahoo, which is the foundation practice of Sunray Meditation Society and Sunray Peacekeepers throughout the world. The Basic Meditation is also available on tape and video cassette, with instruction by Dhyani Ywahoo. For more information, see Appendix C.

4. The Family of Humanity

1. Priestcraft training for those of Tsalagi blood still follows traditional lines. Sunray Meditation Society, a spiritual society founded by Dhyani Ywahoo and based on the teachings of the Ywahoo lineage, trains its ministers by both traditional and modern methods appropriate for those not of Native ancestry.

2. This is a modern Tsalagi teaching tale based on factual events.

3. Some 14,000 Diné (Navajo) and Hopi people are faced with forced relocation from their ancestral homelands under Public Law 93-531, the Relocation Act, enacted by the U.S. Congress in 1974, ostensibly to resolve disputation between Hopi and Diné over use of the Joint Use Area of mineral-rich land on the Diné and Hopi reservation. The true dispute is not between Navajo and Hopi; it is between traditional Indians—who wish to preserve Indian land as the base of Native religion and culture and who therefore oppose industrial development and exploitation of the land—and those who support such development (particularly outside forces, such

271

as mining interests, who stand to profit from such exploitation). To get more information or to offer assistance,
contact: In Defense of Sacred Lands, P.O. Box 1509,
Flagstaff, AZ 86002; telephone (602) 779-1560.

5. Generating Peacekeeper Mind

1. This meditation arises from a traditional teaching story
   for children.

2. This meditation arises from a practice given to us as
   children when we were being taught about the ancient
   temples of our people.

3. The forgiveness ritual is a daily practice among the
   Tsalagi.

7. Diamond Light

1. See Chapter 5, pages 151–155.

2. A twin crystal is one that develops as a composite. A
   sharp V-shaped depression often marks the conjunction
   between the crystal pairs. The three types of twin crystals are contact twins, united by the composition planes;
   penetration twins, two single crystals growing into each
   other; and repeated twins, a parallel grouping of successive crystals.

Appendix A

THE FAMILY OF LIFE

The One Source of Our Being, The Many in the One

1   ONE: White light going to blue. Will. Circle. Quartz crystal.

The primordial force of life, will, born of the void, brings forth the light. Will to be, beginning of manifestation, is symbolized by the circle or egg. To bring people into a direct relationship with their own self-knowledge and the whole from which we have all evolved, large group meditation is used to come in touch with the ever-flowing stream of consciousness which is the divine light giving birth to sound and manifestation. The goal of this understanding is to let people become better attuned to their own will, to take responsibility for shaping the environment around them by correct thought and action so that all is in harmony with the whole. Let all see that in a universe of abundance there is no scarcity, and let each take responsibility for completion of the circuitry to enable the greater good to manifest. As the solar system and galaxy are moving into higher vibration, a consciousness of planetary oneness needs to be actualized. Within each being is a silver cord connecting individual with awakened presence.

As the One seeks to know itself, it observes the flow and becomes two.

2   TWO: Red. Consciousness, Love-Wisdom. Two parallel lines. Ruby.

Duality emerges as the parent of intelligence separated from the One by observing itself. Red and blue—dialectic opposition seeking balance in the birthing of intelligence.

3   THREE: Yellow. Active Intelligence. Triangle. Orange topaz.

As the One perceives itself and gives birth to the two, the two gives birth to relationship, which is the formless manifest into active intelligence. All aspects of the educational process are based upon the principle of the triangle—acknowledging the flow of wisdom within the individual, the group, and the planet, seeing that within the question is the answer, within the problem is the solution, and actualizing that knowledge into correct action. The triangle is the symbol of the family and the material manifestation of nature's plan in order. This is the basis of understanding our interconnectedness to all beings. Individuals can enhance communication among themselves through a direct perception of the Essence which is present in all. Any thought based upon denial leads to a consciousness of scarcity, separation, and destruction. Let us see the continuous flow of energy which sustains abundant harmony in family, group, national, and planetary consciousness.

Family rituals of prayer and meditation are vehicles of transmutation. Proper ritual, attunement to the land, correct relationship to the abundance of the Earth enable one to sense the larger relationship. Basic geometric shapes evolving from the triangle carry inherent messages of a universal nature. Through clear ideation, the energy field of individual, group, and planet is clarified of limiting thoughts, which manifest as impediments of consciousness and the body of expression is made whole (holy).

4 **FOUR:** Orange. Extended family. Healing. Tetrachord, Square. Jasper.

The four distributes the basic concept of healing, attunement to the light, healing body, emotions, mind, and the etheric web, which unifies individual with the monadic presence. The power of right thinking as preventive medicine and divine invocation as tools to healing the family of mankind must be realized.

Calling forth the rays (colors) of healing and seeing their relationship to the organ systems and consciousness are also necessary to healing. The triad of primary color as the birthing of form is messenger to the material form. Each color has qualities of consciousness (as described through each numeral and shape) and relationship to physical organ systems. Each element when burned in the laboratory spectrascope gives off its characteristic color. Humans in perceiving particular colors relate to a common experience. Like the periodicity of the elements, there are aspects of thought and action that also follow the basic laws of harmony. Healing with light, color, and sound, laying on of hands, auric balancing, right thinking and right action are universal disciplines that bring forth the harmony in healing.

5 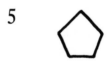 **FIVE:** Green. Neighborhood, village. Mentation, concrete science, knowing. Pentagon. Emerald.

Five relates to knowing. It has an assimilative function, synthesizing the wisdom of eternal presence into physical manifestation. At the level of neighborhood and village, the principle of the council has as its basis invoking and receiving the abundance of dynamic harmony and awakened awareness of service through developing an idea which benefits many in

275

harmony with all beings. The vehicle is group meditation—clearly perceiving the purpose of the parts in the whole, knowing the needs of all through communion with the essence of a question wherein lies the answer.

6      SIX: Rose. Earth, clan. Six-pointed star. Rose quartz.

Six is the ray of devotion to manifestation of the ideal form: as above, so below. Remembering that the thought is energy manifesting, interpreted through the heart and energy receptors of being, we energize the consciousness of abundance and right relationship to the Earth. When love of and devotion to the Earth is carried through with proper thinking and right action, the land responds with abundance. A scarcity mentality will perpetuate the illusion of hunger, poverty, and unbalanced distribution of power.

When the group attunes to receptivity with discrimination, the group can then perceive the ideal form emerging for the good of the entire planet. Thus, through alignment with the higher group self, we can reaffirm the qualities of connection with the whole and express that connection in right action.

7   SEVEN: Violet. Nation. Tetrahedron. Amethyst.

Seven brings awareness of the family of common purpose. The group must take responsibility for transforming community structures from a mentality of separation to one of unity. Acknowledging the part that multiplicity plays in the whole, the family becomes purified of illusions of separation. The method for realizing this end is the council from neighborhood, village, clan, and nation.

8 EIGHT: Indigo. Planetary Consciousness; understanding. Octagon. Blue sapphire.

Planetary consciousness understands the oneness of humanity and realizes the Earth as our home, with all people working in harmony for the benefit of the whole.

The system of economy is based on what is appropriate for the whole and on the constructive ideation that all resources are present, only needing to be moved from one place to another. As the waters flow and the winds blow there is an inherent energy distribution. In the manifestation of planetary consciousness we can move in harmony with those flows. Scarcity consciousness stands in the way of full planetary consciousness, which acknowledges the wisdom of all beings so that the few do not make decisions for the many and legislators are true servants of the people, receptors of the multiple will in alignment with the greater good.

9 NINE: Opalescent. Universal consciousness. Nine-pointed star. Fire opal.

The structure of universal consciousness is three superimposed triangles. It is truly receptive to the oneness of all being in its many manifestations. The Earth is part of a living organism that is being initiated to a higher awareness. As part of a living being, the Earth needs to manifest a unified consciousness in harmony with the whole solar system, so that illuminated minds can travel on beams of light throughout the universe, partaking in communion with the larger family of being.

Appendix B

THE DIRECTIONS AND THEIR ATTRIBUTES

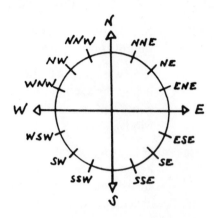

North

Wisdom, will. Tempering; brings forth tests to prepare for meeting the hell of the West, where all thought forms that one has generated are met. Frozen water; potential.

North-Northeast

Wisdom and will combine as love.

Northeast

The birth of intelligence through interaction of will and wisdom.

East-Northeast

A bringing forth of the illumination of the East; the rising sun of consciousness.

East

Illumination; understanding the expression of mind; integration. Raises gentle nurture of Mother Nature in us all. Gentle winds.

East-Southeast

Realization that for illuminated consciousness to manifest seeds of mindfulness must sprout.

279

Southeast	Rays of regenerative energy, like the seed in utero, taking in the consciousness of its purpose and direction.
South-Southeast	Seed's firm implantation; recollection of future growth.
South	Renewal, regeneration for future being; the seed of tomorrow. Primary energy of adolescence. Warm, wet winds.
South-Southwest	Gathering of experience and recognition of responsibility to self and all living creatures; returning sustenance and abundance to others.
Southwest	Vines growing forth; spread of family, clan, based on right relationship.
West-Southwest	Place where we accept our power and decide to share and carry forth in harmony with the present, giving birth to children of tomorrow, fed by traditions of our grandmothers.
West	Assimilation. All experiences of life and karma. Idea forms transmuted in the fire that destroys, giving birth to something new. The door we pass through to death of the ego. Place of our old age. Integration and balancing of experience; dissolution of desires. Yearning to merge fully with spiritual consciousness. Can be taken as the door out of incarnation. Drying, driven winds set ablaze.
West-Northwest	Sharing the wisdom; assimilated experiences are recognized as arche-

	typal patterns of consciousness and shared with the coming generations.
Northwest	Development and arising of true resonance with the elements and the ability to call forth the elements for the good of the community.
North-Northwest	Emblazoned consciousness of full spiral of understanding and relationship to the stars. Recognition of self as a vibrating being creating cause through thought and action.

The ascending spirals of energy, rays of Mother Earth, connect with the South's regenerative aspects of self, rising up through generative organs to meet in the heart as it is illuminated by inner knowledge of our relationship to all. The wind of the North and the lightning of change are drawn forth by this vortex of energy, so that one recognizes clear mind through relationship to heaven and Earth. The lightning nurtures the inner qualities of the physical form. The inner being calls forth from East and West spirals of energy, balancing consciousness and universal motion. One may realize the emptiness of no remainder.

Appendix C

ABOUT DHYANI YWAHOO AND SUNRAY MEDITATION SOCIETY

Dhyani Ywahoo is a member of the traditional Etowah Band of the Eastern Tsalagi (Cherokee) Nation and the twenty-seventh generation to caretake the Ywahoo lineage. She is also founder and director of Sunray Meditation Society, an international spiritual society dedicated to planetary peace. Sunray Meditation Society is affiliated with the Igidotsoiyi Tsalagi Gadugi.

The Sunray teachings are being passed to people throughout the world, with the guidance of traditional Native elders, that we may realize on Earth the ideal of Caretaker Mind and manifest harmony and right relationship in the family of life. The teachings are shared primarily through The Peacekeeper Mission, a program of personal, group, and planetary education and training based on the Ywahoo lineage teachings. The Peacekeeper training gives specific practices of an "Earth Wisdom" nature, to transform obstacles and renew faith and power to create a peaceful world. The training is offered twice yearly at sites in North America and Europe.

Sunray meditation groups meet regularly in many cities in the United States and Canada. The practice is open to all; instruction is provided.

Sunray Tapes and Literature offers audio and video cassettes and written materials on the Sunray teachings and practice. A brochure is available upon request.

A portion of the proceeds of all Sunray activities supports selected Native American projects.

For more information, please write:

Sunray Meditation Society
P.O. Box 308
Bristol, VT 05443

READINGS

Agnew, Brad. *Fort Gibson: Terminal on the Trail of Tears.* Norman: University of Oklahoma Press, 1980.

Blankenship, Bob. *Cherokee Roots.* (Contains indexes of Cherokee tribal rolls.) Gatlinburg, Tenn.: Buckhorn Press, 1978.

DeLoria, Vine. *The Aggressions of Civilization: Federal Indian Policy Since the 1880's.* Ed. with Sandra L. Cadwalader. Philadelphia: Temple University Press, 1984.

——. *American Indian Policy in the Twentieth Century.* Norman: University of Oklahoma Press, 1985.

——. *American Indians, American Justice.* Ed. with Clifford M. Lytle. Austin: University of Texas Press, 1983.

——. *Behind the Trail of Broken Treaties: An Indian Declaration of Independence.* New York: Delacorte Press, 1974.

——. *God is Red.* New York: Grosset and Dunlap, 1973.

——. *The Metaphysics of Modern Existence.* San Francisco: Harper and Row, 1979.

——. *The Nations Within: The Past and Future of American Indian Sovereignty.* Ed. with Clifford M. Lytle. New York: Pantheon, 1984.

——. *We Talk, You Listen: New Tribes, New Turf.* New York: Macmillan, 1970.

Denton, Thetford. *Tsali.* San Francisco: Indian Historian Press, 1972.

Foreman, Grant. *The Five Civilized Tribes.* Norman: University of Oklahoma Press, 1934.

——. *Indian Removal: The Emigration of the Five Civilized Tribes of Indians.* Norman: University of Oklahoma Press, 1932.

——. *Sequoyah.* Norman: University of Oklahoma Press, 1938.

Girard, Raphael. *Esotericism of the Popol Vuh: The Sacred History of the Quiché-Maya.* Pasadena: Theosophical University Press, 1979.

Hansen, L. Taylor. *He Walked the Americas.* Amherst, Wisc.: Amherst Press, 1963.

Katz, William Loren. *Black Indians: A Hidden Heritage.* New York: Atheneum, 1986.

Lewis, Thomas M. N., and Madeline Kneberg. *Tribes That Slumber: Indians of the Tennessee Region.* Knoxville: University of Tennessee Press, 1958.

Momaday, N. Scott. *House Made of Dawn.* New York: Harper and Row, 1968.

_____. *The Names: A Memoir.* New York: Harper and Row, 1976.

_____. *With Eagle Glance.* New York: Museum of the American Indian, 1982.

Mooney, James. *Myths of the Cherokee and Sacred Formulas of the Cherokees.* Nashville: Charles and Randy Elder, 1982.

Shearer, Tony. *Beneath the Moon and Under the Sun: A Poetic Reappraisal of the Sacred Calender and Prophecies of Ancient Mexico.* Albuquerque: Sun Publishing Co., 1975.

_____. *Lord of the Dawn: Quetzalcoatl.* Happy Camp, Calif.: Naturegraph Publishers, 1971.

Strickland, Rennard. *Fire and the Spirits: Cherokee Law from Clan to Court.* Norman: University of Oklahoma Press, 1975.

Wallace, Paul A. W. *The White Roots of Peace.* Philadelphia: University of Pennsylvania Press, 1946.

Wardell, Morris L. *A Political History of the Cherokee Nation, 1838–1907.* Norman: University of Oklahoma Press, 1938.

Weyler, Rex. *Blood of the Land.* New York: Everest House, 1982.

Woodward, Grace Steele. *The Cherokees.* Norman: University of Oklahoma Press, 1963.

INDEX

action, enlightened, 27; *see also*
    Beauty Path
  and communication, 199–203
  and mind, 33
  and skillful means, 47
  and spiritual practice, 76–79,
    82, 95–96
  and Temple of Understanding,
    174–177
  and transformation, 229
  and triangle, 35
actualizing, and spiritual practice,
    46–49, 84, 101
Adawees, star beings, 12, 19, 40,
    95, 132, 153, 171, 228–229,
    243
affirmation, 47–49, 86–87, 97,
    119, 122, 158, 198–200, 215;
    see also compassion
Africa, 15–16, 239
air, 140
Algonquin language, 14, 89
Amazon Basin, Land of the Hum-
    mingbird, 17
amplification of self, and crystals,
    235–263
Andes Mountains, 17
Arkansas, and Tsalagi nation, 4–5
armaments, 12, 27, 80, 207–208
Asga Ya Galunlati, Creator Being,
    19, 29–33, 58–59; *see also*
    God
astronomy, and ancestors, 17–18
attraction, 185–186; *see also*
    magnetization

Aunt Hattie, 193, 232
Aunt Leila, 232
Australia, Rainbow Serpent Moun-
    tains of, 128
Aztecs, xiii, 14

balance, stabilization, stability
  and circle, 37
  and crystals, 236
  and disease, 54
  and emerald, 60
  equanimity, wisdom of, 36–41,
    173–174
  and health, 178–180
  and heart, 212–215
  and Nellie Ywahoo, 164
  and priestcraft, 21–27
  and purpose, 192
  and resolution, 150–151
  and sacred songs, 33
  and spiritual practice, 17–18,
    74–77, 124, 138, 240, 246,
    256–257
  and subtle communication,
    199–203
  and Ywahoo lineage, 2–3
bear, and West, 252
Bear Clan, 184
Bear, Great, and fear and igno-
    rance, 51, 96, 133, 172–173,
    223, 235
Beauty Path, and right action, 34,
    53, 58–59, 66, 77–81, 109,
    115, 118, 123–126, 136, 152,
    177, 180, 198–203, 216, 223

behavior, and Tsalagi teachings, 112

bioresonance, science of, 107–108, 126–139, 246

biorhythms, 243

Black Hills, 128, 138

Black Mesa, 128–132, 138

Blue Mountains. *See* Smoky, Blue, Mountains

body, and Tsalagi teachings, xii, 114–117, 125, 136, 156, 161–168, 203–219, 225–233, 240–243, 249–255, 262–263

Book of Life, 176–177

breath, 40, 102, 121, 130–139, 184, 217, 226–227, 231; *see also* meditation

Brother of the Dark Face, Light Face, 31–32; *see also* Twins

Buddhism, xiii, 88–89, 191

Buffalo, sacred, 172

Buffalo Maiden, 223

bundles, 185
    wisdom, 99–100

Buzzard, Great, and Star Woman, 30

calendar, xiii, 4–7, 17, 18–19, 23, 26–27, 49–50, 77, 129

Canada, 14

Carolinas, North and South, 3
    Cherokee, North Carolina, 171

chants, hymns, sacred, 40
    Earth Chant, 101–102
    and forgiveness, 122–123
    Heart Chant, 197, 261
    and meditation, *see* meditation
    and quartz, 33

Cherokee. *See* Tsalagi

chocolate, 44

Choctaw, and Sacred Seven, 12–13

choice, 120–126, 150, 156–158, 252, 256–257

Christianity, Christ, xiii, 88–91, 239, 251, 257

clan, 183; *see also names of clans;* community, family

Colorado Plateau, 128–130

colors, 35, 102–103, 250–254, 273–277

communication, 59, 199–203, 238–239

community, communities, 67, 125–126, 128–129, 135, 141–144, 162, 236–237

comparison, 213–214

compassion, xii–xiii, 9, 41–46, 79, 100, 107, 113–119, 126, 147–188, 195, 203, 210

conflict, war. *See* scarcity, illusion of

conquerors. *See* domination

consciousness. *See* mind

Corn Mothers, 77–78, 172

Cortés, 4

council, united mind of, 141–144

Council of Elders of the Red Nations of North, South, and Central America (1531), 4, 15

Council of Elders (1978), 194

creation. *See* Great Mystery

creation stories, 29–34

Creek, and Sacred Seven, 12–13

Crescent Moon, teaching of, 219–225

Crystal Ark, 2–3

crystal, sacred (quartz), 22–23, 31–33, 60–70, 127–139, 162, 217, 236–263, 273

crystals, gemstones, and their attributes, 31, 52, 60–62, 75–76, 108, 239, 249–254, 273–277

INDEX

dances, sacred, 229–233
   Dance of the Directions,
      130–131, 170–171
   Eagle Dance, 171
   sun dances, 69, 257
days of week, 253–254
death, xiii, 180–188
Deer Clan, 183–184
   Mother, 101–102
Deerskin Clan Mother, of New
   England, 194–195
desire, 33–70
De Soto, 14–15
destiny, karma, 53, 76, 95
Diamond Body, 197–198, 245
Diné (Navajo), 139
directions (compass), 37, 51, 79,
   95–96, 120, 128, 132–133,
   171–173, 222–223,
   243–252, 257, 279–281
disarmament movement, 69, 117,
   210
DNA spiral, 40, 52, 90, 127
domination, 16–17, 27, 124–125,
   255
doubt, 67, 81, 157, 241, 258
dragons, and Earth energy, 16
dream attentiveness, 153–154
drugs, and abuse of crystals, 236
duty, spiritual. *See* practice

Earth
   and calendar, 27
   and circle, 161
   and communication, 199–203
   energy, 16, 22–23, 51–54
   history, 26
   life forms on, 26, 30
   Mandala, 220–223
   Mother, 164
   and prayer, 47
education, 99, 170
Egypt, 181

Elder Fires Above, three sacred,
   xii, 10, 34–35, 89, 113, 129,
   147, 162–163, 195, 204–205,
   217, 225; *see also* intelligence,
   active; love; will
Elo, 6–7, 29–70, 124–125, 246
Elohi Mona (Atlantis), 11–13, 26,
   124, 129, 181
emotions, 11, 104, 116, 118, 172,
   185–186, 203–219, 251–252
   anger, 62, 104, 118, 142, 185,
      206–212, 258
   envy, 39, 118, 202, 218–219
   fear, 16, 40, 51, 55, 76, 118,
      121, 141–144, 149, 168, 185,
      187, 206–212, 241
   grief, 214, 249
   guilt, 83
   humility, 55
   pride, 12, 106, 255
energy, 16, 22–23, 51–54, 74–76,
   84, 90, 102, 115–116, 126–
   139, 162–164, 185–186,
   197–198, 235–263
equanimity. *See* balance
error, 39–40, 99, 167
ethics, 256; *see also* Beauty Path
Europeans, 13–14, 47
evil, 16, 255–256

faith, 36, 46, 51, 114, 169
family, 37, 111–144, 220–225,
   255; *see also* community
father, 221–224
Fifth World, 18, 26, 50, 77
Fisher, Eonah (grandfather), 3, 14,
   38, 81, 98, 130, 151–155,
   174–177, 231–233, 235
food supply, and origins, 17
Forced Removal. *See* Trail of Tears
forgiveness, 41–46, 55, 100–102,
   122–123, 136–139, 177–
   178, 183, 214

INDEX

Four Corners area, 13
friendship, 113, 120–124, 177–178, 224, 247

Galunlati, the realm of light, 29, 34, 40, 79, 82, 129, 174, 195, 242
gardens, 17, 91–92
  Findhorn, Scotland, 150, 254–355
generosity, gift, 41, 46, 67, 120–121, 168–169, 246
genocide. *See also* Trail of Tears
  Native American, 5–6, 12–13
  Nazi Holocaust, 12
Georgia, 4–5
God, Aqteshna Ana, 89; *see also* Great Mystery
  Eye of, and crystal, 236
gold, 252
good, doing, xii–xiii

harmony, 44–45, 96; *see also* balance, and crystals
healing. *See* medicine
history, xiii
Hoop, Sacred, of life, xii, 5, 20–21
Hopi, 25, 101, 139
Hopi Plateau, 128–131

Igidotsoiyi Tsalagi Gadugi (Three Sisters Society), xi
ignorance, 16, 51, 79, 96, 132, 141
illness. *See* mind, and illness
imagination. *See* mind
Indian. *See* Native American; *names of tribes*
Inquisition, 12
inspiration, 31, 66–67, 124–125, 222, 250
intelligence, active, building, xii–xiii, 9, 27, 46–47, 101, 115–116

intention, xii–xiii, 9, 35–40, 46, 85, 99, 101, 114–115, 156
invention, 22, 27, 51
Iroquois, 13–14
Islam, 88–89

Japanese-Americans, 139
Jerusalem, 128
Judaism, xiii, 88–89
  Star of David, and crystal, 253
Jupiter (planet), 69

Kabbalah, and sacred sounds, 239
karma. *See* destiny, karma
kingdoms, animal, mineral, plant, and priestcraft, 23
Kituwa Society, 15
Kuan Yin, 195

leadership, 16–17, 135, 139, 148–149
light, 34–35, 130–131, 138–144
lightning, 31, 66–67, 127–139
line. *See* symbols, sacred
love, xii–xiii, 27, 44, 60, 98, 101, 116, 186, 203–204

magnetization, and spiritual practice, 48–49, 83–86
mandala, 171
  Crystal, 249–253
  Earth, 220–223
Mars, and calendar, 27, 49, 259
mathematics, 17–18, 23, 50, 239
Maya, xiii, 14, 239
Mecca, 128
medicine
  and crystals, 235–263
  and human body, 114–117, 229–233
  and jasper, 60
  for mental illness, 21–22
  pharmacopoeia, 4, 17

INDEX

and ritual, 123–124
and rose quartz, 60
and sound, 116–117
and Sunray practice, 86
of the Twins, 6
medicine people, 16, 193–194,
 203, 210–211, 247
Medicine Wheel of Life, 37, 51,
 76–79, 172, 223–224,
 249–252
meditation, 67, 85–86, 93–95,
 239, 245, 257–258, 265; *see
 also* practice, spiritual
and breath, 45, 102
Clear Intention, 69–70
Coming Home, 158–160
and communication, 200–201
Crystal, 62–64, 261–262
heart, 212
solar plexus, 211–212
with Sound and Visualization,
 196–197
Temple of Understanding,
 174–177
Three Gems of Most Pure
 Mind, 154–155
and vigil, 54
Vision of Peace, 83
men, and priestcraft, 21–27
Micmacs, Dawn Greeters, 129
migrations, 32, 13–18, 142
mind, 9
child, 36
and communication, 201
and crown of head, 216–218
and crystal, 238–263
and dreams, 53–54, 98–99
and heart, 212–215
and illness, 45, 53–54, 121,
 171, 184–185, 230–231, 242
and peace, Peacekeeper, 38,
 147–188, 191–233
and physical form, 84–85

and spiritual practice, 74–76,
 93, 101
and reality, 74–75
and Temple of Understanding,
 174–177
and Tsalagi origins, 11–12
and Tsalagi teachings, 22, 27,
 30–70, 85, 97, 103–109,
 122–123
and Twins, 32–33
and vigil, 54–57
Mississippi Valley, 14–15
Mother-Father, concept of, 24–25,
 51–52, 76, 103, 130–139,
 164, 166, 195, 197–203, 210,
 217, 222, 199–203, 210, 217,
 222, 253
mound, temple, society, 14–16,
 25–26
music, tones, 33, 40, 61, 74, 101,
 114, 239, 252–253; *see also*
 chant
Muskrat, and Star Woman, 30
Mystery, Great, 19, 77–79, 89,
 157, 164, 166, 173, 191–192

Native Americans
and government, 143
North American history of, xiv,
 1, 3–5, 9–18
and spiritual practice, 89, 138,
 139–144, 237–238, 256–263
New England, 194–195
New York State, 101–102
Watkins Glen, 259
nine hells, ninth hell, 7, 27, 50, 129
nitrogen, and bioresonance, 127, 130
Normandy, and Second World War,
 257
numbers, 273–277
five, pentatonic scale, 95, 100–
 101, 114, 161, 163, 205, 239
seven, 12–13, 20–22, 97

Nuna, Grandfather Moon, 153
Nutawa, Sunlight Arising, 96
Nuwati, "sacred medicine that
permeates all things," 229

Oaxaca, 128
Oconaluftee River, 42
offerings, 19, 54, 62
Oklahoma, 15
Orineida, "subtle mind uniting all
things," 229

Pale One, the, "Keeper of Mysteries," xiii, 2, 18–21, 29,
143–144
Paumonkees, 101–102
peace, 27, 34, 38; see also practice,
spiritual
Peace, Great Tree of, xiii, 27, 38,
58, 79, 90–91, 113, 144, 157,
243
Peace, Most Great, 202, 236
Peace, White, Village, 21–27, 148
Peacekeeper, and spiritual practice,
80–82, 107, 114, 126,
147–188
Peacemaker, the, xiii, 16, 27, 29,
75–76
people, and Native American
names, 166
People of One Fire, 82; see also
Tsalagi
planet, Earth's sister, and Earth
history, 26
planet behind sun, and calendar,
259
Pleiades (Seven Dancers), 1, 9, 12,
25, 27, 49–50, 58, 97, 166,
235, 243
practice, spiritual, 6, 19, 34, 45,
47, 53–70, 73–75, 90–91,
98–99, 102–103, 105–106,
122–123, 122–124, 133–

139, 150, 169–170,
174–178, 196–197,
239–240, 245, 247–249,
261–263
prayer. See practice, spiritual
prejudice, 38, 179
priests, priestcraft, 21–27
Principal People (An Yun Wiwa).
See Tsalagi
prophecy, 12, 37
purpose, life, 76–77, 104–109,
162, 183, 202–203

Quetzalcoatl, xiii

Rainbow Bridge, and practice,
65–69, 156
reaction, 35, 39–40, 140–141
reality, 20–21, 46–47, 74–75, 91,
192, 199, 206, 256
rebirth, 186–188
reciprocity, 247; see also generosity
relationships, and mind, 75; see
also Beauty Path
Code of Right Relationship,
20–21
religion
and Native Americans, xiii–xiv,
1–2, 136
Pale One's teachings, 19–21
priestcraft, 21–27
reminders, seven, of Pale One,
20–21
resolution, 44
complimentary, 43, 150, 209
ritual, 19, 32, 41–42, 54, 123–
125, 136–139, 166,
177–178, 183–185

Saint George, and dragon, 157
Salish, Lummi northwest coastal,
33, 129, 160–161
salmon, 11, 158, 161, 244

sanctuary. *See* Village, Peace or White
Saturn, and learning, 251
scarcity, and conflict, war, 80, 121, 124, 149, 168–169
Scotland, Findhorn, 150, 254–255
sexuality, 26
sin, 32–33, 165
Sirius, 27, 49, 243
Six Nations Confederacy, 16
Sixth Worlds, 18, 26, 50
Smoky, Blue, Mountains, 4–5, 16–18, 42–43, 129
society, and spiritual practice, 73, 88–89, 92, 185–186
sound, 116–117, 121–122, 239; *see also* music
Spain, museums of, and Tsalagi documents, 15
star children, Sacred Seven, 11–12
Star Woman, Mother, Maiden, 9–10, 29–33, 167, 255
stars, and origins, 9–12, 25, 50, 181; *see also names of stars*
Stonehenge, 128
Sun, Children of the, 11–12, 167
sun temples, and Tsalagi history, 3, 25
Sunray Meditation Society, xi, 6, 86, 170–171, 283–284
symbols, sacred, xiii, 9, 35, 37, 46, 51, 60, 91, 119–120, 125, 127, 134, 139–140, 161, 163, 171, 185–186, 198–199, 219, 241, 249, 273–277

teacher, savior, 88–89
teaching, methods of, xii
Tennessee, 3–5
thirteen heavens, 4, 7, 27, 50
thought. *See* mind
thunder, "thunder being," 124

Thunder Bird, and lightning, 31, 126–139, 172
Tibetan Plateau, 128–131
time, xiii, 4, 102
tla (thought) beings, 9
tradition, 79
Trail of Tears, 3, 5, 15, 25, 180
transformation, 60–61, 92–93, 102, 115, 150–155, 194, 203–219
Tsalagi, def. xi
  and accidents, mistakes, 162
  Ani Gadoahwi (Wild Potato) Clan, 3
  children, 3–5, 23, 52, 85, 118, 156, 169, 221–233
  and Dhyani Ywahoo, 2–3, 283–284
  Etowah Band, Eastern Tsalagi Nation, xi, 15
  fifth generation, 1, 5, 7
  history, 9–18, 112–113
  and sacred fire, 25
  and teachings, 5–6
  tribes, twelve original 10–11
  and types of people, 107–108
Turtle, and Star Woman, 30
Turtle Island (North America and the world), 6, 15–16, 79
Twins, 31–32, 255
  Medicine of the, 6

Uk-kuk-a-duk, Ukdena. *See* dragons
unconscious, 16
understanding, 76
  Temple of, 106–107, 174–176
Unto These Hills, 171
U.S. Constitution, 16, 143–144
U.S. government, and "national sacrifice areas," 131
  American Indian Religious Freedom Act (1979), 1–2
  Indian Removal Act (1830), 5

Vatican, 15
vegetables, 17
Venus, and calendar, 27, 49, 259
vigil, 19, 40, 54–57, 77, 106
vision, vision quest, 55, 77, 106, 192–193, 239–240, 247
visualization, 48, 85–86, 118, 195–199
vitamin D₃, 238
voice, power of. *See* affirmation

Walks the Forest, 42–43
Wampanoags, 129
Washington, Joe, 160–161
water, *ama*, 26, 117–118, 131, 138, 140
water lily, 120
Water Spider, 14, 30, 89
Water Woman, Ama Agheya, 133, 195
will, xii–xiii, 9, 35–40, 52–54, 107, 115–120, 147–188
wind, 26, 31, 126–139
wisdom, 76, 95
Fire of, 1, 25–26, 34–35,

96–97, 113, 147–188, 225–228
Magic Lake of, Atagahi, 121, 175
women, and priestcraft, 21–27
World Peace March (1982), 148
worlds, cycle of. *See* calendar, ceremonial
World War, Second, 257

Yuchi, and Sacred Seven, 12–13
Ywahoo, Dhyani, 3, 38, 53–54, 58, 81, 99–100, 169–170, 181–182, 249, 257–259, 283–284
Ywahoo, Eli (great-grandfather), 3, 14, 60, 65, 130, 181–186, 231–233, 235
Ywahoo, Nellie (grandmother), 3, 25, 38, 66, 108, 130, 164–165, 180–188, 193–194
Ywahoo lineage, 2–6, 86, 89, 130–131, 138–144, 166, 236–237

zero, concept of, 4, 17, 19, 37